William of Orange and the Struggle for the Crown of England

William of Orange and the Struggle for the Crown of England

The Glorious Revolution

By Brian Best

FRONTLINE
BOOKS

An imprint of
Pen & Sword Books Ltd

FRONTLINE
BOOKS

First published in Great Britain in 2021 by
FRONTLINE BOOKS
an imprint of Pen & Sword Books Ltd,
47 Church Street, Barnsley, S. Yorkshire, S70 2AS

ISBN: 978 1 52679 522 9

For more information on our books, please visit
www.frontline-books.com, email info@frontline-books.com
or write to us at the above address.

Printed and bound by TJ International

Pen & Sword Books Ltd incorporates the imprints of Pen & Sword
Archaeology, Atlas, Aviation, Battleground, Discovery,
Family History, History, Maritime, Military, Naval, Politics,
Social History, Transport, True Crime, Claymore Press,
Frontline Books, Praetorian Press,
Seaforth Publishing and White Owl

For a complete list of Pen and Sword titles please contact
PEN & SWORD LTD
47 Church Street, Barnsley, South Yorkshire, S70 2AS, England
E-mail: enquiries@pen-and-sword.co.uk

Or

PEN AND SWORD BOOKS
1950 Lawrence Rd, Havertown, PA 19083, USA
E-mail: Uspen-and-sword@casematepublishers.com

Contents

Introduction

This account features the leading figures of the time who saw out the Stuart dynasty from 1660 to 1714. It also covers various Acts passed by Parliament and the wars between the English, Irish, the Netherlands and France. It covers the Popish Plots, the religious conflicts and the dreadful punishments metered out to those who disobeyed the royal decree. It was also a time when diarists kept a true record of their fellow countrymen. The Glorious Revolution of 1688–89, a foreign monarch and the Protestant daughter of a born again Catholic King made one of least-known periods of British history into one of the most important fifty years that shaped democracy in Great Britain and the United States.

The end of the English Civil War left the country impoverished and under the bleakly austere dictatorship of Oliver Cromwell. The incomes of citizens were damaged or bankrupted, while public and private properties were destroyed on a vast scale. Cromwell's New Model Army spent most of the 1650s on campaign, but when he died in September 1658, the Protectorate and the Army went into a swift decline. At one time it was felt that factions of the New Model Army loyal to different generals might wage war on each other, precipitating another Civil War.

When Charles II returned to England on 25 May 1660, sparking the Restoration, the country was in a poor state. It had a small army, a navy that was ranked below France and the Netherlands and a Parliament that was made up of divided sides, mostly Tories and Whigs. It became dominated by the House of Stuart. The English Parliament was a junior partner in the governing of the country and had met only eleven times in the first forty years of the seventeenth century. When Parliament met after William and Mary's enthronement, a historian noted, '... it was nothing less than a landmark moment in the emergence of the modern state'. It was indeed a landmark moment for the English, whose decisions were made by a succession of kings and queens. One of the most recent monarchs was Charles I, who firmly believed in the divine right of kings. Although short in stature and possessing a bad stammer, he was convinced that he was next to God. After his execution on 30 January 1649, Cromwell ran the country as a Puritan republican until his death.

The Restoration in 1660 brought Charles II to the throne, much to the resentment of those who supported the Commonwealth. Nonconformists were deprived by the Act of Uniformity of 1662, which forbade them from holding civil office, and laws against dissenters that were enforced by local Justices of the Peace. The political crisis that followed Charles I's death resulted in the restoration of the monarchy and his eldest son was invited to return to Britain and reclaim his crown.

Charles II was regarded as 'the Merry Monarch' and surrounded himself with close boisterous advisors with the acronym-based names of Lord CLIFFORD, Lord ARLINGTON, The Duke of BUCKINGHAM, Lord ASHLEY and Lord LAUDERDALE, together making a new English word – CABAL. Charles was always short of money, which did not deter him from feeding well, establishing Newmarket for the racing and having thirteen known mistresses. These included Lucy Walters (the mother of the Duke of Monmouth), Barbara Villiers and the famous Nell Gwynne. They quite often bore him children and Charles was pleased to confer dukedoms on them, including James Scott, the Duke of Monmouth. John Wilmot, 2nd Earl of Rochester, a poet and courtier, said of Charles:

> Here lies a great and mighty King,
> Whose promise none relied on;
> He never said a foolish thing,
> Nor ever did a wise one.

During his enforced exile, Charles lived at the court of his cousin, King Louis XIV of France. Later when he became king, he was always at the beck and call of Louis, from whom he secretly accepted bribes. In exchange, he sold his sovereign rights to Dunkirk on 27 October 1662 to France for £320,000, much to the dismay of Parliament.

On 26 January 1661, Charles issued the Royal Warrant that created the first regiments of the British Army. Scotland and Ireland maintained separate military establishments until the Act of Union in 1707.

The new army consisted of two regiments of cavalry, the Life Guards formed from former Cavaliers, and The Blues made up of some of the best New Model Army horse regiments. The infantry consisted of the Coldstream Guards, the Grenadiers Guards, The Royal Scots and the Queen's Royals. The general public, encouraged by the pamphleteers, feared this standing army under royal command would allow monarchs to ignore the wishes of Parliament. It was not until the reign of William III that the near-perpetual wars with other European states saw the British Army being accepted by the public. In 1688, Parliament succeeded in wresting control of the army under a general bill, the first Mutiny Act. Because the Bill of Rights prohibited the existence of a standing army during peacetime without the consent of Parliament, the Mutiny Act was expressly limited to one year's duration. Many other changes occurred during this transition from absolute monarchy to constitutional monarchy. As written in the *Oxford History of the British Empire Companion* series, these were:

> Products of the exigencies and opportunities of the quarter century
> of warfare on the grand scale that commenced with the accession
> of William and Mary.

In 1673, Charles ran out of money and Parliament forced him to agree to the Test Act. These were a series of English religious laws that allowed those of the Church of England to take communion but banned Roman Catholics from public employment. The second Test Act of 1678 forbade Catholics from becoming members of both Houses of Parliament. The members also passed the Exclusion Bill, which was aimed at barring James, Duke of York, from succeeding Charles as king. Charles procrastinated for months and made the prophetic comment to James:

> You may depend upon it that nobody will ever think of killing me
> to make you king.

At the age of fifteen, Mary, the daughter of James, Duke of York, became betrothed to her cousin, the Protestant Stadtholder of Holland, William of Orange. At first Charles opposed the marriage with a Dutch ruler, as he desired that Mary should marry her second cousin, Louis, the

Grand Dauphin, the eldest son and heir of Louis XIV and Maria Theresa of Spain. This would ally his realm with Catholic France and strengthen the ties of a Catholic successor in England. Pressure from Parliament meaning a coalition with the Catholic French was no longer politically favourable; he backed down and approved of the marriage. Mary's father thought that his own popularity would improve among Protestants if he agreed with the Chief Minister, Lord Danby, and the King. When the news was broken to the fifteen-year-old Mary, she was so distraught that she wept all that afternoon and into the following day. On 4 November 1677, William and Mary were married. Their relationship worked out well and they were happy for the few years they were together. After a lengthy period of political machinations, the sharing of the crown was finally decided, and together William and Mary ruled over England, Scotland and Ireland.

Charles, on his death bed, reverted to Catholicism. James succeeded his elder brother to the throne in February 1685 with initial widespread support from the English public but it was the intransigence of James, who wanted to convert his Protestant citizens to the Catholic faith, that led to problems. His Tory allies in Parliament recognised what would happen and protested. James changed tack by associating with the Whigs and Dissenters in an effort to force his plan through Parliament. Finally, in the unlikely partnership of Tories and Whigs, Protestants and Non-conformists, James and his Catholic followers were thwarted in their efforts to force a change from the majority Protestant to the minority Catholic religions. Despite his efforts, most of which set the population against him, he did not relent. Even Pope Innocent XI, who shared a loathing for the Catholic King Louis XIV, was keen to keep his distance from the new English ambassador, Lord Castlemaine, to the Vatican. At the end of four years, the Immortal Seven invited the Protestant William of Orange to take over from the hated James. As James's reign progressively worsened, the population wished for a Protestant change of monarch. It was a situation that would soon change in the following four years.

The final Stuart monarch was Anne, an increasingly corpulent queen who mothered seventeen children, all of whom died before adulthood. She is known mainly for the Act of Union between England and Scotland, thus forming Great Britain. Although she was not a clever woman, her reign saw the emergence of such talents as Jonathan Swift, Alexander Pope,

Joseph Addison and Richard Steele, poets and playwrights; Sir Christopher Wren, the architect of St Paul's Cathedral and other churches in the City of London; and John Locke and Isaac Newton, philosopher and scientist. She is always associated with one of Great Britain's outstanding soldiers, John Churchill, Duke of Marlborough.

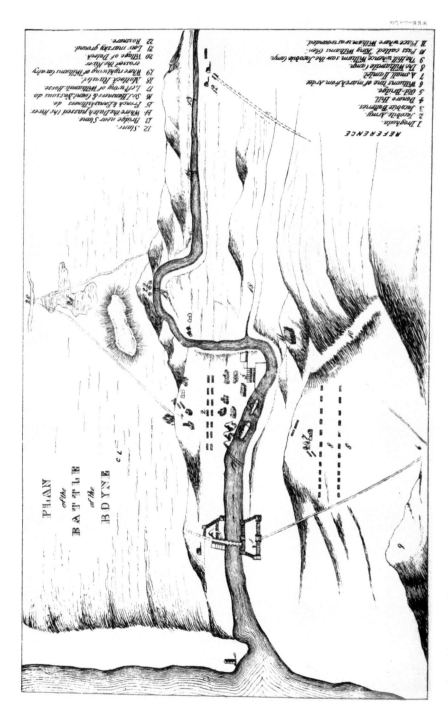

A plan of the Battle of the Boyne, looking south.

Chapter 1

Restoration

One of the outstanding soldiers of the Civil War was George Monck. He was born on 6 December 1608 in Great Potheridge, Devon, the fourth child and second son of Sir Thomas Monck, an impoverished landowner, and his wife, Elizabeth. His father sank further in debt and was unable to provide for his children. George was one who was sent to be brought up by his mother's family, the Smyths in Exeter. As the younger son, at the age of sixteen he was given little choice but to join the army and in his religion he remained a Presbyterian at heart. He volunteered to join an English expedition against the port of Cadiz in 1625, during which he served under his cousin, Sir Richard Grenville, the grandson of the same-named Sir Richard Grenville. The expedition was a disaster and Monck returned to Devon, having at least tasted life on campaign.

A couple of years later he and his brother attacked and beat an under-sheriff who had arrested his father for debt. Monck pursued the under-sheriff and stabbed the man, who later died of his wounds. To escape prosecution, he joined another expedition to La Rochelle in 1627, led by the profligate Duke of Buckingham. Monck was promoted to ensign in Sir John Burroughs's regiment and carried the regimental colours in an unsuccessful attack on a French fort. The following year he was commissioned as captain of foot in a regiment that Grenville had been appointed colonel. Buckingham's ruinously expensive and unsuccessful expedition to raise the siege of the Huguenot stronghold came to nought. Monck's regiment sailed for La Rochelle, only to sail straight back to England. His commander, Buckingham, had gone to the Greyhound Pub in Portsmouth to organise another campaign but, on 23 August 1628, he was stabbed to death by John Felton, an officer who had been wounded in an earlier military campaign and believed he had been passed over for promotion. Most of the population sided with Felton, who they saw as manly, and justified his actions against the effeminate Buckingham. Despite his support, he was tried, convicted and later hanged.

Monck then joined the Dutch to fight against the Spanish Netherlands between 1629 and 1638. In 1637, at the siege of Breda, Monck led a forlorn assault on one of the outworks of the town. Quartermaster Henry Hexham, in his account entitled *Brief Relation of the Famous Siege of Breda*, wrote of Monck's bravery in foiling the attempts of the French mine engineers:

> The first officer then of the English which was to fall up the breach and enter it was Captain Monck, Colonel Goring's Captain, with 20 musketeers and 10 pikes, and after him a work-master [engineer officer] – with certain workmen, to cast up a breastwork behind them, that they might lodge our men upon the top of the horn-work [fortification] ... The English mine [Monck was serving with the Dutch] then being sprung, and taking good effect, Captain Monck, ere the smoke was vanished, hastens up to the breach, and with his commanded men, fell up to the very top of it, where at first he was entertained with some musketry of the enemy.
>
> But they instantly gave back, and he with his commanded men, of which half had slunk away, advanced forward into the work, where he found a stand of pikes [pike-men], of about six or seven score, ready to receive him. And falling pell-mell upon them, whether by order, or out of affection for the Colonel [recently wounded in action], or for a revenge upon the enemy, they gave the word, 'a Goring. A Goring.' and though the enemy was twice their number, yet Captain Abrahall pressing hard upon them, and galled them shortly with his musketeers, yet Captain Abrahall being bravely followed with a Company of gallant men, charged home upon them, and came to push the pike with them. And seeing this advantage that Captain Monck fell upon the left flank of them, and galled them shortly with his musketeers, Captain Abrahall pressing hard upon them, and this brought the enemy into a disorder, and made them give back (retreat). Upon this, the French also falling on upon their right flank from their side, diverse [many] of them were slain, drowned and wholly routed.

He then returned to suppress a rebellion in Ireland in 1642–43, before joining the Royalist Army of King Charles to fight the Parliamentarians. In the battle at Nantwich in 1644, he was captured and imprisoned in the Tower of London for three years, where 'he found it very hard to subsist'. Thomas Gumble wrote in his book *Life of Monck* 1671:

> His elder brother, Thomas, who was not rich, and was actively engaged in the King's cause (Charles I), sent him £50. In a letter begging for another £50, on the score of his great necessities, Monck adds: 'I shall entreat you to be mindful of me concerning my exchange; for I doubt all my friends have forgotten me.' Prince Rupert made an attempt to get him exchanged for Sir Robert Pye, and the king sent him £100, a gift which he has often with gratitude in later days.

The Roundheads recognised that Monck was an exceptional army commander. He was released and made a major general of the Army sent to Ireland to suppress the rebels. After three years of limited success, he sought terms with the Irish and retired from the army. In 1650, Oliver Cromwell brought him back into the New Model Army and put him in command of a foot regiment to suppress the Scottish royalists. He fought with Cromwell in the Battle of Dunbar on 3 September 1650 and remained in Scotland as Commander in Chief. He spent most of the Interregnum in Scotland, suppressing minor outbreaks by Royalist uprisings in the Highlands and also the gangs of the 'moss-troopers', who raided into Cumbria and Northumberland.

When Cromwell died in September 1658, the Protectorate died a slow death, as did the New Model Army. In late 1659, General George Monck moved his army south and reached the River Tweed. He stopped for three weeks at the border village of Coldstream, where he raised a new regiment he named the Coldstream Guards, For example: which makes this regiment the oldest in the British Army Or something similar the oldest in the British Army.

Monck had initially supported Cromwell's son, Richard, but when Major General John Lambert dissolved the Rump of the Long Parliament by force in October 1659, Monck refused to recognise the new military regime. The Rump Parliament was the English Parliament after Colonel Thomas Pride removed the Long Parliament. This was when the New Model Army soldiers prevented Members of Parliament from entering the House of Commons.

He ordered that the Rump was restored once again in December and led an army 335 miles from Scotland to London. Pepys wrote in his diary for February 1660 that:

> In early 1660, General George Monck marches into London and, with his army of 7,000 paid soldiers, holds the whip hand as the most powerful men in the country. He isn't all-powerful, however, and so he manoeuvres politically among the Puritans in the Rump and in the Army on the one hand, and popular sentiment against the Rump and for restoring the Monarchy on the other. Monck eventually demands that the moderate, 'secluded' Presbyterian members of Parliament be allowed to take their seats. As a result, celebrations immediately explode that night across London and in the countryside, with bonfires and roasting rumps.

John Lambert was arrested and sent to the Tower on 3 March 1660. He escaped by descending a silk rope aided by six men, who took him away by barge. He was later recaptured on 22 April at Daventry by Colonel Richard Ingoldsby, a regicide, and hoped to win a pardon. Lambert was a vain man and with his cousin Cromwell's death, imagined he was entitled to succeed him. He was later taken to Castle Cornet, Guernsey. In 1667 he was transferred to Drake's Island off Plymouth until he died of insanity during a severe winter in 1684.

The Long Parliament lasted from 1640 until 1660 and was dissolved in March 1660 and a newly elected Convention Parliament was assembled. This was a 'free Parliament' with no oath of allegiance to the Commonwealth or the Monarchy. It was predominately Royalist Tory, which assembled and invited Charles II to return to England as king. In the Declaration of Breda of 4 April 1660, the terms were drawn up by Charles's three chief advisors, Edward Hyde, James Butler and Nicholas Monck. A clergyman, Nicholas Monck was the brother of George Monck, and he helped phrase the declaration in which the King promised:

> A general pardon for crimes committed during the English Civil War and Interregnum for all those who recognised Charles as the lawful king; the retention by the current owners of property

purchased during the same period; religious toleration; and the payment of pay arrears to members of the army. And that the army would be decommissioned into service under the crown. Further, regarding the two latter points, the Parliament was given the authority to judge property disputes and responsibility for the payment of the army. The first three pledges were all subject to amendment by acts of parliament.

George Monck realised that the country was in danger of entering another civil war and, with his formidable army, created the situation favourable to the return of Charles II. The declaration was written in response to a secret message sent by Monck, who was in effective control of England. On 1 May 1660, the contents of the declaration were made public. Monck urged that the King should also emphasise 'amnesty, liberty of conscience and other measures'. Monck was the chief architect of the Restoration of the Stuart monarchy and was amply rewarded. The next day Parliament passed a resolution inviting Charles to England and to receive his crown, and by 8 May Charles was proclaimed King. On the advice of Monck, the Commons rejected the formation of a committee to investigate the conditions the King had offered. When Monck entered London with his army, he made his headquarters at the Bull's Head tavern as he waited for Charles to enter the city. Six years later, the 1666 Great Fire destroyed all the taverns along Cheapside; the Half Moon, the Mitre and the Standard, and included the Bull's Head. On 25 May, Charles landed at Dover and was greeted on the shore by Monck. Samuel Pepys had sailed to The Hague and waited for a few days until King Charles and his brother were ready to sail. On their arrival at Dover, Pepys wrote in his diary dated Friday, 25 May 1660:

> By the morning we were come close to the land, and everybody made ready to get on shore. The King and the two Dukes (York and Berwick) did eat their breakfast before they went, and there being set some ship's diet before them, only to show them the manner of the ship's diet, they eat of nothing else but pease and pork and boiled beef ... Great expectation of the King's making some Knights, but there was none. About noon yet he would go in my Lord's barge with the two Dukes. Our Captain steered, and my

Lord went along with him. I went, and Mr Mansell and one of the King's footmen, with a dog that the King loved, which dirtied the boat, which made us laugh, and me think that a King and all that belong to him are but just as others are, in a boat by ourselves, and so we got on shore when the King did, who received by General Monck with all imaginable love and respect at his entrance upon the land of Dover … A canopy was provided for him to stand under, which he did, and talked awhile with General Monck and others, and so into a stately coach there set for him, and so away through the town towards Canterbury, without making any stay at Dover.

The next day, Monck was knighted at Canterbury and invested with the Order of the Garter. On 7 July, he was raised to the peerage with the titles of Baron Monck of Potheridge, Beauchamp and Teyes, Earl of Torrington and Duke of Albemarle and given the estate of New Hall in Essex. His brother, Nicholas, was also rewarded and appointed Bishop of Hereford. On 29 May 1660, John Evelyn wrote in his diary of the King Charles entrance into London:

This day came in His Majesty Charles II to London, after a sad and long exile, and calamitous suffering both of the King and Church: being 17 years. This was also his birthday. And with triumph of above 20,000 horse and foot, brandishing their swords and shouting with unexpressable joy, the ways strewn with flowers, the bells ringing, the streets hung with tapestries, fountains running with wine … for such a Restoration was never seen in the mention of any history, ancient or modern, since the return of the Babylonian Captivity, nor so joyful a day, and so bright, ever seen in this nation.

For four days in January 1661, Thomas Venner was the last leader of the Fifth Monarchy Men and thirteen followers who had tried unsuccessfully to overthrow the new Parliament of King Charles. They believed that the death of Charles would welcome the coming of Jesus and that Christianity would rule the world. Venner was executed by being hanged, drawn and quartered and his head was impaled on a spike at the southern end of London Bridge along with other rebels. The Fifth Monarchy Men were easily routed by Monck's Regiment of Foot and a squadron of Cuirassiers. These two regiments were incorporated in the Royal army of Charles as regiments of Foot Guards and Horse Guards.

Some of the demobilised soldiers and officers of the New Model Army were sent to Portugal in support of the Portuguese Restoration War in their fight for independence from Spain. The English army numbering 3,000 proved to be a decisive factor and helped Portugal to win back her independence. In the Battle of Ameixial on 8 June 1663, the Spanish were vanquished from Portugal. For King Charles it was an expedient way of ridding his country of the New Model Army and also marrying the Portuguese princess Catherine of Braganza on 14 May 1662. On a spring day in April 1661, King Charles was crowned. Making sure he had a good view, Pepys departed at four in the morning to wait until eleven o'clock:

And a great pleasure it was to see the Abbey raised in the middle, all covered with red, and a throne and footstool on top of it, and all the officers of all kinds, so much as the very fiddlers in red vests. At last come the Dean and Prebends of Westminster, with the Bishops (many of them in cloth of gold copes), and after them the Nobility, all in their Parliament robes, which was a most magnificent sight. Then the Duke and King with a sceptre (carried by my Lord Sandwich) and sword and orb before him and the crown, too. The King in his robes, bareheaded, which was very fine … The crown was put upon his head, a great shout begun, and he came forth to the throne, and there passed more ceremonies as taking the oath, and having things read to him by the Bishop, and his lords (who put on their caps as soon as the King put on his crown) and bishops came, and kneeled before him.

And three times the King at Arms went to the three open places on the scaffold, and proclaimed, that if anyone could show any reason why Charles Stewart should not be King of England, that now he should come and speak. And a General Pardon also was read by the Lord Chancellor and medals flung up and down by my Lord Cornwallis, of silver, but I could not come by any. But so great a noise that I could make but little of the musique, and indeed, it was lost to everybody.

Pepys retired to bed that night, very drunk.

One of the first acts made by King Charles and the Church of England was the Worcester House Declaration, which attempted to reconcile Episcopalians and Presbyterians. Charles II's Coat of Arms was placed on most of the church's chancel arches, reminding the authorities that Anglicanism had been established by the Restoration monarchy. One result of Anglicanism was an uprising in the north of England in 1663. Known as the Farnley Wood Plot, it was hatched by Parliamentarians from the Civil War. Their aim was to capture the Royalist strongholds in Leeds and:

> To re-establish a gospel ministry and magistracy; to restore the Long Parliament; to relieve themselves from the excise and all subsidies and to reform all orders and degrees of men, especially the lawyer and clergy.

The plot failed to get off the ground due to the lack of support. Rather harshly, the twenty-six who did turn up were arrested as traitors and suffered the horrors of being hanged, drawn and quartered.

The Second Anglo-Dutch War started in 1664, provoked by the escalation of commercial tensions rather than any territorial provocation. The Dutch had installed themselves for many years in Batavia (Indonesia) and exploited the rich trade in spices and precious stones from the islands. The Dutch East India Company sent a Return Fleet back to The Netherlands in 1664, which was the richest cargo ever. It consisted of spices such as pepper, cloves, nutmeg, mace and cinnamon; also, ebony, silk, indigo, pearls, rubies, diamonds and porcelain. Avoiding the Channel, the fleet managed to reach the Dutch ports despite being attacked off southern Norway in August 1665. The English Channel was seen as too dangerous with both French and English privateers patrolling these waters. By 1666, the English were anxious to destroy the Dutch navy before it became too strong and threatened the collapse of English trade. In fact, the Dutch invested in the largest ship-building programme in its history, which put the English navy in the shade.

The impressive George Monck commanded a far greater public respect and confidence than the King, who was regarded by many citizens as a dilettante. In fact, there was more substance to Charles than was realised. He was a far more kingly type than his brother, James, Duke of York, who would succeed him. Despite his lifestyle, he managed to guide England through many troughs until his final years.

By the summer of 1667, still reeling from the effects of a plague and fire, the English Royal Navy was in a reduced state owing to a lack of funds to keep the fighting ships in prime condition. It also saw the worst naval defeat in home waters inflicted on the English fleet as it lay at anchor off Chatham Dockyard on the River Medway. In June 1667, the Dutch navy, under the command of Willem van Ghent and Michiel de Ruyter, bombarded and captured Sheerness on the Isle of Sheppey. Many Dutch officers doubted the success of an attack on the fleet in Chatham given the treacherous shoals in the Thames estuary and the River Medway. They were greatly helped by two English pilots who had defected; one a dissenter named Robert Holland and the other an unnamed smuggler. Seizing the opportunity to catch the English fleet as it lay at anchor, they sailed up the Medway, from where they attacked the fortifications at Chatham and Gillingham. They also managed to overcome the chain barrier that was strung across the river from Upnor Castle of the west bank to Gillingham on the east bank.

Only on the Dutch navy's arrival did Charles instruct the newly appointed Admiral George Monck to go to Chatham and take charge of matters. Monck first went to Gravesend, where he noted that there were few guns in the town and at Tilbury on the other bank. Not enough to prevent the Dutch reaching London. He then travelled to Chatham on 11 June and was dismayed to find that there were only twelve of the 800 dockyard workers left. Also, out of thirty sloops only twelve were present. The rest had been used to remove the personal possessions of the officers. He found that there were no munitions or powder and the 6in-thick chain that blocked the Medway was not protected by batteries. Monck immediately ordered that artillery should be moved from Gravesend to Chatham.

As the cannon would not arrive soon, he ordered a squadron of cavalry and a company of soldiers to reinforce Upnor Castle. He also ordered that blockships should be sunk in the approaches to Chatham, which was successfully achieved. Monck then decided to sink blockships in Upnor Reach, presenting another barrier. The chain was a problem, as it was some 9ft below the surface. Monck got around this by building stages near the shores to raise the chain. All to no avail, as the Dutch still managed to reach Chatham Harbour.

With the English navy suffering from a lack of crews, the Dutch sent in fire ships, which destroyed the *Matthias* and *Charles V*; the *Monmouth* was the only major warship to escape. Two capital ships and ten ships of the line burned and some thirty more were sunk to prevent their capture. It was a great degradation for the English population, and Pepys wrote in his diary of the unpreparedness that the Dutch raid had exposed:

> Never were a people so dejected as they are in the City all over at this day, and do talk most loudly, even treason; as, that we are bought and sold, that we are betrayed by the papists and others about the King. They look upon us as lost; and remove their families and rich goods in the City and do think verily that the French, being come down with his army to Dunkirk, it is to invade us – and that we shall be invaded.

To the King's humiliation, the flagship *Royal Charles* was towed back to the Netherlands and put on display. Charles begged the Dutch not to show his flagship to visiting dignities, to which, surprisingly, they agreed.

Seeing the burning ships, Monck ordered all sixteen remaining warships further along the Medway to be sunk to prevent them being captured. This made a total of about thirty ships sunk by the English. On 13 June, the whole of the River Thames as far as London was in a state of panic, with many wealthy citizens leaving London carrying their valuable possessions. The Dutch tried to repeat their success with other ports but were repelled. For a few years the English fleet was handicapped by the Dutch raid, but by 1670 a new building programme was started and restored the English Navy to its former power.

On 9 May 1670, a daring and botched theft took place at the Tower of London, when Thomas Blood, dressed as a clergyman, attempted to steal the crown jewels. In an elaborate con, he involved three men and an actress to fool the elderly keeper of the new jewels. The previous collection had been either sold, the jewels and pearls removed, or the gold melted down into hundreds of coins by the Mint. The dismantlement of the royal regalia was regarded by Oliver Cromwell as 'symbolic of the detestable rule of kings and monuments of superstition and idolatry'.

Blood and his gang were almost immediately caught as they left the Tower and imprisoned. Condemned to death, Blood asked for an audience with the

King. In his lilting Irish manner he managed to receive a pardon from the King, who had been amused by this confidence trickster. There may have been a reason for this extraordinary reprieve as the Duke of Buckingham was the King's favourite and together they may have instigated the theft with the hope of receiving more money from the public purse. Buckingham also thoroughly disliked James Butler, Duke of Ormond, and called upon Thomas Blood to perform the killing of the duke.

In December 1670, Ormond was driving up St James's Street when he was dragged from his coach by Blood and his gang and taken along Piccadilly with the intention of hanging him at Tyburn. Ormond put up resistance and managed to escape. To the disgust of Ormond's son, the attempted killing had been instigated by Buckingham. Blood was captured and not only pardoned, but given property in Ireland. In 1679, Blood had a disagreement with Buckingham, his former patron, who sued his criminal accomplice for £10,000. Unable to pay, Blood was imprisoned but was freed from prison within a few months. Two days later, on 24 August 1680, he fell into a coma and died at his home in Bowling Alley, Westminster. He was buried in the churchyard of St Margaret's Church, and his tombstone reads:

> Here lies the man who boldly hath run through
> More villainies that England ever knew
> And ne'er to any friend he had was true
> Here let him then by all unpitied lie
> And let's rejoice his time was come to die.

For all Blood's criminal activity, his son, Holcroft Blood, became a distinguished military engineer, rising to the rank of brigadier general and, in 1704, commanded the artillery at the Battle of Blenheim.

On 1 June 1670, Charles II and Louis XIV signed the Secret Treaty of Dover, which forced England into the Third Anglo-Dutch War and ended the hostilities between England and France. It required Charles to convert to the Roman Catholic Church, something that was hidden from the public for a century. Charles promised to declare himself a Roman Catholic, something he did not do until he was on his deathbed in 1685. In return, Louis gave Charles £200,000 annually to re-Catholicise England and support French policy against the Dutch Republic. It was not until 29 April 1672 that England and France declared war on the Dutch Republic, with France invading the Netherlands. It was France's mission to reduce the Dutch Republic to a second-rate power and Louis planned to attack on land and sea. He occupied the Overijssel, Gelderland and Utrecht but was pulled up short when the Dutch opened the dykes and flooded the land of the Holland Province. In 1673, the Anglo-French fleet confronted the Dutch fleet at the Battle of Kijkduin but came off second best, being badly mauled and forced to withdraw. Also, in 1672, the Dutch declared war against Munster and Cologne. The Dutch call the year *het rampjaar* (the disaster year), and fortunately, Charles's small army was not called upon to invade.

Chapter 2

The Great Fire

Within five years of the start of Charles II's reign he was confronted with two monumental catastrophes; the Great Plague and the Great Fire of London. The bubonic plague was the largest since the Black Death in 1348 and it began its deadly spread from spring 1665, lasting to early 1666. It was the last bubonic plague to occur in England, and it killed an estimated 100,000 people in eighteen months, almost a quarter of London's population. It started in St Giles-in-the Fields, one of the poorest of the neighbourhoods in the City. To avoid the plague, the King and his Court left London in July and stayed at Hampton Court. They then went on to Oxford, where Parliament had moved, and kept clear of the pestilence. The disease was transmitted by fleas that lived on rats. It rapidly spread to other towns throughout the country, with the chances of survival very slim. Daniel Defoe wrote in his book, *A Journal of the Plague Year*, which was published in 1722, that the virus had reached London and the population:

> Were immediately overwhelmed with it, and it came to violent
> fevers, vomiting, insufferable headaches, pains in the back, and so
> up to ravings and raging with those pains.

Samuel Pepys recorded in his diary in October 1663 that the plague had reached Amsterdam brought by a ship from Algiers. The same ship travelled on to Hamburg, passing on the virus, and so began the spread of the bubonic plague on the Continent. England attempted a form of border control as its first line of defence. From as early as 1663, the presence of plague in the major trading ports of Amsterdam and Hamburg raised concerns within the English Privy Council. With its terrifying symptoms of buboes, dark spots and fever-induced madness, the plague was the disease of nightmares and so a plan was developed to prevent it reaching British shores. They proposed to isolate ships heading for England by quarantining at Hole Haven, Canvey Island, in Essex. This was a good distance from London and also there was a creek around Canvey Island that could accommodate one hundred vessels. In his diary of 23 November 1663, Pepys recorded that it was a decision the English had never taken before.

A pair of naval vessels patrolled the Thames Estuary, intercepting incoming ships that were either English or foreign. Those ships from infected ports or with crews showing symptoms of plague would be ordered to turn back or sent straight to Hole Haven for thirty days quarantine. Impounded ships were cleansed, all cargo was aired onshore, and crews were isolated aboard their ships. If anyone died, their body was thrown overboard. At Tilbury, a second line of defence inspected incoming ships once more and only those vessels issued with a certificate of health could pass. In this way, London was doubly guarded. By 1664, as the continental plague appeared to worsen, the quarantine period was increased to a full forty days and further foreign ports were blacklisted. Away from London, the offshore quarantine procedure was rolled out across other key ports in England and Wales.

Despite these small deviations, the quarantine proved relatively successful; there were 24,000 plague deaths in Amsterdam in 1664 and only a handful in England. Sadly, with the 1665 Anglo-Dutch war declared, the focus naturally shifted away from quarantine and towards military matters. Within a month, the first case of plague occurred in London. Soon the Bills of Mortality spiralled to 70,000, although the true figure was thought to be about 100,000. The strict quarantine measures put in place in England from 1663 until the outbreak of war with the Dutch certainly appeared to hold the plague at bay. Forty days exceeded the disease's incubation period and Hole Haven was remote from London's dense population so quarantined ships were never close enough to the wharves for rats, the main source of the disease, to invade London.

Although the King returned to Whitehall in February 1666, London remained unsafe, with death carts still on the streets. What caused the most worry was the east wind that blew the dry, dusty air westward carrying the plague. At least forty-six pamphlets and books relating to the plague were published between 1665 and 1666. The most obvious message in the publications was of an image of a skeleton clad in royal robes and this was very significant because the Restoration had only recently replaced the Civil War and Interregnum. By equating the monarchy with death when death reigned supreme, this underlined the power and authority of the crown. Some pamphlets carried antidotes, including one:

> Take the Top of a Garlic–head, or half a quarter of a walnut, and
> a corn of Salt, eat every morning containing so a month together.
> This is good against worms in young and old.

One city that was badly affected was York. The plague victims were taken outside the walls and buried in the embankments, which have never been disturbed for fear of another outbreak. Trade between London and other plague towns ceased and the economy suffered. A small village in Derbyshire called Eyam, just 6 miles north of Bakewell, was subject to the bubonic plague with a strict lockdown of residents. The local rector, William Mompesson, persuaded his parishioners not to flee the village but to stay until the plague had run its course. A bale of cloth had been brought from London and was infested with fleas, which put the villages in danger of an outbreak. The inhabitants quarantined themselves for over a year so it would not spread to other villages. The inhabitants of Eyam would place money in six holes drilled into the boundary stone to pay for food and medicine left by their neighbours. By the end of the plague, three-quarters of Eyam's villagers had died but, by their vicar's conviction, they had saved their neighbours.

This catastrophe was followed by the Great Fire of London of 1666, brought on by a long hot summer that left London dry and tinder-prone. The fire started at the bakery of Thomas Farriner on Pudding Lane shortly after midnight on Sunday, 2 September. The baker was appointed by the King to supply ship's biscuit to the seamen in His Majesty's navy. He also baked loaves of bread for the inhabitants of the City. The fire started in Farriner's ovens and quickly spread out of control until Thursday, 6 September. Appointed secretary to the new commission of Admiralty and, as such, administrative head of the navy, the evergreen Samuel Pepys noted in his diary on 2 September:

> By and by, Jane comes and tells me that she hears that above 300
> houses have been burned down tonight by the fire we saw, and
> that it is now burning down all Fish Street by London Bridge.
> So I made myself ready presently and walked to the Tower; and
> there got up upon one of the high places ... and there I did see the

houses at the end of the bridge all on fire, and an infinite great fire on this and the other side of the bridge.

So down I went, with my heart full of trouble, to the Lieutenant of the Tower, who tells me that it began this morning in the King's baker's house in Pudding Lane, and that it hath burned St Magnus's Church and most part of Fish Street already. So I rode down to the waterside and there saw a lamentable fire. Everybody endeavouring to remove their goods, and flinging into the river or bringing them into lighters that lay off; poor people staying in their houses as long as till the very fire touched them, and then running into boats, or clambering from one pair of stairs to another. And among other things, the poor pigeons, I perceive, were loath to leave their houses, but hovered about the windows and balconies, till they some of them burned their wings and fell down.

Having stayed, and in an hour's time seen the fire rage every way, and nobody to my sight endeavouring to quench it. I went next to Whitehall … and there up to the King's closet in the Chapel, where people came about me, and I did give them an account that dismayed them all, and the word was carried to the King, so I was called for, and did tell the King and the Duke of York what I saw; and that unless His Majesty did command houses to be pulled down, nothing could stop the fire. They seemed much troubled, and the King commanded me to go to my Lord Mayor from him and command him to spare no houses.

I hurried to St Paul's, and there walked along Watling Street. As well as I could, every creature coming away laden with goods to save and here and there, sick people carried away in beds. At last I met my Lord Mayor in Cannon Street, like a man spent, with a handkerchief about his neck. To the King's message he cried, like a fainting woman, 'Lord, what can I do? I am spent; people will not obey me. I have been pulling down houses, but the fire overtakes us faster that we can do it.' So he left me. And I him, and walked home; seeing people all distracted, and no manner of means used to quench the fire. The houses, too, so very thick thereabouts. And full of matter for burning, as pitch and tar in Thames Street; and warehouses of oil and wines and brandy and other things.

The indecisiveness of the Lord Mayor of London, Sir Thomas Bloodworth, in creating firebreaks caused the fire to spread at an alarming rate, destroying the wood-frame houses crammed together within the City. The conflagration gutted some 13,200 houses, eighty-seven parish churches, St Paul's Cathedral and most of the buildings in the City within the old Roman city wall. It is estimated that 70,000 homes were destroyed out of 80,000 inhabitants. On 4 September, Pepys was getting concerned with the direction of the fire and wrote in his diary:

Sir W[illiam] Pen and I to Tower Street, and there met the fire burning three or four doors beyond Mr Howell's, whose goods, poor man, his trays and dishes, shovels &c., were flung all along Tower Street in the kennels (gutters), and people working therewith from one end to the other; the fire coming on in that narrow street, on both sides, with infinite fury ...

Only now and then walking into the garden, and saw how horridly the sky looks, all on fire in the night, was enough to put us out of our wits; and, indeed, it was extremely dreadful, for it looks as if it was at us; and the whole heaven on fire. I after supper walked in the dark down Tower Street, and there saw it all on fire, at Trinity House on that side, and the Dolphin Tavern on this side, which was very near us; and the fire with extraordinary vehemence. Now begins the practice of blowing up houses in Tower Street, those next to the Tower, which did frighten people more than anything, but it stopped the fire where it was done, it bringing down the houses to the ground in the same places they stood, and them it was easy to quench what little fire was in it, though it kindled nothing almost.

W. Hewer this day went to see how his mother did, and comes late home, telling us how he hath been forced to remove her to Islington, her house in Pye Corner being burned; so that the fire is got so far that way, and all the Old Bayly (Baily), and running down Fleet Street; and St Paul's is burned, and all Cheapside.

The City was where the poor, the refugees and radicals lived. The wealthy people preferred to live away from the polluted slums within the City walls, especially after the previous year when it was ravaged by the bubonic plague. Most aristocrats and wealthy businessmen preferred to live to the west, in the Westminster district and the King's court at Whitehall. There was tension between the impoverished City and the wealthy West End. The City was a stronghold for republicanism during the Civil War, and there had been several republican uprisings during the 1660s. Many of the City authorities were of a generation who could remember Charles I's grab for absolute power that led to the Civil War. They refused offers from Charles's son for his soldiers to come and help. Even in such an emergency, the idea of unpopular Royalist troops entering the City was something the authorities would not sanction. Charles viewed the Great Fire from the Royal barge and took control from the ineffectual Lord Mayor, but already the fire was out of control. The City officials were adamant that the King should play no part in bringing control of the fire and left it to burn itself out. The author Neil Hanson wrote of the City's disdain for the Stuart House:

> He (Charles) had reason enough to hate the City that had led and financed the evolution against his father and signed his death warrant. The King was reminded of it every day, for he could never look upon the Banqueting Hall in Whitehall without recalling the events of the afternoon of 30 January 1649.

Despite being rebuffed by the City's officials, Charles and James did take part in trying to stem the spread of the fire. John Evelyn praised James for his efforts, writing in his diary:

> Labouring in person, and being present, to command, order, reward, and encourage workman; by which he shewed his affection to his people, and gained theirs.

The conflict between the Monarchy and the City rumbled on into the 1680s. When Henry Cornish and Slingsby Bethel, both Whigs, stood as joint sheriffs, Charles decided to force two men of his choosing to stand for the election. On 29 July 1680, Charles's chosen candidates lost and Cornish and Bethel were declared elected. Cornish and other members of the City sailed up to Windsor to present a petition to the King summoning parliament. Charles, in a fit of pique, refused to receive the deputation.

While the blaze consumed everything in its path, order broke down and the homeless blamed the fire on foreigners. Dutch and French immigrant groups were singled out and some became victims of lynching and beatings by the mob. By Tuesday, the fire had destroyed St Paul's Cathedral and had crossed the small Fleet River. This threatened the King's Court at Whitehall but the strong east winds died down. On the east side of the City, the garrison at the Tower used its store of gunpowder to create effective firebreaks and stopped the fire spreading.

The disaster caused overwhelming social and economic problems. The cost was partially born by a tax on coal brought into the City. Evacuation and resettlement was encouraged by Charles, who feared a rebellion from the many refugees, particularly as they had been so harshly treated. He called upon Christopher Wren, who drew up plans to build fifty-two churches in the City. Despite several ideas for a different layout, the City was reconstructed on the same street plan used before the fire. His great masterpiece was St Paul's Cathedral, which was delayed but was consecrated for use on 2 December 1697, although not totally completed until 1711.

By 1680, Wren had completed his task of building the required number of churches in the City. Another conspicuous column was built in Pudding Lane as a monument to commemorate where the fire started. Alexander Pope, a Catholic, wrote somewhat bitterly:

> Where London's column pointing at the skies/Like a tall bully, lifts its head and lies

Wren was appointed as King's Surveyor of Works in 1669 and played an important part in rebuilding the City of London. He was knighted by the King in 1673 and is responsible for other outstanding architectural jewels such as the Royal Hospital in Chelsea, the Royal Naval College in Greenwich and the south front of Hampton Court Palace, built for William and Mary. On 10 August 1675, King Charles laid the foundation stone for the construction to begin on the Royal Greenwich Observatory on the ridge in Greenwich Park overlooking the Thames.

Later that year, a devastating fire destroyed the town hall and 624 houses in Southwark on the south bank of the Thames. Nine years later, another fire followed, rendering the market town of Northampton a sea of ashes.

On 20 September 1675, in St Mary's Street and in six hours quickly consumed the town. According to a witness:

> The market place (which was a very goodly one), the stately church of Allhallows, two other parish churches and above three-fourth parts of the whole town was consumed and laid in ashes.

As with the City of London, Northampton was rebuilt with stone and bricks. Daniel Defoe visited the town in 1724 and described it as:

> The handsomest and best built town in all this part of England … finely built with brick and stone, and the streets made spacious and wide.

Chapter 3

The Popish Plot

The Roman Catholic religion was set against a background of the English Reformation of 1533, when King Henry VIII sought an annulment of his marriage to Catherine of Aragon to marry Anne Boleyn. The refusal of the Pope to grant a divorce led to Henry breaking away from Rome and establishing the Protestant Church of England. The subsequent development of a strong anti-Catholic sentiment among the mostly Protestant population of England lasted for over 150 years.

Between 1678 and 1681, a bogus anti-Catholic plot was hatched by a thoroughly unpleasant individual, Titus Oates. Born in 1649, he was the son of a schoolmaster at Oakham and was expelled from Merchant Taylors School in London. The Popish Plot was the brainchild of Rutland-born Titus Oates, a homosexual, tub-thumping dissenting preacher, who was regarded by his Cambridge University tutor as 'a great dunce, ran into debt; and, being sent away for want of money, never took a degree'. Pretending to have a degree, Oates still managed to obtain a licence to preach from the Bishop of London and he became a priest in 1670. His appearance was described as having:

> The speech of the gutter, and a strident and sing-song voice, so that he seemed to wail rather than speak. His brow is low, his eyes small and sunk deep in his head; his face was flat, compressed in the middle so as to look like a dish or discus; on each side were prominent ruddy cheeks, his nose was snub, his mouth in the very centre of his face, for his chin was almost equal in size to the rest of his face. His head scarcely protruded from his body and was bowed towards his chest.

He became a curate at Sandhurst in Surrey, where he defamed a local schoolmaster, who brought charges against him of perjury. He managed to escape imprisonment and fled to London. In March 1673, he was appointed as curate to the village of Bobbing in Kent. He was soon removed after complaints about his drunkenness and unorthodox religious opinions. He returned to his father's home in Hastings, where he soon accused his father's enemy, William Parker, of sodomy. Parker appeared before the Privy Council, which exonerated him and Oates was fined £1,000 in damages. Oates quickly disappeared and, in 1675, was assigned as chaplain on HMS *Adventure* which was bound for Tangiers. On his return to London, he was accused of buggery, which was a capital offence, but was spared because of his clerical status and dismissed in 1676 from the Royal Navy. The following year, he was arrested in London to face trial for the outstanding 1675 perjury charges. With the help of an actor friend, he joined the Catholic household of the 7th Duke of Norfolk as an Anglican chaplain to those members who were Protestants. This was a short-lived appointment in which he infuriated his employers and was dismissed.

In 1677, he was received into the Catholic Church and, although a new Catholic, he could not read Latin. Perversely, he co-wrote with Israel Tonge, an unhinged man, a series of anti-Catholic pamphlets but, despite this strange reversal of faith, he was sent to study at the Jesuit house in St Omer, in France, and the Royal English College in Valladolid, Spain. By 1678, he was expelled for blasphemy and anti-monarchy. He returned to England with fictitious evidence that convinced gullible officials of Catholic plots. In what became known as the Popish Plot, he accused Jesuits of plotting to assassinate King Charles II. He later explained that he joined the Catholics to discover the secrets of the Jesuits. Charles learned of this alleged plot against his life, but was unimpressed by Oates. Instead he handed the matter over to one of his ministers, Thomas, Earl of Danby, who had Oates questioned by the Privy Council. Oates furnished the Council with forty-three allegations against various Catholic members, including 541 Jesuits and many nobles. He accused Sir George Wakeman, Queen Catherine of Braganza's doctor, and Edward Colman, the secretary of James's wife, Mary Beatrice, Duchess of York. Wakeman was acquitted but Colman had corresponded with Father Ferrier, the confessor to Louis XIV, and this was enough to condemn him. There was no proof of any conspiracy against the King, except the perjured testimony of Oates and his confederate, William Beloe. The jury believed that Colman must have been guilty of treason and found him guilty. On 3 December 1678, Colman was taken to Tyburn, where he faced the terrible fate of being hanged, drawn and quartered.

Others whom Oates accused included Dr William Fogerty, Archbishop Peter Talbot of Dublin, 1st Baron John Belasyse and Samuel Pepys. With Danby's help, the list grew to eighty-one accusations, which included those who had helped Oates in the past. A company of soldiers was given to Oates so he could arrest those he had accused. On September 1678, Oates and Israel Tonge swore an affidavit to an Anglican magistrate, Sir Edmund Berry Godfrey, detailing their accusations. Although Godfrey accepted Oates's deposition, he was not entirely convinced of its contents.

On 17 October 1678, a baker and a farmer spotted a pair of gloves and a walking stick on the waste ground on the south side of Primrose Hill. Searching, they found the body of Sir Edmund Godfrey in a ditch. His death rapidly became a *cause celebre* and was conveniently blamed on the Catholic plotters. He had been strangled and stabbed with his own sword. In his *History*, the Bishop of Salisbury, Gilbert Burnet wrote:

> His body was found in a ditch, about a mile out of town, near St Pancreas Church. His sword was thrust through him. But no blood was on his clothes, or about him. His shoes were clean. His money was in his pocket. But nothing was about his neck and a mark was all round it, an inch broad, which showed he was strangled. His breast was likewise all over marked with bruises: and his neck was broken ... There were many drops of white wax-lights on his breeches, which he never used himself. And since only persons of quality, or Priests, use those lights, this made all people conclude in whose hands he must have been.

One of the unlikely suspects of the Popish Plot was Samuel Pepys. By then he had spent six years at the Navy Office working with efficiency, rooting out corruption and helping to build ships. In 1678, Lord Shaftsbury, who disliked the diarist, implicated Pepys in the mysterious murder of Sir Edmund Berry Godfrey. Pepys was able to produce proof that had rock-solid alibi. Shaftsbury then accused Pepys's clerk, Samuel Atkins, who was imprisoned but, thanks to Pepys, was able to furnish a firm alibi. Six months later, Pepys's enemies brought into England a criminal and blackmailer named John Scott. He was also a map-maker and is likely to have sold maps of the south coast of England to the French. Pepys tried to have Scott arrested for Godfrey's murder. This was rather tenuous on Pepys' part as he thought he saw Scott disguised as a Jesuit at Somerset House. In retaliation, Scott hurled a series of accusations at Pepys, who was not a Catholic, but it still did not prevent him being imprisoned in the Tower on the absurd charge of treason. Scott had travelled from Long Island, New York, and ended up in Paris where, using his trickery, he persuaded the French that he was a cartographer. He also had support from the Exclusionists, which included Shaftsbury. Pepys was further charged of popery by his dismissed butler, who he had caught in bed with his favourite maid. The butler was on his deathbed and anxious to absolve his conscience by withdrawing his accusation. This deathbed confession did little for Pepys, incarcerated in the Tower. After several weeks furiously writing to those men who would support him, he was released on bail but then re-arrested and sent to Marshalsea Prison. For two years he vehemently denied any part in Godfrey's murder or any other crime. Scott, meanwhile, was regarded as a likely witness and was able to travel to France and the Netherlands. Pepys wrote of Scott:

> He is a fellow who I thank God is not of my acquaintance, but he is so despicable a vile reputation in all places where he has lived that a real criminal would be fortunate to suffer by his means.

Then Pepys had a piece of luck. Scott got into an altercation with a cab driver, John George Butler, used his sword to stab him and killed him. Nor bothering to hang around and be arrested, Scott fled to France and disappeared from justice. Fortunately for Pepys, Charles had dissolved Parliament and prevented a new one being formed for another eighteen months. Pepys was released and returned to being Secretary to the Navy.

The Godfrey murder was not resolved until 21 December when Miles Prance, a Catholic servant to Catherine of Braganza, was arrested and taken to Newgate prison. He was confined to the coldest cell, 'Little Ease', where he was put in chains. He was denied a fire in the bitter winter weather, and nearly froze to death. The government was so keen to make him confess that it even threatened him with the rack, which had been illegal for more than fifty years. Probably the threat of torture loosened Prance's mouth, for he owned up to the murder. He said that the main instigators were Thomas

Gooden, head of the secular English clergy, and two Irish priests named Kelly and Fitzgerald. They had witnessed Godfrey's murder in the court-yard of Somerset House, where he had been strangled and his neck broken. Prance named the killers as Robert Green, Henry Berry and Lawrence Hill, who were promptly arrested. Godfrey's body had been taken to Hampstead and flung in a ditch on Primrose Hill. He also appears to have been impaled on his own sword. Prance seemed a credible witness, although the evidence was not plausible. To Oates this was a murder that he could exploit and he launched a public campaign against the Papists, alleging that the Jesuits had killed the magistrate.

The three men were sentenced to death and, on 5 February 1679, they were hanged on what became known as 'Greenberry Hill' named after Green, Berry and Hill. Later, Prance's story was discredited; he pleaded guilty to perjury and had let three innocent men go to their deaths. When James came to the throne in 1685, Prance was again put on trial for his part in the Rye House Plot. He was found guilty of perjury, ordered to stand in the pillory and to be whipped. His patroness, the Dowager Queen Catherine, pleaded that the last of these two punishments should be withdrawn as he had returned to the Catholic faith. He confessed to the false testimony against the three innocent men and, in 1688, he fled to France.

Edmund Godfrey had stipulated in his will that he should have a pauper's burial. Instead, he received an unofficial state funeral attended by thousands of mourners. Commemorative daggers were made with the legend 'Momento Godfrey, 12 October 1678' along the blade. He had been transformed into a Protestant martyr alongside Cranmer, Latimer and Ridley. His funeral and sermons made him briefly popular and it was less to investigate the Popish Plot than to exclude James, Duke of York, from succeeding to the Crown. On 2 November, Anthony Ashley-Cooper, the Earl of Shaftsbury, declared in the Commons that James should be removed from the King's presence, which received considerable support. The next day it was agreed that James would not attend the Privy Council and its committees. The Commons moved to introduce a new Test Act that would exclude the Catholics, including James, from the Court as well as Parliament. Opposition from the Lords and pressure from Charles and James saw that James was exempted from the Bill, which was passed by just two votes.

Oates was riding on the crest of a wave and there was no stopping him with his baseless accusations. During the early 1950s in America, Senator

Joe McCarthy fuelled fears of widespread Communist subversion. His reign was brief but has left the term McCarthyism, broadly meaning demagogic and unsubstantiated accusations, as well as public attacks on the character or patriotism of political opponents. It was very reminiscent of the machinations of Titus Oates.

On 24 November 1678, buoyed by his popular success, Oates claimed that Catherine of Braganza was working with Charles's physician to poison her husband. The King interrogated Oates and caught him out on a number of falsehoods, including an interview Oates had with the Regent of Spain, Don Juan, in Madrid. Charles had met Don Juan and Oates's hopelessly inaccurate description of his appearance convinced the King that he had never seen him. Charles ordered Oates's arrest but a few days later, with the threat of a constitutional crisis, Parliament was forced to release him. Incredibly, he later received a state apartment in Whitehall with an annual allowance of £1,200. As the philosopher David Hume pointed out, in this fevered atmosphere, 'Parliaments are hot, and the Juries were easy in this prosecution.'

In 1678, the Catholic Lord William Stafford was implicated by Oates and sent to the Tower Of London on 31 October, along with four other Catholic peers; Earl of Powis, Lord Arundell, Lord Belasyse and Lord Petre. Anti-Catholic feelings were at their height in 1680, when Stafford was put on trial in November for impeachment. Oates presented evidence against Stafford, who said he had seen a document from the Pope naming Stafford as a conspirator. Stephen Dugdale, who had perjured himself on numerous occasions by giving false evidence against men who would go to their deaths on the scaffold, testified that Stafford had paid him £500 to kill the King. A third witness, Edward Tuberville, said he had visited Stafford in Paris and also had been asked to kill Charles.

Stafford was denied counsel and forced to conduct his own defence, furnishing witnesses who refuted the outrageous allegations. One such witness, Richard Gerard, was arrested before the trial and, unable to defend Stafford, died in jail. The Oates's prosecution had already made up its mind and Stafford was convicted. He was beheaded on 29 December 1680 on Tower Hill.

Oates was the man of the moment and basked in his anti-Catholic publicity. He even applied to the College of Arms to furnish him with a coat of arms. It was also rumoured that he would marry the daughter of

Anthony Ashley-Cooper, 1st Earl of Shaftsbury, one of the members of the *cabal*. By 1681, his self-publicity was running out of steam. After nearly three years and the execution of fifteen innocent men, public opinion was turning against him. His final high-profile victim was the Catholic Archbishop of Armagh, Oliver Plunkett. He presented numerous pleas for mercy but Charles considered it was too politically dangerous to spare him. Even Louis XIV pleaded for the execution to be stopped but Charles, who knew Plunkett to be innocent, felt unable to find any means of preventing Parliament from passing a series of repressive edicts against Catholics. Lord Essex belatedly pleaded for Plunkett's life, to which Charles turned on him, saying:

> His blood be on your head – you could have saved him but would not. I would have saved him and dare not.

Plunkett was hanged, drawn and quartered at Tyburn on 1 July 1681; the last Catholic martyr to die in England.

Oates exploited the Protestant fear of Roman Catholicism to the extent that the government gave him complete judicial power. From 1679 to 1681, the opposition to the Crown appeared to be very strong and the Whigs secured majorities in the Commons for the Exclusion Bills in October 1680, January 1681 and March 1681. William Scroggs, the Lord Chief Justice of England and Wales, began to declare more people innocent and the backlash against Oates turned into an avalanche. On 31 August 1681, Oates was told to leave his apartments but refused. Feeling he could do no wrong, he even denounced Charles and his Catholic brother, James, until he was arrested for sedition. He was fined £100,000 and imprisoned for three years. Suddenly Oates's life of Catholic accusations collapsed.

When James acceded to the throne in 1685, he had Oates retried for perjury. The presiding judge was the notorious George Jeffreys and he handed Oates a particularly severe sentence. He was stripped of his clerical dress, imprisoned for life and sentenced to be 'whipped through the streets of London five days a year for the remainder of his life'. Oates was taken from his cell wearing a hat, on which was printed, 'Titus Oates, convicted upon full evidence of two horrid perjuries'. He was put in the pillory at the gate of Westminster Hall, now New Palace Yard, where passers-by would pelt him with eggs, excrement and rotten vegetables. This continued the following day until on the third day he was stripped, tied to a cart and whipped from Aldgate to Newgate. The flogging resumed the next day from Newgate to Aldgate. Short of execution, his penalty was so severe that it was planned to kill Oates by ill treatment. Somehow he managed to survive his three-year imprisonment until William and Mary came to the throne, when he was released. According to the journalist and printer, Henry Muddiman:

> He had seen Titus Oates, very fat and trim, walking through St James's Park, on his way to interview William of Orange. Oates had been illegally released but had taken up residence in Axe Yard, remaining there for several years in order to be near the House of Commons, and the best account of his friends at this time has been left to us by another cheat and imposter, William Fuller, who was Oates's lodger two years later on.

William Fuller was a plausible conman who made the most outrageous accusations. After 1688, Fuller associated with the gullible Mary Beatrice and the Jacobites, while gaining favour with Prince William of Orange. He was a tenant of Oates, but debt and falsifying Jacobite plots saw him imprisoned. In 1692, the House of Commons declared that 'he was an imposter, cheat and false witness' for having revived the story that Mary Beatrice had falsely given birth to a Catholic heir to the throne. Unable to prove any of the stories he had written, he was put in a pillory, whipped and fined. He continued his nefarious ways until old age. Once again he was imprisoned in Newgate prison, where he died in 1720. Henry Muddiman continued:

> These friends of Oates were, first and foremost, John Tutchin and John Arnold of Llanvihangel Crucorney, the priest hunter, Member of Parliament for Monmouth in the last three Parliaments of Charles II, as well as in the Convention; and Aaron Smith, the solicitor, of Rye House Plot fame. Arnold was, Lord Ailesbury writes, 'a vile fellow who cut his own throat in 1679, when Oates's plot was failing, in order to give verisimilitude to his tale that he had been set upon by Papists and thus give fresh life to the plot'. But we are chiefly concerned with Tutchin, who was probably one of Oates's lodgers, and in any case was continually in and out of Oates's house … He himself said his birth-place was London, and

since he was expelled from a school at Stepney for theft, his state-
ment was probably accurate ... his marriage at St John's, Coleman
Street, upon 30 September 1686 to Elizabeth, daughter of John
Hicks, the Nonconformist minister ...

Much to William III's eternal disgrace, Oates was pardoned and given a
pension of £260 a year. The rest of his life was marked with lawsuits, debt
and fruitless intrigue. He entered the Baptist Church but his ranting was too
much for the authorities and he was expelled. On 12 July 1705, he died in
London, by then an obscure and forgotten figure.

Chapter 4

The Rye House Plot and Other Conspiracies

The Rye House Plot foreshadowed the bloody rebellions of Monmouth and Argyll and the bloodless Glorious Revolution. The plot involved the assassination of the Royal brothers, Charles and James, as they returned from the horse racing at Newmarket. The fact that it failed with no one getting killed led to a mass scramble for the safety of the Netherlands. According to Forde Grey, later the Earl of Tankerville, who wrote a lengthy confession that was later published in book *The Secret History of the Rye House Plot and of the Monmouth Rebellion*, the main plotters were the Duke of Monmouth, the Earl of Essex, Lord Shaftsbury, Lord William Russell, Sir Thomas Armstrong, Algernon Sidney, Robert Ferguson and Lord Forde Grey. There were about thirty-two other conspirators, who discussed the means to rid the country of Charles and his openly Roman Catholic brother, James. They secretly met at Thanet House and the Monmouth residence in Soho Square, while several other London houses were used during 1682.

They met with a rebellion in mind rather than an assassination. There were discussions around Monmouth of an uprising in September 1682, but it never came to fruition. A group known as the Council of Six pursued the struggle to control the City of London rather than kill the Royal brothers. The actual assassination plot was masterminded by Robert West, a lawyer from the Middle Temple and a Green Ribbon Club member. His associates were Aaron Smith, John Ayloffe, Christopher Battiscombe and Israel Hayes. The philosopher John Locke arranged a safe house for West in Oxford. Richard Rumbold was also implicated as he purchased the arms. During the spring of 1683, there were further contacts between Monmouth's party and West's group about drafting a manifesto and there were disagreements over which a republican or a monarchical constitution should be accepted.

The plan had been bandied about for some years among the Whigs and Dissenters, but when the Duke of Monmouth became involved, despite the high office accolades his father had bestowed on him, he was willing to remove his uncle James and take the crown for himself. The government cracked down on this plot, not because it led anywhere but because it failed in its intention to remove Charles and James. There was a strong opposition to the Stuart monarchy during this fraught decade, with a declining Charles and the prospect of a Catholic James taking the throne.

On 1 April 1683, a plot was put in motion to kill the two Royal brothers as they returned from Newmarket. Charles spent seven weeks each year in the town, watching the racing and meeting his many mistresses. On Thursday evening, 22 March, a fire broke out in stables near St Mary's Church, which put pay to the racing. Charles and James, with their entourage, left early, so avoiding the assassination attempt at Rye House. They stayed at Cheveley Park Stud on the outskirts of Newmarket and made their leisurely way back to Whitehall. An extremist Whig group wanted to re-establish a republican government of the Cromwellian style but, due to a major fire in which half of Newmarket was burned to the ground, it was abandoned. Instead the Rye House Plot went ahead.

Charles and James's coach approached a narrow road close to Rye House. The plan was to conceal men in the grounds of the house and ambush the royal coach as it passed by along the narrow road. With good cover, a small force would easily accomplish their goal and disappear quickly. Rye House was a fortified medieval mansion surrounded by a moat and leased to a republican and Civil War veteran, Richard Rumbold. According to Bishop Gilbert Burnet, in an interview with the old Cromwellian soldier, he told him that:

> He had a farm near Hodsden (Hoddesdon in Hertfordshire) in the way to Newmarket. And there was a moat cast round his house, through which the King sometimes passed in his way thither. He said, once the coach went through quite alone, without any of the guards about it; and that, if he had laid anything cross the way to have stopped the coach but a minute, he could have shot them both, and have rode away through the grounds that he knew so well that it should not have been possible to have followed him.

A total of thirty-six plotters were rounded up; twelve of them were put to death and the rest were imprisoned. The leaders, William Lord Russell and Algernon Sidney, were hanged, drawn and quartered because it had been a treasonable offence. There was only one female put on trial, who was named as Elizabeth Gaunt, and she was treated to a show trial. She was on the fringe of the conspiracy and, according to Bishop Burnet, she spent 'her life in acts of charity, visiting the gaols and looking after the poor of what persuasion so ever they were'. She was sentenced to be burnt at the stake, the last woman executed for a political crime in England. The philosopher David Hume wrote that James Burton escaped to Holland but after his arrest in 1685 he implicated Gaunt, who had helped him escape, in order to secure his freedom. Hume wrote:

> He received a pardon as a recompense for his treachery and she was burnt alive for her charity.

Ten weeks later, Josiah Keeling, a Baptist, supplied information about the Rye House Plot, in the hope that it would bring about an end to the persecution of religious dissenters. Keeling turned informer and made contact with Secretary of State Sir Leoline Jenkins to reveal details about the intended assassination, in which he played a minor role. Keeling's testimony was used at the trials of Thomas Walcott, Charles Bateman and Algernon Sidney. The incriminated conspirators thought it best to confess, although none had committed murder, in the hope that they would be pardoned. The last charge was in 1685, when Bateman was hanged, drawn and quartered. Keeling was pardoned, paid £500 and given a position in the victualling office on Tower Hill, but he lost the latter with the fall of James II in 1688.

On 13 July 1683, John Evelyn wrote of a dreadful event in his diary:

> I was visiting Sir Thomas Yarbrow and Lady in Covent Garden, that astonishing news of the Earl of Essex having cut his own throat was brought to us, having now been but three days prisoner in the Tower. And this happening on the very day and instant that Lord Russell was on his trial, and had sentence of death: This accident exceedingly amazed me, my Lord Essex being so well known by me to be a person of so sober and

religious deportment, so well at his ease, so much obliged to the King.

It is certain the King and Duke were at the Tower and passed by his window about the same time this morning, when My Lord asking for a razor, he shut himself into a closet, and perpetrated the horrid act. It was wondered yet by somehow it was possible he should do it, in the manner he was found; for the wound was so deep and wide, as it were, which cut through the gullet, wind-pipe and both the jugulars, it reached to the very vertebrae of the neck, so as the head held to it by very little skin as it were, which tacked it from being quite off.

William Howard, 3rd Baron Howard of Escrick, was another conspirator who easily gave way at his interrogation and informed on William Russell, 1st Viscount Stafford. He gave accounts of meetings held at John Hampden's and Russell's houses, which led to Russell's conviction. He also implicated Henry Booth, 1st Earl of Warrington, who was tried by his fellow peers and was pardoned. According to John Evelyn, Howard was one of the most detested and despised men of his age and referred to as 'that monster of a man'.

Another idea was to support Archibald Campbell, 9th Earl of Argyll, in a military rebellion in Scotland, which turned out to have little support. In 1683, Argyll travelled to the Netherlands, leaving his agent, Abraham Holmes, a fanatical Anabaptist, in London. Holmes was implicated in the Rye House Plot, among many such conspiracies in which he was involved. Holmes would visit the Cock & Bottle in Aldersgate, collecting notes and passing on correspondence between Argyll and London's Whig conspirators as they finalised the details of the Rye House Plot. Government sources learned of the plot by intercepting letters addressed to a 'Master West' and delivered to 'Mr. Staple's Southwark Coffee House' in Bartholomew Lane, half-a-mile from St Paul's. When questioned by the authorities, Leonard Staples, the coffee house's proprietor, explained that he accepted the delivery of the letters, which Holmes 'constantly called for and paid for'. He claimed never to have seen Mr West, the addressee. This is hardly surprising, as Mr West was an alias employed by Holmes. Another of Holmes's identities was 'Peter Harvie', a supposed linen weaver, whose letters (actually from the Countess of Argyll) were addressed to a cider seller in Bow Churchyard and passed on to the Netherlands in a similar manner. Holmes's job was to collect these letters and then send them on to other agents of Argyll and Monmouth in the Low Countries. The correspondence was written using a simple cipher, with letters and words substituted for numbers. These ciphers were further disguised through pseudonyms: 'brand' stood for Scotland, 'birch' England, and there were disguised references to dubious 'parcels of goods' that were hoped would 'please the merchants'. Holmes was arrested and subjected to lengthy interrogation in which the King took a close interest: the King told Holmes:

> You know this business concerns me and the safety of my three kingdoms, I am resolved to carry it on very vigorously, therefore say the truth.

Under examination, Holmes freely divulged much of the information contained in the letters (although he must have suspected that the alphabetic cipher had already been worked out – both the letters and the keys to decipher them had been in his possession). Holmes admitted that the letters were conveyed to and from the Netherlands aboard the *Success*, a merchant ship out of Colchester, and confessed that he was engaged in Argyll's scheme to raise £10,000 in England to pay for weapons to use in armed rebellion. He acknowledged that the 'parcel of goods' referred to were political writings, aimed at stirring sedition among the King's subjects. Holmes, however, refused to reveal the identities of any persons referred to in the letters who had donated money to Argyll's cause.

Holmes was committed to the Gatehouse prison for high treason. While there, he divulged more information to the authorities, including the use of his alias 'Harvie'. Whether such admissions softened the Crown's attitude toward him is unclear. It is possible they thought Holmes was more useful to them if he were free to act as Argyll's agent, sending and receiving correspondence that they were confident they could intercept and decipher. It is still uncertain whether Holmes was released or if he affected an escape, but by 1684 he was in the Netherlands, where he was joined from London by his son, Blake, and they became part of the group of dissenters and Whigs that had gathered around Argyll and Monmouth.

One of the plotters who exiled himself to Bremen in 1683 was Sir William Waller, the son of Sir William Waller, the famous Civil War general, who became the leader of a group of political exiles. The English ambassador said that he was called 'the governor' and 'They style Waller, by way of commendation, a second Cromwell'. Waller accompanied William of Orange to England in the Glorious Revolution but William chose to overlook him in his government. He died in poverty in 1699.

Chapter 5

James's Failed Reign

Triggered by the Popish Plot in 1681, the Exclusion Bill was introduced in the House of Commons, which effectively prevented James from becoming the next king. Charles managed to outmanoeuvre his opponents and dissolved the Oxford Parliament, which was also known as the Third Exclusion Parliament. It met for one week in the former Royalist stronghold, which was Charles I's capital during the Civil War, and, despite popular support for the Bill, it was quashed by Charles, who dissolved Parliament. Charles proved to be a shrewd politician but was defeated by Parliament, who introduced two Test Acts banning Roman Catholics from taking office.

In 1682, James returned to England, having been exiled in Brussels and Edinburgh. He assumed the position of Lord High Admiral in the Royal Navy but Charles forbade his brother from fighting. Although James was forthright, he was also stupid and 'managed affairs, but with great haughtiness'. In February 1685, Charles suffered a stroke while shaving. Burnet wrote that:

> The King, who seemed all the while to be in great confusion, fell down all of a sudden in a fit like an apoplexy: He looked black. And his eyes turned in his head.

James was at his brother's bedside and arranged for a Catholic priest, John Huddleston, to administer the Sacraments. Coincidentally, it was Huddleston who helped Charles escape from the battlefield at Worcester in 1650. Charles said that Huddleston had saved his life twice; first his body and then his soul. Charles lingered until he died on 6 February 1685, when his younger brother ascended the throne as James II.

Living an impoverished exile in France during the 1650s, James served under one of the greatest military commanders of the age, Henri de La Tour d'Auvergnem, Viscount de Turenne. He fought at the siege of Arras in 1654 and the defensives of Merdyck and Nieuport. James led the cavalry and fought with distinction at the Battle of the Dunes, or the Battle of Dunkirk, in 1658, eliciting praise from Prince Louis Condè:

> If ever there was a Man of the World without fear, it was the Duke of York.

Sadly, as he grew older, his military prowess deserted him. James converted to Roman Catholicism in 1668 but the expected change of religion when he succeeded as monarch did not happen immediately. In fact, the first year of his succession was surprisingly peaceful. He declared before the Privy Council and the new Parliament made up of Tories that he would reassure them in respect of law, of property and of religion:

> I shall make it my endeavour to preserve this government both in church and state as it is by the law established. I know the principles of the Church of England are for the monarchy and the members of it have shown themselves good and loyal subjects; therefore I shall always take care to defend and support it. I know too that the laws of England are sufficient to make the king a great monarch as I can wish; and as I shall never depart from the rights and prerogative of the crown, so I shall never invade any man's property.

Parliament was strongly Royalist and Protestant but determined to give James the benefit of the doubt and even voted him a generous income. For James, his intention was precisely opposite, for he vowed he would replace the Anglicans with Catholics in Parliament, the Privy Council, the ecclesiastical commission, the judiciary and the officers in the standing army. This shift in the King's declaration after a few months of his reign upset the Protestants and changed the mood in the country considerably. James would have an uphill battle to convert the citizens from Protestant to Catholic, for by 1680, Catholics formed just 1.1 per cent of the English population, while in Scotland it was even lower.

Parliament refused to repeal the Test Act, which had excluded Catholics from public office. James got around this by prevailing on the Catholic judiciary to allow him to override the Act whenever he wished. Parliament soon realised that James, far from being their friend, was their mortal enemy. An uncoordinated alliance with opposition to James had been formed. There were former soldiers of Cromwell's New Army, now mostly in their late thirties and forties, and religious groups that had been persecuted under the Act of Uniformity discouraging the restoration of the Anglican Church. There were also Whig and political opposition groups that had been deprived of their parliamentary seats. Finally, there was staunchly republican element from the Interregnum that wanted the monarchy removed, although, despite the opposition, there was little co-operation between the disparate groups. The only hope was that the popular Duke of Monmouth would have a unifying influence.

During the late 1650s, James had been attracted to Anne Hyde, the daughter of Edward Hyde, the Earl of Clarendon, soon to be the Lord Chancellor. Soon Lord Clarendon would be driven from power and forced into exile in the Netherlands. Gilbert Burnet wrote of James's father-in-law:

> Clarendon's enemies – notably Henry Bennett, Earl of Arlington, and George Villiers, Duke of Buckingham – were determined to ensure he did not return from exile and resume power. They were eager to drive from office and from the court all who might support Clarendon's return, among whom James and Anne were the most conspicuous. To this end they sought to make Charles jealous of his brother's influence and ambitions and to supplant him from the position as heir presumptive. One possibility was that Charles might vest the succession in his son James Scott, Duke of Monmouth, but there was no doubt that Monmouth was illegitimate, so a more promising expedient seemed to be for Charles to divorce the Queen on the grounds of sterility.

A changed political landscape would bring fresh perils, culminating in the Glorious Revolution. With the collapse of the Interregnum, Charles returned from exile, landing at Dover on 25 May 1660. About this time, Anne Hyde discovered that she was pregnant, and James pestered his brother until he relented and gave permission for them to marry. In a private ceremony on 3 September, the couple were wed, but it was not until 20 December that James acknowledged Anne as his wife. On 22 October she gave birth to a son. She had a difficult time at court and was sneered at for being a commoner.

She behaved herself with courage and dignity, but James's philandering made Anne take to comfort eating and she became increasingly large. Over the next eleven years Anne Hyde gave birth to seven children. None of the sons survived, but the couple's eldest daughter, Mary, and her younger sister, Anne, were Protestants and both grew up to be monarchs.

Hatred of popery reached new heights among Protestants, which was fanned by the succession of James II. Nell Gwyn called James, 'Dismal Jimmy'. He was pious, lustful, arrogant and a poor monarch. An avowed Catholic, he was scarred by smallpox and afflicted by a stutter. Unlike his older, more amenable brother, he was teased by his ugly mistress, Catherine Sedley, who at the court of George I met the mistresses of Charles II and William III. She had an acerbic wit and exclaimed to Louise de Kerouaille and Elizabeth Hamilton:

> God! Who would have thought that we three whores should meet here?

Previously she had said, 'It cannot be my beauty, for he must see that I have none; and it cannot be my wit, for he has not enough himself to know that I have any.'

James also had another mistress, Arabella, sister of John Churchill, who was described as 'a tall creature, pale-faced and nothing but skin and bone'. In Thomas Macaulay's words, her family's feeling about Arabella's seduction of James came as remarkable as it 'seemed to have been a joyful surprise that so plain a girl had attained such high preferment'. Charles said the ugly mistresses must be a penance imposed by his brother's confessor.

In early 1669, James contacted and became friendly with Joseph Simons, a controversial Jesuit Provincial attached to the Court. By 1672, James had converted to the Catholic faith, something that would be his undoing. He did continue to attend the Church of England services for another four years. In 1676, the Pope acknowledged his conversion. With the death of Anne Hyde, James took a second wife, the fifteen-year-old Catholic Mary Beatrice of Modena. They were married by proxy in a Roman Catholic ceremony on 20 September 1673 and it was not until 21 November that Mary arrived in England. With his brother's death in February 1685, James wanted a quick coronation on 23 April and was crowned with Mary Beatrice at Westminster Abbey.

The new Parliament was assembled in May and was given the name 'Loyal Parliament', which was initially favourable to the new king. The Catholics made up no more than one-fiftieth of the English population but the filling of important positions upset the balance. As the year passed, James allowed Roman Catholics to occupy the highest offices in England, which rankled with the Anglicans. The Earl of Sunderland replaced office-holders at court with Catholics and the King began to lose the confidence of his Tory supporters.

In May 1686, James sought to obtain a ruling from the English common law courts that he had the power to dispense with the Acts of Parliament. He dismissed judges who disagreed with him, as well as the Solicitor General, and elevated enough judges to rule in the King's favour. On 12 February 1687, the Declaration of Indulgence was issued in Scotland. On 4 April 1687, James issued the Declaration of Indulgence, also known as the Declaration for Liberty of Conscience, in which he did away with the law that punished Catholics and Dissenters. It was published that April, and James ordered that it should be read in every church, starting in London on 20 and 27 May, then on 3 and 10 June in all parts of the country.

In August 1687, William of Orange sensed there was popular discontent with James's government and sent his half-uncle, William Nassau de Zuylestein, to England to console Mary Beatrice of her mother's death. In fact, he had gone to spy the mood of the English population. The following summer de Zuylestein was sent as envoy to congratulate Mary Beatrice on the birth of her son, James Francis Edward. He wrote a letter to William giving an account of London's population being sceptical of the manner in which the birth was broadcast.

James frequently made things worse for himself by his inability to accept opposition. In April, he ordered the fellows of Oxford's Magdalene College to elect Anthony Farmer, widely believed to be a Catholic, as President. As he was ineligible under college statues, he was rejected. This caused a rift between the King and the Anglican establishment that contributed to the Glorious Revolution. The writer, Thomas Macaulay, described Farmer as a 'lascivious drunk and womaniser who preferred to be down at the local tavern along the River Thames near Oxford'. In his place, the academics voted in Dr John Hough, a popular choice with the fellows, and an opponent of Catholicism and absolutism. William Levett, President of the College, declared of Farmer:

Frequent complaints were brought to me by some of the masters that he raised quarrels and differences among them; that he often occasioned disturbances, and was a troublesome and unpeaceable humour.

James was outraged that his appointment had been overruled and demanded that the fellows apologise for 'defying him'. When they refused, he had them replaced with Catholics. William Sancroft, the Archbishop of Canterbury, felt he could not remain silent in what he saw as James's attempts to undermine the Anglican Church. On 13 May 1688, together with the bishops Jonathan Trelawney of Bristol, William Francis Lloyd of St Asaph, Francis Turner of Ely, Thomas White of Peterborough, Thomas Ken of Bath and Wells and John Lake of Chichester, they sent a petition asking to be excused from reading the Declaration from the pulpit. Those not present but who approved this course of action were the bishops of Winchester, Gloucester and Norwich. They included their support for fellow Protestants provided that it was settled by Parliament, not Royal Prerogative.

On 20 May, only seven churches in London read the Declaration, with the congregation walking out in at least three of them. In the country, only 200 out of 9,000 churches complied and from James's point of view it was an unmitigated disaster. The fact the opposition was led by the Archbishop of Canterbury, who believed that the Declaration was unconstitutional, further infuriated James. He had the seven bishops indicted for seditious libel. On 18 May they were arrested and taken down the Thames to the Tower of London to await trial. They had to wait until 29 June before they were taken from the Tower to the King's Bench, Westminster Hall, to face charges of sedition. James was confident of victory and had stuffed the judiciary over the past three years with Catholic loyalists. However, the four presiding judges included Powell and Holloway, who favoured the bishops; Lord Chief Justice Wright was unusually moderate, and only the Catholic Sir Richard Allibond was hostile. Lawyers for the bishops argued their petition simply confirmed a ruling established by Parliament and thus could not be considered a libel. In their summing up for the jury, three judges refused to comment on whether James was entitled to use his dispensing power and focused on the issue of libel. On 30 June, three judges voted in favour of the bishops, who were acquitted of all charges.

The acquittal resulted in wild celebrations throughout London, much to James's annoyance. The only one to disagree was, who tried to procure the bishops' conviction. He even referred to it later when he instructed a Croydon jury to speak against the verdict.

Sometime in September 1687, Mary Beatrice announced she was pregnant. Princess Anne, Mary's sister, wrote that their stepmother's belly, or rather, lack of it, was in fact 'a false belly'. It was not until 10 June 1688 that Mary Beatrice produced a male heir and raised the prospect of a Catholic succession. With the country set against James and his Declaration, it seemed opportune for his wife to produce such an heir. According to Protestants, a substitute was brought into the birth chamber in a warming pan and introduced as the Catholic Prince of Wales. Another theory was that the child was from Richard Talbot, Earl of Tyrconnel and a 'Mrs Gray', who was immediately sent to a convent in Paris, from where she escaped. She was captured and maybe killed by the Jesuits, who were eager for an English Catholic heir. Although this conspiracy theory is almost certain to be false, it does muddy the water as to who would be the next heir. The small stuffy birth room was filled with Jesuits, who surrounded the cradle of their future king. The child was named James Francis Edward Stuart, later to be called the Old Pretender. It was an unexpected birth and one that would complicate the succession into the new century. Mary Beatrice had suffered from gynaecological problems leading to her inability to give birth and the arrival of a healthy male heir answered her prayers, albeit in a very doubtful method. James was thought to be impotent due to venereal disease, so the birth was widely greeted with scepticism by the population. A pamphlet circulated in 1688 entitled *An Account of the Reasons of the Nobility and Gentry's Invitation of His Highness the Prince of Orange into England* went into intimate details of Mary Beatrice's pregnancy. It noted that she continued menstruating and that her breasts did not swell or leaked milk. It appeared too much of a coincidence, with James's popularity at an all-time low, that a Catholic male heir should suddenly appear.

In 1687, King James undertook a tour of the west and north-west areas of England arguing for his Declaration. The King's brusque and authoritarian manner did not inspire confidence among his subjects and the disastrous tour was cut short. His arrogant manner united the country against him, and Bishop Gilbert Burnet later wrote of James's downfall:

One of the strangest catastrophes that is in any history; a great king, with strong armies and mighty fleets, a great treasure and powerful allies, fell all at once, and his whole strength, like a spider's web, was … irrecoverably broken at a touch.

James had achieved an unenviable fame as the worst of the English sovereigns, and the redeeming features in his character are not easy to discover. He had a real love of cruelty, and his heart was pronounced by Marlborough, who knew him well, to be as hard as marble. The time was approaching for King James to be replaced.

Chapter 6

The King's Illegitimate Son

Five months into his reign, James II learned that his nephew, James Scott, the Duke of Monmouth, was planning an invasion to overthrow him. As the Protestant illegitimate eldest son of Charles II, he claimed to be the rightful heir to the throne by displacing his uncle James. Proving initially to be a moderate Catholic, James had lulled the majority of Protestants into a false sense of security and began elevating fellow Catholics into higher positions. He would later take a right-wing Catholic stance and insist that England would be a Catholic kingdom.

James Scott was born in Rotterdam in the Netherlands on 9 April 1649, where his mother, Lucy Walter, had joined her lover, the eighteen-year-old Prince Charles, son of Charles I. Monmouth's Welsh-born mother was described by the diarist John Evelyn as a 'brown, beautiful and bold but insipid creature' and known as Mrs Barlow. It is not certain that Prince Charles was the father, for in 1648 Lucy had been the mistress of Colonel Robert Sidney, the younger son of the Earl of Leicester. James Scott was known as Jemmy and had inherited his good looks from his mother. In late 1651, Charles made it clear that their relationship had ended. This did not faze her for she took up with Theobald, 2nd Viscount Taaffe and Henry Bennett, Earl of Arlington, and gave birth to a daughter named Mary. Later Lucy married William Sarsfield, the brother of Patrick Sarsfield, 1st Earl of Lucan.

For about four years Lucy was involved in one scandal after another, which caused much embarrassment to the exiled royal court. By 1656, she was persuaded by the King's friends to return to England as she was aware that Charles, who was in Brussels, wished to claim paternity of their son. With the Interregnum in force, mother and her maid, Ann Hill, were imprisoned and examined in the Tower of London. Learning little, the two women and the teenaged Monmouth were later deported back to Flanders.

Once back in Europe, she travelled to Brussels and resumed her extravagant lifestyle. In 1658, in a botched kidnapping by Edward Progers, Charles's confidential page, Lucy was persuaded to hand over James into the care of William Crofts, 1st Baron Crofts, who passed him off as his nephew. James took the name Crofts until he married. His mother followed him to Paris and died there in September or October 1658, probably from venereal disease. In 2012 a DNA test was conducted on Monmouth's direct descendant, the Duke of Buccleuch, which revealed that he shared the same Y chromosome as a distant Stuart cousin, providing strong evidence that Monmouth was the son of Charles II.

James later went to live with his grandmother, Henrietta Maria, and his aunt, Henrietta Anne, known as Minette, the youngest child of Charles I. Both were devout Catholics and placed James under the instruction of Father Geoffe of the Oratorian College of Notre Dame des Verlus. It is not at all certain that he took to the Catholic religion for later he received education from Thomas Ross, a Scottish Protestant. He later attended school at Petit Ecoles, but his education was sketchy, which he regretted as he grew older.

The Restoration took place in 1660, when Charles II came to the throne after the failure of the republican Interregnum. Henrietta Maria brought James to London, and he was described by Samuel Pepys as 'Mr Crofts, the King's bastard, a most pretty spark of about fifteen years old'. Charles took to his son and, on 14 February 1663, he created him Duke of Monmouth, with the subsidiary titles of Earl of Doncaster and Baron Scott of Tynedale. At this time he was married to Ann Scott, 4th Countess of Buccleuch, on 20 April 1663. The day after their marriage they were showered with more titles. Ann produced six children but half of them died in infancy. Monmouth separated from his wife, whom at his death claimed 'never to have much cared for'. Ann outlived Monmouth by more than fifty years and died in 1732 aged eighty.

Monmouth lived openly with his mistress, Henrietta Wentworth, who John Evelyn the diarist referred to as 'that debauched woman'. Monmouth bought Moor Park in Hertfordshire in April 1670 and built a house that was completed in 1678–79. It was later reconstructed in the Palladian style around 1720, and today it stands on what was Ruislip Moor, which is where the name Moor Park originates. Monmouth toured the south-west of England in 1680 and was greeted wholeheartedly by the citizens of Chard and Taunton, towns where he would later recruit men to bolster his army. He was happy to live a life of leisure as long as his father remained on the throne. The Rye House Plot of 1683, and Monmouth's part in it, is open to speculation. It is unlikely he would have been involved in the murder of his own father but may have offered some protection for his friend, John Hampden. When the plot was discovered, he was served with a subpoena to give evidence against Hampden, but it is not clear whether he submitted to the writ. Monmouth swore that he had nothing to do with the Rye House Plot, but Charles no longer trusted his son. He was spared during the trials in 1684 and he went into self-imposed exile in the Netherlands.

In November 1683, Hampden gave evidence before the 'murder committee' of the House of Lords investigating the trials of the Whig leaders in the Rye House Plot, and admitted that he was on the fringes of the conspiracy of the Council of Six. He was sent to the Tower on 8 July 1683 after a witness had testified that the first meeting of the Council had been held at Hampden's house in Bloomsbury. Hampden was spared execution and imprisoned with the proviso of paying £40,000 imposed on him; an outrageously expensive sum.

After the failure of the Monmouth rising in 1685, Hampden was again brought to trial on the charge of high treason and condemned to death. An estate in Buckinghamshire and his manor in Preston, Northamptonshire, were seized by James I. The sentence was not carried out as Hampden found £6,000 to secure a pardon and was set free.

In 1688, it was Hampden who coined the phrase 'Golden Revolution' when William, Prince of Orange, launched his non-violent invasion. Hampden felt William's invasion was a continuation of the Council of Six, which was made up of Robert West, Aaron Smith, John Ayloffe, Christopher Battiscombe, Israel Hayes and Richard Nelthorpe.

Hampden formed an attachment with Monmouth's wife, Lady Ann Monmouth, and it was said that they spread rumours that led to her husband's execution. After the Rebellion, Hampden appeared again in society and was described as a 'great beau'. William of Orange, who felt Hampden was mad, dismissed any thought of him being ambassador to The Hague. Hampden became a Whig member of the Convention Parliament, one that assembled without the King. In April 1689, he took the chair of a committee that called for a war against France, but used such inflammatory words that he was replaced by a different chairman.

In 1690, he was defeated as the Member of Parliament for Wendover in Buckinghamshire, and suffered bouts of depression during the next five years. Not only did the Whigs shun him but he was unable to attain any senior office. On 7 December 1695, in a fit of depression, he botched the slashing of his throat, lingered for three days, and died.

In adulthood Monmouth's contemporaries claimed he bore a stronger resemblance to Robert Sidney than the Bourbon-looking Charles. These rumours probably sprang from his brother, James, Duke of York, who feared his nephew's claim to the throne. In 1665, at the age of sixteen, Monmouth served under his uncle James in the English fleet during the Second Anglo-Dutch War. It was political issues that drew the two countries into conflict rather than commercial trading. The Great Fire of London in September 1666 meant the Navy Board was unable to pay the fleet and discharged many sailors without paying their wages. This resulted in the fleet being unable to send out its ships to fight the Dutch. The war ended in September 1667, and Monmouth returned to England and took command of a troop of cavalry, something he relished.

In 1669, he was promoted to Colonel of the King's Life Guards, one of the most senior appointments in the army. George Monck, 1st Duke of Albemarle, died in 1670 and the twenty-one-year-old Monmouth became the senior officer. With the outbreak of the Third Dutch War in 1672, a brigade of British troops was sent to serve with the French Army in repayment for money paid to his father. During the 1673 campaign, Monmouth, who enjoyed army life, was prominent during the Siege of Maastricht, and gained a considerable reputation as one of England's boldest soldiers.

Joining Viscount Turrenne, the French commander, the Duke of Monmouth and John Churchill distinguished themselves as the finest officers in the English army. They were part of the army that marched on Maastricht and its outlying forts. The Dutch viewed Maastricht fortress as its most important as it dominated the River Meuse. It was manned with some 11,000 mercenary troops from Germany and Sweden, which the Dutch were happy to pay. The French reached Maastricht on 16 May 1672 but instead of attacking, they occupied the other forts along the Rhine, thus extending the French supplies. It took the Prince of Orange six months to reach Maastricht. By November 1672, instead of staying at Maastricht, he took part of the garrison with him and continued on to Charleroi, the French city at the start of the supply route to the army.

The French King, Louis XIV, thoroughly enjoyed sieges and even brought along his wife and two mistresses to join in his pleasure. The French had the skilful engineer Sebastian Le Prestre de Vauban, who directed the operation against the town of Tongeren in the east of what is now Belgium. His siege works required large numbers of unpaid workers and some 20,000 local agricultural labourers were conscripted to dig his trenches. Gradually the French advanced and their artillery destroyed the Tongeren Gate. On 25 June, as the French troops were being relieved at daybreak, the Dutch detonated a mine, killing about fifty attackers. Immediately the French and English recaptured the ground lost to the Dutch. Monmouth attacked from the left flank, Charles de Batz de Castelmore, better known as Count d'Artagnen, came in from the right, while the 2nd Musketeer Company assaulted from the front. In the confused fighting, the defenders were driven back and several English officers were killed. Others were wounded, including John Churchill, soon to oppose Monmouth at the Battle of Sedgemoor. D'Artagnen was killed by a stray shot as he pushed his way through the barrier. He is famous as Alexander Dumas's fictionalised version of d'Artagnen in *The Three Musketeers* and their subsequent screen adaptations.

In between wars, Monmouth was appointed Lord Lieutenant of the East Riding of Yorkshire and Governor of Kingston upon Hull. In March 1677, he was also made Lord Lieutenant of Staffordshire and also appointed Master of the Horse As one of Charles's favourites, Monmouth returned to England in 1674 and was designated Chancellor of Cambridge University, something he did not expect to be, given his poor education. King Charles ordered that all military orders should be brought to Monmouth for examination, which effectively made him in command of the Army. Despite his youth, he relished his responsibilities, which included the movement of troops and the suppression of riots.

In the confusion of the many wars fought on the near-Continent that resulted in the 1678 Franco-Dutch War, Monmouth, now with the Dutch Army, was made commander of the Anglo-Dutch brigade, fighting for the United Provinces. In the battle at St Denis in August, he distinguished himself, adding more plaudits to his reputation, and he found himself fighting on the Dutch side against his former ally, France. The only British troops involved were six regiments of the Anglo-Scots Brigade, while Monmouth took command of the English Horse. As an expert rider, he took part in several cavalry charges and was highly praised for his bravery.

In 1679, he returned to England and his father sent him to Scotland to raise a small militia to oppose the Presbyterian Covenanters in Scotland. The battle took place on 22 June, at Bothwell Bridge, which crossed the River Clyde. Monmouth's force numbered about 5,000 and opposing them were 6,000 poorly armed men of Covenanters. After some resistance by the Covenanters on the south side of the bridge, Monmouth's men broke through and scattered their enemy. Many were brought to trial and sentenced to exile in North America and the West Indies. A core of hard-line Presbyterian rebels remained and were known as the Cameronians, after their leader, Richard Cameron. They were later pardoned by William III in 1689 and later became one of the Scottish regiments, the Cameronians or Scottish Rifles, of the British Army.

As the years passed, Monmouth's relationship with his father reached a low point after the Rye House Plot. He had moved to the Continent with his mistress, Henrietta Wentworth, and never saw Charles again. On Charles' death in February 1685, he wished to claim the crown from his uncle, James II. He had taken refuge in the Dutch United Provinces and was persuaded by his supporters to fight a hopeless war that was doomed to failure before it even started.

Chapter 7

The Monmouth Rebellion

While in exile, Monmouth seemed content to go hunting, womanising and living with his mistress. He had moved from Brussels to the Netherlands, where there was a large colony of refugees escaping from the rule of James II. Many plots were hatched but none were put into action. Monmouth shied away from any involvement but the conspirators needed a leader to unify them. Monmouth was popular with the English and he recalled the warm reception he had received in the West Country, which eventually converted him to the plotters' cause.

The leading conspirators were Nathanial Wade, a barrister from Bristol, with a republican background. His father, John Wade, had been a major in Cromwell's New Model Army and was later appointed Governor of the Isle of Man. Wade disagreed with the other plotters about the proposed proclamation of Monmouth as king, but despite this contradiction, he was made one of Monmouth's commanders.

Robert Ferguson was a fanatical Presbyterian minister known as 'The Plotter'. It was he that drew up Monmouth's proclamation and was most in favour of him being crowned king. Thomas Hayward Dare was a wealthy goldsmith and a Whig politician from Taunton. He had been jailed during a political campaign calling for a new parliament and also was fined £5,000 for uttering seditious words against James. After his release from jail, he made his way to the Netherlands. He was appointed banker for the Monmouth invasion. The last conspirator was Archibald Campbell, the 9th Earl of Argyll, who had already been involved in the Rye House Plot. Condemned to death in 1681 in a dubious charge of treason and libel against the King, he escaped from Edinburgh Castle disguised as a page and made his way to London. Charles learned of his whereabouts but refused to do anything about it as Campbell was a Protestant. As events were becoming uncomfortable, Campbell decided to escape to the Netherlands. He made great efforts to convince Monmouth of the viability of a joint invasion, claiming he could count on a large number of men among his tenantry on his estate. On 2 May 1685, he sailed from Vliestroom in three small ships carrying about 300 men. Monmouth promised that he would start his own invasion within some days but did not sail for another three weeks. The Earl of Argyll attempted to raise a rebellion in Scotland but could not find sufficient troops. He realised that there was less support than he hoped and in the end he was left to lead his men around the west of Scotland. Apart from a couple of skirmishes, there was no uprising and there was to be no crossing the border into England by splitting James's army and supporting Monmouth. He was finally captured and taken to Edinburgh. Like his father, he was executed on the maiden (parade ground) in Edinburgh on 30 June 1685.

On paper the Monmouth Rebellion seemed to be a perfect *putsch* but, as with most detailed plans, it went horribly wrong. For one thing the rebels were short of money to purchase weapons and ships to make the crossing. Monmouth resorted to selling his family jewels and those of his mistress. Other donations came from the supporting groups. The duke needed to protect his ships and spent £5,000 on hiring the Dutch frigate *Heldevenberg*, the most expensive item on his list.

On 30 May 1685, Monmouth set sail from Tessel in Holland with three small ships, four light field guns, 1,500 muskets and eighty-two supporters, including Lord Grey of Warke and Andrew Fletcher of Saltoun. After a ten-day voyage covering 400 miles, the three ships reached Lyme Bay. Mooring off the fishing village of Seaton, they sent a small rowing boat ashore carrying Thomas Dare and a companion. They were to make their way to Taunton to bring the message that the Duke of Monmouth had landed. After the first day Monmouth had 300 men rally to his flag and by 15 June it had increased to 1,000 men. One of Monmouth's officers wrote of his arrival in Lyme:

We have so many men coming to the colours, that as the sun rose this morning, there are already over 800 carrying arms for his grace. As I watch the road, more and more men are streaming into town from the country. While recruits arrive, our stores of powder and shot, together with the stacks of muskets and pikes are being unloaded at the Cobb (the harbour at Lyme). I have sent my old friend John Kidd, now Captain, and once gamekeeper at Longleat towards Axminster, for we have information that the Devonshire

Militia have been mustered. My watch is now over the Dorchester Road for the Dorset Militia Troop are reported to be in that place. As the sun sets, I believe near one thousand and five hundred men have joined our Army today. For Young Dare has told me that the Duke's Red (sash) now has 500 in its ranks, whilst Holmes has nearly the same, with the White close to 350. To my surprise and joy, even the Yellow Regiment is now being formed. In addition, we had over one hundred and fifty horse come in already, these being under Colonel Fletcher and Major Manley.

The local customs official, Samuel Damsell arrived on the beach and questioned the fishermen as to the identity of the three ships. He then rode into Lyme and told the mayor, Gregory Alford, who urged Damsell to ride to London. Armed with this intelligence, Damsell and a companion rode from Lyme to London, covering 200 miles in two days. Along the way, he warned the militias not to join the rebels. On arrival in London, he went to the home of Lord Winston Churchill, who took Damsell to tell the story to King James. To confront the rebels, James called upon John Churchill to take command of the infantry of the King's army, but the leadership of the campaign was given to French-born Louis de Duras, Earl of Feversham.

At Lyme Bay, a fisherman came aboard the *Heldevenberg* to sell fish. He was later hanged for providing sustenance to the rebels. It was time for Monmouth to land and he made towards Lyme. The local militia had fled the town, leaving one man to answer the call to arms, but he immediately came over to Monmouth's side. Monmouth took possession of the forts around the area and raised his standard to the east of the town. His proclamation was read to the residents in the market square in Lyme, who hailed Monmouth as a saviour of the Protestant cause. He published a:

> Declaration for the defence and vindication of the protestant religion and of the laws, rights and privileges of England from the invasion made upon them and for delivering the Kingdom from the usurpation and tyranny of us by the name of James, Duke of York.

This manifesto was printed by London printer, William Disney, on 15 June in pamphlet form in English, French and Flemish. On the

Monday, he was arrested and accused of high treason for printing and publishing:

A most vile and Trayterous Paper against His most Sacred Majesty and Government: Intituled The Declaration of James Duke of Monmouth, and the Noble-Men, Gentlemen and others now in Arms, &c.

Between twelve and one o'clock in the morning, an investigator, accompanied by some musketeers and two or three other men, burst in on Disney, who was dressed in a shirt. He asked for his breeches but when these were searched, they found a dagger in the pocket. They also found a brace of pistols and a large hanger in the shape of a scimitar. The investigator made his way into the printing room and found 750 pamphlets, and fifty that were incomplete, with the Duke of Monmouth's declaration. The evidence was apparent and Disney had little to say for himself. He stood trial at Marshalsea in Southwark on 25 June, accused of high treason. There was only one sentence that could be passed and that was he was to be hanged, drawn and quartered on 29 June on Kennington Common with his 'quarters' displayed on the City Gates of London.

Thomas Dare arrived back from Taunton riding a particularly fine horse and accompanied by a troop of locally raised cavalry. Andrew Fletcher, a Scottish politician, who had been educated by Gilbert Burnet, the minister at Saltoun and later the Bishop of Salisbury. Both men had been forced to leave Scotland in 1683 seeking exile in the Netherlands, where Fletcher became a confident of Monmouth, while Burnet became close with the Prince of Orange and was with him when he landed in 1688 in Tor Bay.

Fletcher wanted to strike the county militia while they were being formed up and appropriated Dare's fine horse. Dare was outraged and a heated argument broke out. Dare tried to whip Fletcher, a man with a short temper, who produced a pistol, with which he shot and killed him. Dare was a popular local man and Monmouth was forced to send Fletcher back to the *Heldevenberg* anchored at Lyme Bay. Monmouth did not realise that James's navy had sailed from Portsmouth and had trapped Monmouth's vessels in Lyme Bay. Losing Fletcher, he had lost an able cavalry leader and the death of Dare robbed him of his most influential supporter. Monmouth's army had grown but was filled with inexperienced farm labourers whose weapons consisted of curved scythes lashed to end of long poles. Old weapons from the Civil War were made good by local blacksmiths, but there was little in the way of artillery, with just four light cannon served by a Dutch gunner. The few experienced soldiers were men in their forties who had served with Cromwell and acted as instructors. In five days, Monmouth's force had increased to 3,000 with volunteers coming in from the surrounding towns and villages in Somerset, Dorset and Devonshire.

On 14 June, Monmouth sent a small force to Bridport to the east of Lyme. With Lord Grey commanding 400 infantry and forty cavalry, they approached the small town in the early hours of the morning. Taking the outlying pickets by surprise, the small force went on to confront the main militia force made up of 1,200 foot soldiers and 100 mounted men, camped to the east of the town. Volleys of musket shot were exchanged and the fight seemed deadlocked. With the rebels in the High Street, shots were fired from the Bull Inn midway along the street. With Lord Grey's men trapped at one end of the town, the cavalry wheeled about and rode for Lyme. Colonel Samuel Venner, although wounded, gave orders to retreat, which was orderly, and Venner and Wade managed to lead the foot soldiers back to Lyme.

The following day, Monmouth prepared to leave Lyme and march on to Axminster. Arriving at the town, he spotted Lord Albermarle's militia approaching from the west. Albermarle had lost faith in his militia, most of whom wanted to join Monmouth's army, so he ordered a retreat. Monmouth resumed his march on to Taunton, so missing the opportunity of capturing weapons and ammunition. Instead he found:

> The Streets so thronged with People. We could scarce enter ...
> their Houses, Doors and Streets garnished with green Boughs,
> herbs and Flowers, all the Emblems of Prosperity.

He was also presented with twenty-seven banners by 'The Maids of Taunton', girls from the local school. The greeting was very heartening but Monmouth had a lingering doubt in his mind; he had support from the lower and middle classes but had few from the nobility. After some discussion with his commanders, he was persuaded to proclaim himself king, 'out of tenderness and for the interest of our loving subjects, and not upon any motives arising from ourself'. The proclamation of Monmouth as king failed to have the desired effect, with the Tory nobility regarding him as illegitimate and an imposter to the crown. It also upset the many Whig republicans, who wished for the return of the republican Commonwealth. Without a proper battle, the Rebellion was running out of steam.

On the Royalist side, John Churchill had reached Chard, while Lord Albermarle had moved to Wellington with his militia force, which had regrouped after the Axminster debacle. After three days, Monmouth left Taunton on 21 June with Bristol as his main objective. Despite discovering a small cache of weapons in St Mary's Church, Monmouth had to reject the men who volunteered with a paucity of weapons. By now Monmouth's army had grown to 7,000 but was disorganised and lacking in weapons and horses. His force headed for Bridgewater on the River Parrott and was received by the town mayor, Alexander Popham, and the local magistrates. The duke stayed in Bridgewater Castle while his men camped in the surrounding fields. The next morning, the rebels moved on to Glastonbury, passing through the small town of Westonzoyland, which skirted Sedgemoor. With the weather deteriorating to constant rain, the Somerset Levels were becoming water-logged. Monmouth decided to take Bristol, being the second largest city after London. It had a history of dissidents and rebels, which would have increased his army, supplied plenty of weapons and given him a strong base from which he could attack London.

By 24 June, he was at Pensfold, just 12 miles from Bristol. It was noticed that there was a dull glow in the sky above Bristol, which was a ship that had caught fire in the docks. It was widely believed that the Duke of Beaufort had threatened to burn Bristol and its shipping if Monmouth advanced on the port. Monmouth sent Captain Tilley with a squadron of horsemen to Keynsham to inspect and repair the damaged bridge over the River Avon. As they approached, the Gloucester Horse Militia fled the town. The bridge was not as damaged as first thought and Tilley and his men managed to repair it enough for Monmouth's army to cross and made camp in Sydenham Mead. He then received intelligence that Bristol had been occupied by Henry Somerset, Duke of Beaufort. There were some inconclusive skirmishes between the two opposing cavalry squadrons, which gave the impression that Bristol was under the control of a much larger militia force.

Monmouth was to make several mistakes during his short-lived rebellion and Bristol was one of them. He decided to recross the bridge but then faced an uncoordinated cavalry attack from Colonel Theophilus Oglethorpe with about 100 men on a scouting patrol from the south. Oglethorpe had been lieutenant colonel of the Royal Dragoons in 22 June 1679, and commanded the advance guard of the Duke of Monmouth's army at the defeat of the Scottish Covenanters at Bothwell Bridge. Coming from the Bristol area, Colonel John Parker, having forded the Avon, rode along the south bank with 150 of Faversham's troops. The rebels managed to repel the two squadrons of cavalry, who were not aware of the other's intentions. Monmouth believed that it was the opening phase of a Royalist attack. Although Monmouth still wanted to capture Bristol, his men were in a poor condition with worn-out shoes after marching 100 miles. He decided to strike camp, despite assurances from Bristol that he would not encounter any resistance. By this time he was desperately short of money and lacking arms. His decision to march to Bath and find support in Wiltshire was the turning point of the campaign. One of James's supporters, Sir John Reresby remarked:

> Had Monmouth obtained a victory it was much to be feared that
> the disaffected would have risen in such numbers in several parts
> of England as to have made the crown precarious.

Monmouth abandoned his dinner and the departure was swiftly made. The ragged foot-sore volunteers dragged themselves through the pouring rain to Bath. Unbeknown to Monmouth, John Churchill had arrived with a strong cavalry force and Feversham had occupied Bath, so the rebels were greeted with the closed gates of the town. There was little alternative but to turn south to the small village of Philips Norton (now Norton St Philip), where Monmouth sought refuge in the local inn, The George, which was to be his temporary headquarters. That evening an attempt was made on his life when a musket was fired at him through the window. The shot went wide but the bullet was alleged to be a silver button. The assassin vanished in the confusion and was unable to claim the reward of £5,000 as he had missed.

The Earl of Feversham learned that Monmouth's army had reached Philips Norton and sent a 500-strong force under the Duke of Grafton, Monmouth's stepbrother, to engage the rebels. Feversham was still waiting for his artillery and said he would soon join Grafton. Monmouth's sentries saw Grafton's force in the distance and laid a trap. Hiding behind the hedgerows lining the road into the village, the rebels shot at Grafton's men as they passed and it was only John Churchill's cavalry that managed to extricate Grafton's men. The rebels chased and fired at the retreating Royalists and lost the protection of the hedgerows and walls. Retreating back to Philips Norton, they prepared to move to Frome during the night. There is some doubt about the casualties; Grafton is said to have suffered 100 dead and wounded, while Monmouth's men lost eighteen. This was the only victory that Monmouth's men could claim.

With neither side wishing to fight a conclusive battle, the Royalists retreated east to Bradford-on-Avon and the rebels south to Frome. Monmouth's soaked and dwindling army reached Frome. Here they received a warm welcome but it was spoilt by the news that the Earl of Argyll's army had been defeated in the west of Scotland. Monmouth's small force was diminished by more desertions, leaving him with just 3,500 men. With the heavy rain and a declining army, Monmouth's morale began to slide and he even began thinking of abandoning his cause. He discussed disbanding his bedraggled army and heading for Poole to catch a ship to take him back to the Netherlands. His advisors were divided but his closest friend, Ford Grey, 1st Earl of Tankerville, persuaded him to fight on. With little chance of victory, Monmouth's rag-tag army were in no condition to fight. The planned march on London was no longer possible and, with more Royalist reinforcements arriving from London, Monmouth's options were very limited.

From Frome, the army headed for Shepton Mallet but the Royalist army moved into the town in its wake. A proclamation was read in the market square that offered a pardon for any rebels who would lay down their arms and return home. Monmouth and his officers tried to keep news of a pardon from their men, fearing desertions on a large scale. After another short march, Monmouth reached Wells and, with little in the way of ammunition, the lead roof on the cathedral was stripped and made into shot. Remembering Cromwell's destruction of the churches, the more militant rebels started to desecrate the carvings and statues and smash the windows. Lord Grey and a group of officers intervened and spared the cathedral from greater damage.

The following day, 2 July, the rebels headed back to Bridgewater. Lacking in artillery, Monmouth ordered some of his troops to travel to nearby Minehead and collect some cannon. His reception in Bridgewater was lukewarm and the number of new recruits was disappointing. Only a few miles from Bridgewater were the regiments of the Royalist army, who were camped on Sedgemoor. Monmouth decided that a night raid on the camp would cause confusion and scatter the Royalists. Although it would be a victory, there could not be any follow-up.

The Royalist troops were led by Lord Feversham and Colonel John Churchill, camped just beyond the Bussex Rhine, one of the many drainage ditches in the Somerset Levels. The infantry forces included 500 men of First Regiment of Foot (the Royal Scots), known as Dumbarton's Regiment; two battalions of the King's Royal Regiment (Grenadier Guards) and 600 men of the second Regiment of Guards (the Coldstream Guards). Also there were five companies of the Queen's Dowagers', or the Tangier Regiment (2nd Foot), known as 'Kirkes Lambs' and five companies of the Queen Consort's Regiment (King's Own Royal Regiment). These were all disciplined and battle-hardened soldiers who would be unlikely to retreat. In a separate nearby camp was the Royal Train of Artillery bivouacked along the Bridgewater road, with 420 men of the Royal Cavalry (the Blues and Royals) and three troops of the King's Horse Guards (Lifeguards). With such an experienced gathering of soldiers, Monmouth's untrained and ill-equipped men stood little chance of winning. Lord Feversham had made his headquarters at the village of Westonzoyland with the camp to the west of him. Expecting a battle the following morning, the Royalists settled down for the night.

That night, in a last desperate attempt to salvage something from his abortive rebellion, Monmouth launched a surprise night attack from the least expected direction, across the marshy wastes of Sedgemoor. Leaving Bridgwater at 10 pm on 5 July, the small army of 3,500 men was guided by Richard Godfrey, a servant of a local farmer who knew the area well. The night was misty and dark. Making their way north-east to Knowle Hill, they turned right down Bradley Lane and Marsh Lane, skirting the hamlet of Chedzoy. Heading east, they found their progress slowed by the mud and the numerous drainage ditches as they made their way towards the Royalist camp. Monmouth knew the layout of the Royalist camp, which he had seen through his telescope from St Mary's bell-tower.

The cavalry under Lord Grey was guided by local graziers, who would wade through the Langmoor Rhine. The sound of men wading through the Rhine alerted a Royalist patrol. Both sides were now fully awake through the sound of firing. By that time the infantry had come to the Bussex Rhine in front of the Royalist camp, and they were aware of horse men charging towards them. It became apparent that it was Lord Grey's men fleeing in some disorder. Nathaniel Wade and some of the other officers managed to rally the pikemen into some semblance of order before advancing through the Bussex Rhine.

The sentries and pickets did not hear the rebels advance, thinking they would take the easy option on the road from Bridgwater. Instead of rushing the Royalist camp, Monmouth's men hesitated at the wide Bussex Rhine. A pistol was fired either by accident or deliberately, which further alerted the Royalist camp. The drummers began beating a call to arms as the soldiers grabbed their weapons. Firing into the night, both sides settled for a long-distance firefight with the two sides exchanging musket and cannon fire with little effect. Unable to cross the wide but shallow Bussex Rhine, Monmouth's men milled around in confusion. The rebels fired indiscriminately, using up powder and shot. The rebel cannon did cause some casualties but it was the only arm that did so, thanks to the Dutch gunner. The Royalist cannon were out of range and badly sighted, and took little part in the night fight.

At daybreak, the Royalists were able to see the shambolic ranks of Monmouth's men and advanced. The rebels broke and fled the 3 miles back to Bridgwater pursued by John Churchill's cavalry. Lord Grey was not a natural cavalryman and on two occasions he had fought, he had been defeated. During the Sedgemoor battle, Grey was taken prisoner by the King's forces and condemned for high treason. He was granted a pardon when he gave evidence against his former colleagues and was even restored to his honours. Many were caught trying to cross what is now called Moor Drive Rhine and were either killed or taken prisoner. The Royalist cannon, now able to see the enemy, fired on the helpless rebels. Colonel Oglethorpe and his cavalry charged but were repulsed by rebel pikemen. The Royalist troops waded through the Bussex Rhine and charged the disorganised ranks of rebels. Within a short time, the battle was over.

Lord Feversham celebrated the victory by hanging twenty prisoners from a nearby tree. He was summoned to London to receive congratulations from King James and in his place, Colonel Piercy Kirke of the Tangier Regiment and his men set about to ravage Somerset. With psychopathic tendencies, Kirke hanged twenty prisoners in Taunton. He sold pardons to the richer rebels and was rebuked by James, who preferred to have them hanged. Other captured rebels were summarily hanged from trees around Bridgwater. Other rebels were rounded up and 500 crammed into St Mary the Virgin Church in Westonzoyland. From there they were incarcerated in local jails. For days, the Royalists continued to ruthlessly hunt down fugitives throughout the West Country. Some small pockets of rebels managed to hide in the woods and moors, but few managed to escape.

One of Monmouth's leading conspirators was Nathanial Wade, who, on horseback managed to reach Lynmouth, where he attempted to board a ship. He was arrested and taken to Newgate Prison in London. He would seem to be in line for execution but he was allowed to turn king's evidence on 19 October. He cited testimony against Henry Booth, 1st Earl of Warrington, who he accused of participation in the Monmouth Rebellion. His judge was the notorious George Jeffreys, but surprisingly Booth's defence received an acquittal. King James granted Wade a free pardon on 4 June 1686 and he died in 1718.

Chapter 8

Monmouth's Capture and Execution

Monmouth managed to escape from Sedgemoor with three other officers. In a letter written by the Earl of Shaftsbury, he wrote of Monmouth's escape:

> That after the defeat of the Duke of Monmouth at Sedgemoor, near Bridgewater, he rode, accompanied by Lord Grey to Woodyates, where they quitted their horses; and the Duke having changed clothes with a peasant, endeavoured to make his way across the county to Christchurch. Being closely pursued, he made for the Island, and concealed himself in a ditch which was overgrown with fern and under wood. When his pursuers came up, an old woman (Amy Farrant) gave information of his being in the Island, and of her having seen him filling his pockets with peas. The Island was immediately surrounded by soldiers, who passed the night there, and threatened to fire the neighbouring cotts (cottages). As they were going away, one of them espied the skirt of the Duke's coat, and seized him. The soldier no sooner knew him, than he burst into tears, and reproached himself for the unhappy discovery. The Duke when taken was quite exhausted with fatigue and hunger, having had no food since the battle but the peas which he had gathered in the field. The ash tree is still standing under which the Duke was apprehended, and is marked with the initials of many of his friends who afterwards visited the spot.

When Amy Farrant found that she had given away Monmouth's hiding place, she was overcome with remorse. Shaftsbury wrote:

> The family of the woman who betrayed him were ever holden in the great detestation, and are said to have fallen into decay, and

to have never thriven (thrived) afterwards. The house where she lived, which overlooked the spot, has since fallen down. It was with the greatest difficulty that anyone could be made to inhabit it.

Another account was written anonymously that filled in some of the information:

Upon the 7th about five in the morning, some of the Lord Lumley's said scouts riding in the road near Holt Lodge in Dorset, four miles west of Ringwood in Hampshire, just at the turn of a cross way, surprised and seized two suspected persons, which, when the Lord Lumley came up, proved to be Lord Grey and Hollyday the guide. Lord Lumley now commenced a strict examination of the cottages scattered thickly over this heathy (heath) country, and called on those to assist him who were acquainted with the locality. Sir William Portman was informed of the capture that had been made, and hastened to the spot, with as many of his horse and foot as he could suddenly get together. As Lord Lumley was making enquiries of the cottagers, a poor woman, Amy Farrant, directed him to a hedge, over which she had seen two men go. This hedge proved to be part of the outbounds of several enclosed fields, some overgrown with fern and brakes, and others sown with rye, peas and oats. The assembled militia were placed around these outbounds, at short distances from each other, while horse and foot performed their assigned duty – that of beating about within.

When the Duke had left his horse at Woodyates Inn, he exchanged clothes with a shepherd, who was soon discovered by local loyalists and interrogated. Dogs were then put on to the Duke's scent. Monmouth dropped a gold snuff-box, full of gold pieces, in a pea-field, where it was afterwards found. From Woodyates Inn the Duke had gone to Shag's Heath, in the middle was a cluster of small farms called the Island. Amy Farrant gave information that the fugitives were concealed within the island.

The Duke, accompanied by Busse and Brandenburgher, remained concealed all day, with soldiers surrounding the area and threatening to set fire to the woodland. Brandenburgher deserted him at 1 am, and was later captured and interrogated, and is believed to have given away the Duke's hiding place. The spot was at the north-eastern extremity of the Island, now known as Monmouth's Close, in the manor of Woodland, the property of the Earl of Shaftsbury.

At about 7 am, Henry Parkin, a militia-soldier and servant of Samuel Rolle, discovered the brown skirt of Monmouth's coat as he lay hidden in a ditch covered with fern and brambles under an ash tree, and called for help. The Duke was seized. Bystanders shouted out, 'Shoot him! Shoot him!', but Sir William Portman happening to be near the spot, immediately rode up, and laid hands on him as his prisoner. Monmouth was then in the last extremity of hunger and fatigue, with no sustenance but a few raw peas in his pocket. He could not stand. And his appearance was much changed. Since landing in England, the Duke had not had a good night's rest, or eaten one meal in quiet, being perpetually agitated with the cares that attend 'unfortunate ambition'. He received no other sustenance than the brook and the field afforded.

The Duke was taken to Holt Lodge, in the parish of Wimborne, about a mile away, the residence of Anthony Etterick, a magistrate who asked the Duke what he would do if released, to which he answered, 'that if his horse and arms were but restored to him at the same time, he needed only to ride through the army; and he defied them to take him again'.

The magistrate ordered him taken to the Tower of London, from where he wrote a letter to dowager Queen Catherine and his uncle, James, pleading for a pardon. It was hard to imagine what he could have expected but he went ahead and wrote a grovelling letter:

Your Majesty may think it is the misfortune I now lye under makes me make this application to you, but I do assure Majesty it is the remorse I now have in me of the wrong I have done you in several things, and now in taking up arms against you ... my misfortune was such as to meet with some horrid people that made me believe things of your majesty and gave me so many false arguments that I was fully lead away to believe that it was a shame and a sin before God not to do it. But Sire, I will not trouble your Majesty at present with many things I could say for myself, I am sure would move your compassion the chiefest being only to beg of you that I may have that happiness as to speak to your Majesty for I have to say to you, Sire, that I hope may give you a long and happy Reign. I am Sure, Sir, when you hear me, you will be convinced of the zeal I have for your preservation, and how heartily I repent of what I have done … I shall make an end in begging your Majesty to believe so well of me that I would rather die a thousand deaths than to excuse anything I have done, if I did not really think myself the most in the wrong that ever any man was and had not an abhorrence for those that put me upon it, and for the action itself … Therefore Sir, I hope I may live to show you how zealous I shall ever be for your service, and could I say but one word in this letter you would be convinced of it, but it is that consequence that I dare not do it. Therefore Sir, I do beg of you once more to let me speak to you, for then you will be convinced how much I shall be your Majesties most humble and dutiful – Monmouth.

With no reply and a last resort, Monmouth betrayed his noblemen supporters in Cheshire. He wrote to his uncle four days later, in which he revealed:

I forgot to tell your Majesty, that it would be necessary to send some troops down into Cheshire for there are several gentlemen there that I believe were engaged …

He did not reveal the name of Cheshire lord Charles Gerard, Earl of Macclesfield, although to save his skin he would have done so. Macclesfield got wind of the message and fled to Holland, where he became friendly with the Prince of Orange. He returned to England in 1688, the Glorious Revolution, as commander of William's bodyguard.

The dowager Queen Catherine of Braganza persuaded James to grant Monmouth an audience. On 14 July, Monmouth saw a glimmer of hope as he prostrated himself before James and pleaded for a pardon. In his cold arrogant manner, James passed a slip of paper to Monmouth to sign. It was to remove all traces of opposition to his rule, which stated that Charles II had not married Lucy Walter as Monmouth had insisted all his life. Once this was signed, James had Monmouth removed back to the Tower to be executed the following day.

On 15 July 1685, Monmouth was led out on to the scaffolding on Tower Hill. The crowd was large and many were sympathetic to the Duke.

As the illegitimate son of Charles II, Monmouth was 'granted the honour' of being beheaded by the most incompetent butcher of the time – Jack Ketch. He gave Ketch six guineas before laying his head upon the block and asked his executioner to perform his work well. However, Ketch had already botched the execution of Lord William Russell, either with sadistically nuanced skill or just plain lack of dexterity.

Ketch flung down his axe saying 'that he could not do it as my heart fails me'. The sheriff yelled at him to take up the axe and do your duty. Disconcerted, Ketch inflicted five blows with his axe. Ketch's first blow was off target. Russell raised his head from the block and said, 'You dog, did I give you ten guineas to use me so inhumanly?' Several more inaccurate blows were delivered, with the crowd becoming more outraged.

Ketch was moved to publish a pamphlet entitled *Apologie*, in which he excused his performance. He claimed that Lord Russell had failed to 'dispose himself as was most suitable and that he was distracted while taking aim on his neck'.

A final mention of Monmouth's demise; there were few paintings of him so they stitched his head back on his body and painted him asleep. John Evelyn, diarist and witness, wrote:

> He (the Duke) would not make use of a cap or other circumstance, but lying down, bid the fellow to do his office better that to the late Lord Russell, and gave him gold, but the wretch made five chops before he cut his head off; which so incensed the people, that had he not been guarded and got away, they would have torn him to pieces.

Ketch had been the executioner for over twenty years and it may have been that either his eyesight was poor or he was too old to wield the axe. He took part in the Bloody Assizes and beheaded Lady Alice Lisle, the last woman to be decapitated. The seventeenth-century Punch and Judy shows featured the public executioner Jack Ketch, who was always bettered by Mr Punch. He died in 1686 after being replaced by his apprentice, Pasha Rose, a butcher.

Chapter 9

Sedgemoor and its Aftermath

Colonel Piercy Kirke was commander of a large troop of cavalry named 'Kirke's Lambs', which later became the 2nd (The Queen's Royal) Regiment of Foot. Stationed in Tangiers, they were infamously known for their ferocity in 'fighting against the enemies of the Christian faith'. The troops under Kirke had the Pascal Lamb painted on their banners to teach the heathens a lesson, hence the term 'Kirke's Lambs'. After the destruction of the Tangier fortress and town, Kirke returned with the rest of the garrison in 1683. During Monmouth's Rebellion, Kirke replaced Feversham in the aftermath of the Battle of Sedgemoor. Within three days, he had hanged eleven of his prisoners and it is believed that as many as one hundred were killed at the hands of Kirke and his men. Thomas Babington Macaulay wrote of Kirke:

> He was a military adventurer whose vices had been developed by the worst of all schools; Tangier ... Within the ramparts of his fortress he was a despotic prince. The only check on his tyranny was the fear of being called to account by a distant and a careless government. He might therefore safely proceed to the most audacious excesses of rapacity, licentiousness and cruelty. He lived with boundless dissoluteness and procured by extortion the means and indulgence. No goods could be sold till Kirke had had the refusal of them. No question of right could be decided till Kirke had been bribed. It was not Kirke's corruption that the government disapproved but his leniency for those rich enough to satisfy his lust for money.

Kirke was the son of a court official serving both Charles I and his son, Charles II. In 1673, he was with the Duke of Monmouth at Maastricht and accompanied two campaigns with General Turenne on the Rhine. He was promoted to command the 2nd Tangier Regiment and became Governor of Tangier. Although he distinguished himself as governor, he offended those who saw his crude manners and impulsiveness. In 1684, the English destroyed Tangier harbour, her defensive works and completely evacuated the city.

Kirke was promoted to brigadier in Feversham's Royalist army. In the aftermath of Sedgemoor, the rebels were hunted down and treated very cruelly by Kirke's regiment. Some innocents were included and were hanged without any sort of trial. Kirke was considered by Charles I as Governor of the Dominion of New England. That was until James II withdrew the appointment due to his controversial behaviour in the Monmouth uprising. Reacting to this rebuff, Kirke sided with William of Orange and took a notable part in the Glorious Revolution. Gilbert Burnet wrote:

> Kirke, who had commanded long in Tangier, was become so savage by the neighbourhood of the Moors there, that some days after the battle, he ordered several prisoners to be hanged up at Taunton without so much as the form of law, he and his company looking on from an entertainment they were at. At every new heath another prisoner was hanged up. And they were so brutal that observing the shaking of the legs of those whom they hanged, it was said among them they were dancing, and upon the music was called for. This was both so illegal and so inhuman that it might have been expected that some notice would have been taken of it. But Kirke was only child for it.

With William and Mary on the throne, Kirke was promoted to lieutenant general and commanded the relief of Londonderry by breaking the Jacobite Irish Army siege of the city. In December 1688, the Irish Army commanded by James II hoped to enter the city via the gate, but thirteen apprentices rushed to close and lock the doors. This was seen as an act of rebellion by James and the following year he set about besieging the city. He actually appeared before the Londonderry walls and after several attempts to scale them he called for the city to surrender. Near to starvation, they were supplied with food from the ships that arrived to save them. The siege lasted from 18 April to 28 July 1689 as part of the Williamite War. Kirke was also prominent at the Battle of the Boyne and commanded the capture of Waterford that same year. His last campaign was in Flanders in 1691 but he died in Brussels that same year.

Many rebels who escaped the Sedgemoor Battle were captured and faced the Bloody Assizes. Abraham Holmes had been involved in anti-Royalist plots before and could not resist the chance to fight against the hated King James. He had been born in County Durham in 1629 and joined Robert Lilburn's Northern Army in 1644 as a fifteen-year-old. By 1646, he was serving in the south of England, having followed Lilburn into Oliver Cromwell's New Model Army. He converted to the Baptist faith and became prominent in army politics when he signed 'The Vindication of the Army', asserting the rights of Cromwell's soldiers against the moderate Members of Parliament at Westminster.

He returned to Scotland for the Civil War's final battle at Dunbar. He remained with Monck in Scotland as part of the occupying English forces. In 1651, he was appointed Justice of the Peace in Edinburgh. By 1654, his radical views were well known but he refused to become involved in a plot to remove Oliver Cromwell as Protector. He was a fanatical Anabaptist and opposed to all governments. With the collapse of Richard Cromwell's Protectorship in 1659 he gained promotion to lieutenant colonel, and in May 1659 he signed a petition to secure the rights and liberties of the people. Holmes was a major with one of the foot regiments and they were amalgamated into the Guards, and he was with Monck when the army moved south to London to restore law and order. They also supported the elections that led to the restoration of the monarchy and the return of Charles II.

In December 1659, he anticipated Monck's purge on the pro-Rump officers. His attempt to hold Ayr in support of the English army came to nought and he was formally dismissed in 1660. Holmes's Anabaptist faith fell afoul of the Restoration of Charles II and the religious conformity it demanded. During the 1660s, he began to associate with republicans and was known as 'a person of dangerous consequence'. In 1664, he was arrested for suspected sedition and imprisoned for three years in Windsor Castle, He and his companions successfully petitioned for a crime they had never heard of being arraigned against them and were released.

It was another fourteen years before he surfaced again, this time to help shelter Archibald Campbell, the Earl of Argyll. Dressed as a manservant of his stepdaughter, Argyll had managed to escape from Edinburgh Castle. He made his way to London and was given shelter by Holmes, before he could be smuggled to safety in the Netherlands. During this time, he was Argyll's agent, passing correspondences between the Earl and the Whig conspirators as they finalised details of the Rye House Plot. This was at a time when coffee houses were used to hatch plots, and the one that Holmes used was Mr Staple's Southwark Coffee House. He would collect these letters and send them on to other agents of Argyll and Monmouth in the Netherlands. With the King's spies frequenting the coffee houses, it was inevitable that Holmes was arrested. He was subjected to a lengthy interrogation by Charles, who took a close interest. Holmes readily divulged the contents of the letters, although he never mentioned the identities any of the conspirators. He did confess to Argyll's scheme to raise £10,000 to purchase weapons for an armed insurrection but remained silent on the donors.

He was committed to the Gatehouse prison for high treason, and, under torture, divulged more information to the authorities. Then there was a change about keeping him incarcerated; whether it was his confession or whether he was more use outside that in prison. Either way, he was released or escaped to the Netherlands, where he was joined by his son, Blake. They became part of the group of Dissenters and Whigs who supported Argyll and Monmouth. When Charles died on 6 February 1685, plans were discussed to overthrow the Catholic James through armed rebellion.

Holmes, as an experienced army officer, was given command of the Green Regiment of Foot, with his son Blake as captain. Having landed at Lyme and considerably increased their army by the surge of volunteers, Monmouth marched through Somerset with Bristol as his target. Unfortunately, he received faulty intelligence that Bristol was occupied by Royalist troops and turned south. Passing through the small village of Philips Norton, they ambushed a Royalist mounted patrol in which Blake was killed, and Holmes severely wounded in the arm. On the night of 5 July, Monmouth attempted to surprise the Royalist camp on Sedgemoor. Among the enemy troops facing the Green Regiment was Holmes's old regiment, the Coldstream Guards. Alerted by the rebels, the Royalists annihilated Monmouth's army. Holmes was in the forefront of the infantry attack and had his horse shot from under him and was captured. When Lieutenant Colonel John Churchill demanded his identity, Holmes refused to answer. He was stripped and taken to a nearby house. His wounded arm gave him so much pain, that he took a kitchen knife and amputated it. It is doubtful that he would have survived for very long as gangrene and the crude manner of the amputation would have killed him. Sent to London, he was interrogated by James, who got little from him. He showed no remorse and refused to demonstrate any loyalty to the Crown, reportedly saying:

> I am an aged man, and what remains to me of life is not worth a falsehood or baseness. I have always been a republican, and I am one still.

Holmes was tried at Dorchester by the odious Judge Jeffreys and then conveyed to Lyme to be executed at the place where he landed. A curious event happened when the horses that were to pull the cart to the gallows could not be made to stir. Replacements were found and they reared and stamped upon the sledge until it broke. Elderly and infirm, Holmes was a broken figure near to death as he attempted to ascend the scaffold. It is reported that he sat at the foot of the gallows and declared to the crowd his reasons for supporting Monmouth. He apologised to the presiding sheriff, saying:

> The Protestant religion was bleeding and that while God had not graced his cause with victory, he doubted not but that God would make use of the others that should meet with better success. You see I am imperfect, with only one arm, I shall want assistance to help me up on this Tragical Stage.

Other Baptists who landed with Monmouth were the twins, Will and Benjamin Hewling. They were captured but, for some reason, they were executed in different towns; Will in Lyme and Benjamin in Chard. Their maternal grandfather, Watkins Kyffin, pleaded that they should not be quartered, which was granted after a bribe of £3,000 was paid, and they were buried whole. Judge Jeffreys was furious that the bribe was not paid to him but to the London authorities. He told Will his grandfather deserved death as much as he did. His brother, Benjamin, was petitioned by one of Jeffreys' relatives but it did no good as James refused to stay the execution and Benjamin faced the gallows. According to the reports at the time:

> the grave losses sustained by the churches in Somerset and Dorset, still affected them four years later, and so when the churches of all England were represented at London in 1689, the West did not give its usual lead, which it only recovered after ten years. Some real harm was done, the effects of which persisted for nearly a century.

Chapter 10

The Bloody Assizes

The judicial system that followed was a harsh and calculated course that was entirely disproportionate to the sentences metered out to the simple foot soldiers that had joined Monmouth's foolhardy cause. Six weeks after Monmouth's execution, James sent probably his most infamous judge to punish Monmouth's rebels; Judge George Jeffreys. He was born at Acton Park, near Wrexham, on 15 May 1645. His education in 1652–59 was at his grandfather's old school, Shrewsbury. He then attended St Paul's (1659), Westminster (1661), and Trinity College, Cambridge, which he left without graduating. When he was eighteen, he was sent to study law and was fortunate to arrive two years before the Great Plague of 1665, the worst case since 1348, which created a number of useful openings in the legal profession. When the possibility of patronage with the Duchess of Portsmouth came his way, he was introduced into the realms of the Court.

Jeffreys became a close friend and drinking companion of Will Chiffinch. He was a pimp to Charles II, a page to Charles's bedchamber, Keeper of the King's Jewels and Keeper of his Private Closet. Like many in Court, he received backhanders, including a secret pension from the French Court. This made him the closest of all the King's servants and his influence at court is said to be incalculable. His own apartment in Whitehall joined the King's and was a convenient place for secret meetings. It was also an escape route for the King by the backstairs and up the Thames to Holyport, only a stone's throw from Windsor Castle. Chiffinch had rented Old Philiberts' Manor as a rendezvous for Charles's many mistresses, including Nell Gwynne, who was there on a semi-permanent residence for some time. Chiffinch died at Old Philibert's Manor in July 1691, an appropriate place for him.

Through Chiffinch, Jeffreys was appointed by Charles as Lord Chief Justice, a role he relished. He became renowned for his bullying manner and bad temper, which was undoubtedly caused by kidney stones. He was advised to imbibe plenty of alcoholic drinks to ease the stones but all it did was to make him even more irascible. The diarist John Evelyn, who almost liked Jeffreys, described him 'of nature cruel, and a slave to the Court'.

The first Court of the Autumn Assizes was on 25 August at Winchester. William Savage wrote eloquently about the travesty of Alice Lisle's trail and Judge Jeffreys' hounding of her. The trial cast a shadow on English Justice, with Jeffreys siding with the prosecution in condemning her to death. She was a woman of sixty-eight who had to wait through the day while the trials of murderers and thieves were heard. Although she had found refuge for one of the fugitives, she had not taken part in the Monmouth Rebellion. Finally, at five in the afternoon her case was heard by Jeffreys. He had a particular dislike for Alice Lisle's husband, who was at the trial that condemned Charles I to death. John Lisle was not one of the signatories to the death warrant but was included with those regicides. In the aftermath of Cromwell's Commonwealth, Charles II sought vengeance on those twenty men still alive who had condemned his father to death. He sent out men to hunt down those he considered guilty. In the end, he pardoned all but nine, who he executed.

On 11 August 1664, John Lisle, was walking in the churchyard of St Francois in Lausanne, Switzerland, when he was accosted by three Irish Royalists. Miles Crowley drew back his cape and fired his carbine at point-blank range, killing Lisle. Fighting off Lisle's guards, Crowley's companions, John Cotter and John Rierdan, acted as bodyguards and made their escape.

Two men who fled from Sedgemoor were John Hicks and Richard Nelthorpe, who made their way to seek refuge at the Lisle house at Ellingham. Hicks was a non-conformist preacher who practised in Keynsham and joined Monmouth at Shepton Mallet. He believed Monmouth to be the legitimate heir to the throne but did not join his army. He was also associated with Thomas Blood, who stole the crown jewels in 1671 from the Tower of London, but no charge was made. Nelthorpe was a lawyer who was involved in the Rye House Plot. He managed to escape from Scarborough with Nathaniel Wade and arrived in Amsterdam at the end of June 1683. With the Staats-General about to arrest them, they travelled to Vevey in Switzerland but, when he learned of Monmouth's plans to land in the West Country, he offered his services. Along with Hicks, he was arrested at Moyles Court and taken to London. Under torture, he refused to divulge his associates and was executed before the gate of Grey's Inn on 30 October 1685. These two men, although not in Monmouth's army, sought refuge overnight at the Lisle house. A witness, William Savage, kept an account of Lady Lisle's trial, which was extraordinarily one-sided:

> The proceedings began in the normal way, for Alice Lisle was called to the bar and the charge laid before the Jury that she aided and assisted Mr Hicks a known traitor for Monmouth's Rebellious Army, therefore guilty of High Treason. To this, the noble lady pleaded, 'Not Guilty.'
>
> Now the old lady was very deaf and gave the support of Mr Browne to repeat the case to her. Also, her being frail in the frame, the Judge allowed her to be seated for the whole indictment. The Lord Chief Justice Jeffreys opened by reminding the Jury that the Lady was the widow of Lisle, that murderous regicide and follower of Cromwell. Furthermore, that one Mr Hicks, whom she had sheltered, was a conventicler preacher and one of the most active instruments in bringing about the horrible rebellion ...
>
> At this juncture, the poor Lady stood and declared herself against the Rebellion but Judge Jeffreys told her to be silent.

There followed a long interrogation of James Dunne, who had taken a letter to Lady Lisle and helped John Hicks and Richard Nelthorpe from Warminster to Moyles Court at Ellingham, Hampshire. Under cross-examination, Jeffreys showed his bilious side by browbeating the witness with such offensive comments as:

> Why you vile wretch! Didst thou not tell me, that thou pulledst up the latch? But, it Seems the Saints have a charter for Lying; they may Lie and Deceived, and Deceive and Rebel, and think God Almighty takes no notice of it. A Turk has a better Title to an Eternity of Bliss than the Pretenders to Christianity; For he has more Morality and Honesty in him. Sirrah! I charge you in the presence of God, tell me one true, what other Persons did you see that night?

He followed this up with:

Thou art a strange prevaricating, shuffling, snivelling, lying rascal ... How hard then Truth is to come out of a lying Presbyterian Knave! ... O blessed Jesus! What an Age do we live in? What a generation of Vipers do we live among? Sirs, is this that you call a Protestant Religion? Shall so Glorious a Name be applied to such Villainy and Hypocrisy? Thou wicked wretch, I charge you once more, as you will answer it at the Bar of the Great Judge, tell me, what that Business was you and the Prisoner talk'd about?

Jeffreys managed to force Dunne to confess that Lady Lisle knew that John Hicks was a non-conformist preacher. By now the sun had set and with it being a late warm evening, Lady Lisle had fallen asleep during the proceedings. She was woken up but had no idea what had proceeded and declined to question the witness. All she would say was that Mr Hicks was a non-conformist preacher and that he was looking for refuge as a dissenter. His companion was Richard Nelthorpe, a wanted conspirator of the Rye House Plot, and she sent word to Colonel Penruddock for their arrest. She also said she was set against the Monmouth Rebellion, that her son was an officer in the Royalist Army and was a loyal supporter of James II. Judge Jeffreys started his summing up the case against Lady Lisle by picking up on her references to Dissenters and non-conformists:

For they are to blame for the death of King Charles I. I will not say what hand her husband had in the death of that blessed martyr, she has enough to answer for in this case, what she was in former times.

In his final words to the jury, he assured them the Alice Lisle's testimony was, 'As plain a proof can be given and as evident as the sun at noon day.' The jury was warned that they should ignore the prisoner's age and her sex and return a verdict of guilty. An anonymous witness wrote:

For all those present, it was clear that the poor Lady knew of Mr Hicks, not as a fugitive from high treason but one from religious persecution and no evidence was offered to prove that point. Indeed, Mr Hicks had not yet been tried or proven to be a traitor. For, before retiring, the Juryman asked Justice Jeffreys if

Lady Lisle could be tried for treason when Mr Hicks had not been convicted of treason. To which Jeffreys replied that, 'it was all the same, that certainly there could be no doubt Mr Hicks committed treason!'

After a quarter of an hour, the Jury returned and the Juryman stated that they were still in some doubt if Lady Lisle knew Mr Hicks was in the (Monmouth's) Army and therefore the verdict was 'Not Guilty'. With this, Jeffreys flew into a rage shouting, 'There is a full proof, as proof can be; but you are the judges of the proof, for my part I thought there was no difficulty in it.'

Jeffreys then lectured the jury on the evidence proving Lady Lisle's guilt and concluded with 'Come, come gentlemen this is plain proof of guilt' and asked the jury to retire once more to find Alice Lisle guilty. Again they came back with the verdict of 'Not Guilty'. Beside himself with rage, Jeffreys ordered the jury to retire and come back with a guilty verdict. Jeffreys told them to come back with his correct answer, 'If they don't return with the correct verdict, shall themselves be tried for high treason.' Within minutes the jury came back with a 'Guilty' verdict. Now with the verdict delivered, Jeffreys said to the court:

Gentlemen, I did not think I would have had any occasion to speak after your verdict but finding some hesitancy and doubt about you; I cannot but say I wonder it should come about, for I think in my conscience the evidence was as full and as plain as could be, and if I had not been among you and she had been my own mother, I should find her guilty.

On 28 August, Jeffreys called Alice Lisle to the bar to deliver his verdict. In a long and rambling harangue he referred again to John Hicks as 'a canting, whining, Presbyterian, fanatical profession of Mr Hicks'. Pointing to Lady Lisle, he accused her of the sad and dismal effects of disloyalty and 'from all the rest of the deplorable mischief's that attend licentiousness and debauchery'. After his rant, he then pronounced the sentence on the elderly Alice Lisle. She would be tied to a hurdle and dragged to the Winchester Market Place, where her body would be burnt at the stake. It was later discovered that there was not enough kindling to start a fire, so an appeal was made to

King James. It is of interest that gentry and nobility would be beheaded, which was deemed more dignified, than hanging for the commoners. James reversed the sentence to beheading.

On 2 September, Alice Lisle, stepped from the upper window in the Eclipse Inn and on to the scaffold. Because of her age, it was said she died with dignity without regretting leaving the religious tensions behind. Her headsman was Jack Ketch, the inept executioner, but this time he only took one blow to part Alice's head from her body. Alice Lisle was the only person to be executed at Winchester but it would lead to hundreds more throughout the West Country. The Assizes greatly damaged the Stuart cause, particularly the death of Alice Lisle.

Judge Jeffreys reached Dorchester the next day and began the trials at the Oak Room in the Shire Hall, which was aptly draped with scarlet. Jeffreys and his fellow judges, Sir William Montague, Sir Crosswell Levinz, Sir Francis Withens and Sir Robert Wright, spent five days condemning men who had sided with Monmouth. On the first day sixty-eight men pleaded guilty by the advice of the prosecuting counsel; thirty pleaded not guilty, but only one was acquitted. One unfortunate man named Mathew Bragge, a lawyer, became embroiled in this dreadful bloodletting. His crime was to show Monmouth's rebels a house belonging to Roman Catholics that may have held arms. Unable to find any weapons, the soldiers stole Bragge's horse, his cane and gloves as a gift to the Duke. This left Bragge to walk home to his village of Sadbarrow. He later surrendered to the authorities but it did him no favours, for Jeffreys declared 'if any lawyer or parson came under his inspection they should not escape'. Bragge was shown no leniency and was convicted and hanged the next day.

At Taunton, the eight- to ten-year-old girls from the local school had handed a banner and Bible to Monmouth. They were encouraged by their schoolmistress, Mary Blake, who later died of smallpox while in prison. One of her pupils, an eight-year-old, was subjected to a brutal tirade by Jeffreys, who returned the child to prison, where she died. Although Jeffreys was a Protestant, he overwhelmed his victims with scornful mockery and sarcasm. One prisoner pleaded that he was a good Protestant, to which Jeffreys responded with:

Protestant! You mean Presbyterian; I'll hold you a wager of it. I can smell a Presbyterian forty miles.

When someone tried to plea for another prisoner, saying he was 'a poor creature of the parish', Jeffreys responded with: 'Do not trouble yourselves. I will ease the parish of the burden.' He then ordered the man to be hanged at once.

Simon Hamlyn was a notable case tried at Taunton. He was a dissenter but had nothing to do with the rebellion and ended up becoming another victim of Jeffrey's predilection for hanging. Hamlyn lived a few miles outside Taunton and visited the town to warn his son to stay clear of the rebels. He was arrested and brought before Jeffreys, but the Mayor of Taunton, Bernard Smith, tried to intervene saying that Simon Hamlyn was entirely innocent. Jeffreys waved the appeal, saying: 'You have brought him on. If he be innocent, his blood be upon you.' The pardon was made but by that time it arrived, Jeffreys had Hamlyn hanged.

On 23 September, the last day of the Bloody Assizes, the judiciary reached Wells. There they tried Charles Speke, a filacer (a legal officer of the superior courts), whose crime was shaking Monmouth's hand as he rode through Ilminster. Despite testimony that it was another Speke who had been an active member of Monmouth's army, Jeffreys refused to show any mercy and stated Charles Speke 'shall die for his namesake'.

The executioner Ketch said that with one assistant he could hang, quarter, and boil only thirteen people a day. In the five days, 251 were sentenced to death. The others were executed at Dorchester, Lyme, Bridport, Melcombe, Sherborne, Poole and Wareham. At Exeter only one day was necessary; nineteen pleaded guilty while two were convicted and executed at once. The rebellion's main town was Taunton, and after two days, out of 505 indicted, only six pleaded not guilty. The last mass trial was at Wells, where 541 pleaded guilty; one was tried, condemned and executed, all in one day. Of all these, a warrant to execute 239 was signed in September. The hangman was kept busy until December, and by the end of the year heads and quarters, boiled in pitch, were hanging at the gates, bridges and crossroads all over the West Country. They stayed there until they were removed and buried in the autumn of 1686. These ghastly trophies made the West Country seem like an abattoir.

Some say Jeffreys only performed his legal duties, but was in reality a corrupt and cruel judge. He bribed two of Monmouth's imprisoned men to testify against Edmund Prideaux, who had extensive estates in Cornwall, to gain their release. In the end, Jeffreys managed to collect £15,000 from

Prideaux; it was the largest bribe paid for an innocent life during the Bloody Assizes. Another example of Jeffreys' corruption was a condemned man, Roger Hoare, whose parents paid £1,000 in ransom. Lord Grey of Warke, one of the ring leaders of the Monmouth rebellion, was captured, yet his life was spared. Owning such large estates, he was forced to pay a bond of £40,000 for his release.

It seems that the total number executed was 320, for many died from smallpox in the fetid cells of prison before they could be hanged. Jeffreys began by handing death sentences to 251 rebels, which outraged many of the citizens. The brutality of the deaths lived for long time in the memory of its population. Many were hanged, drawn and quartered, and their parts were displayed around the town and some of the surrounding villages. This horrifying sight of heads and quarters dipped in black pitch and salt were displayed in public in the villages where the prisoners had come from.

Hundreds were transported to the Leeward Islands, Barbados, Jamaica and Carolina. They were slaves of the courtiers of James II and were worked to death on the sugar plantations and mines until malaria or other tropical diseases struck them down. Those that survived were pardoned in 1686 and allowed home. The British historian Thomas Babington Macaulay wrote:

> More than 300 hundred prisoners were to be tried. The work seemed heavy; but Jeffreys had a contrivance for making it light. He let it be understood that the only chance of obtaining pardon or respite was to plead guilty.

Twenty-nine did so and were immediately sentenced to death the following day. Some historians sought to mitigate Jeffreys's severity by pointing out that he was a Protestant serving a Catholic King. It was felt that he had to prove that he had no sympathy for the Protestant plotters by the ferocity of the punishments he handed out. He was ordered to report back to James the executions and transportations he had enforced. He was described by one contemporary as a man who:

> was renowned as not just passing judgement but behaving as though he was the prosecuting council. He would hector witnesses, insult and undermine them. For the most part they were country people and they crumbled.

It has been estimated that about a quarter of the male population of south Somerset marched with Monmouth and about 1,000 died at Sedgemoor. Throughout the West Country, some 1,000 were tried at the assizes, while many more hid in the woods and subsisted on what they could find. The trials were held at such major towns as Dorchester, Wells, Bath and Taunton, with executions carried out in the villages where the rebels came from. For instance, Axminster, Dunster, Porlock and Castle Cary executed two men each, while three from Minehead were hanged. On 12 October, Thomas Northmore, barrister, witnessed many of the executions in Somerset and Dorset and wrote:

> On Saturday next [the 14th] at Axminster is the last execution to be done and one more then at Honiton unless reprieved … Three were executed at Honiton Saturday last. There was a great delay, therefore, in carrying out the rest of the Somerset executions, and in the meantime a kindlier executioner than Ketch stepped in and anticipated the hangman [with] Smallpox was raging in the gaol of Somerset and Dorset with a fury … In Dorchester gaol, where [John] Tutchin was imprisoned, eighteen out of forty prisoners died from this disease during the period from November 1685 to February 1686. Amongst them was Mary Blake, Captain of the Taunton virgins, who had presented Monmouth with a Bible. She was buried at All Saints, Dorchester, on 26 November 1686.

John Whiting, the Quaker, imprisoned in Ilchester gaol, said of the smallpox outbreak:

> That it is rife amongst the rebel prisoners in the gaol in the autumn, and as fresh parties of rebels were rounded up long after the month of September and imprisoned for future trial, the overcrowded state of the gaols increased the spread of the disease.

Whilst Whiting was in prison at Ilchester he tells us that the execution of the rebels took place, though he does not specify the date. There were eight executed, says he quartered, and their bowels burnt on the market place before our prison window – a spectacle he naturally took steps to avoid seeing. But Jeffreys' warrant ordered twelve men to be executed at Ilchester, not eight. Did four men die from the smallpox in the gaol?

Once more, Lord Jeffreys ordered six men to be executed at Bath. The execution was delayed until 18 November, on which day only four were dispatched. It is impossible not to conclude that, owing to the delay, two had succumbed to smallpox:

> The Sheriff's own warrant for the execution has survived and is so minute in its repulsive details that it seems desirable to set it out in order to show what a horrible thing an execution for high treason was in the time of our ancestors.

John Hicks, who had stayed overnight at Lady Lisle's house, was arrested under the charge of encouraging others to join Monmouth's rebel force. He was tried at Wells, where some 500 were accused and sentenced the same day. He was executed in Glastonbury and, thanks to the intervention of Bishop Ken of Wells Cathedral, he was buried at Glastonbury Church. Hicks made a last speech to his wife on the scaffold, in which he said:

> My dear, be very cautious not to speake one word. Lest it be wrested in a wrong sense, which may ruin you. Farewell my dear, farewell in the Lord, until we meet to be married to Him forever. My heart is as full of love to thee as it was the first day I married thee, and if God spared my life it should have been as fully manifested until Death.

His daughter, Elizabeth, who had been vocal and active in the anti-Jacobite causes, married radical Whig John Tutchin, who held strongly anti-Catholic views. He became associated with Daniel Defoe, who had participated in Monmouth's Rebellion but escaped punishment. He and Defoe had a falling out in 1702, with Defoe representing a more Whiggish Puritan attitude, while Tutchin was more democratic and Cromwellian. Alexander Pope became involved and wrote a poem, 'The Dunciad', and took Defoe's side. In 1704, Tutchin escaped to France but returned soon after and accused the Royal Navy of secretly selling food for the French navy. He was imprisoned for sedition and on 23 September 1707 he suffered terrible injuries in custody, possibly torture, from which he died.

At Lord Stonewell's house at Cothelstone, the sheriff was able to save the expense of a gallows as Richard Bovett and Thomas Blackmore were hanged from the great gateway at the entrance to the avenue leading to the property. Sir Charles Lyttleton wrote that the executions went on daily in other parts of the country, and 'the countryside looked like a shambles owing to the quarters displayed in every direction'. When the four judges had travelled through the West Country and completed their bloody tour, the counties of Somerset, Dorset, Devon and Cornwall were horrifically changed. The guideposts along the highways were converted into gibbets from which blacked corpses swung in chains and every church tower was bedecked with the executed heads of the victims of the Bloody Assizes. In Devon and Somerset, quarters and heads were sent to Honiton, Axminster, Colleton, Ottery St Mary, Crediton, Bideford, Barnstaple, Torrington, Tiverton, Plymouth, Dartmouth and Totnes. No town was exempt from the dreadful exhibits they displayed.

In one month, Jeffreys and his companions had done as their king commanded, but they had also wrecked James's credibility, from which he never recovered. Two hundred and fifty pickled heads and one thousand quarters of corpses were displayed at crossroads, bridges and churches, until James ordered their removal.

George Jeffreys, despite his loyalty to James, never hid his contempt for Catholicism. In the last months, as the government drifted without leadership, Jeffreys was rewarded with the post of Lord Chancellor. He had been given the presidency of the Ecclesiastical Commission, a body under the royal prerogative to control the governance and coercion of the Church of England. The Ecclesiastical Commission accused the Bishop of London and the academics of Oxford and Cambridge of being 'overly Protestant'. This body came to an end with William's Glorious Revolution. Thomas Babington Macaulay wrote:

> Jeffreys made all the West an Aceldama; some places quite depopulated and nothing to be seen in them by forsaken walls, unlucky gibbets and ghostly carcasses. The trees were loaden almost as thick with quarters as leaves; the houses and steeples covered as close with heads as at other times with crows or ravens. Nothing could be like hell than all those parts; nothing so like the devil as he. Cauldrons hissing, carcasses boiling, pitch and tar sparkling

and glowing, blood and limbs boiling and tearing and mangling, and he the great director of all.

When James fled the country, Jeffreys remained behind, being the only high legal authority left. However, when William's huge retinue approached London, Jeffreys decided it was time to follow the King abroad. He disguised himself as a sailor, to the extent of shaving off his fierce eyebrows, and was apprehended in a Wapping public house. He had been recognised by a surviving victim of his harsh sentencing and was roughed up. Arrested, he was dragged to the Lord Mayor, before taken 'for his own safety' to the Tower of London. Here he remained for five months before dying painfully of kidney stones (pyelonephritis) on 18 April 1689. As with most of the prisoners in the Tower, he was buried in the Chapel Royal of St Peter ad Vincula (St Peter in Chains): A passing that few mourned.

A general pardon was issued in 1686, but the West of England could not forget the grisly body parts displayed throughout the counties. It would not be until late 1687, when James II fled to France and Protestant William and Mary ascended the throne, that the country could rejoice.

Chapter 11

Invitation to Rule England

William, the Prince of Orange, was Stadtholder of the Low Countries or the Netherlands. He was born at The Hague on 4 November 1650, two days after his father's death from smallpox. He grew to be small, slightly hunchbacked with a hooked nose and suffered from asthma. His mother, Mary, was the eldest daughter of Charles I. She had married William II but showed little interest in her son or Dutch society. Mary was in constant conflict with her son's paternal grandmother, Amalia of Solms-Braunfels, over the naming of her son; she wanted Charles, after the name of her brother, and an English education, while Amalia insisted on William and a resurgence of the House of Orange. The frequent quarrels between Mary and Amalia disturbed William's childhood and he became reserved; something that would shape his adulthood. It can be said that the young William did not have the experience of a childhood. His early years were sombre and lonely, with no paternal warmth. William was brought up by Cornelius Trigland in the Calvinist faith, which was devoid of pleasure. From 1659, his education at the University of Leiden proved to be exceptionally outstanding as he quickly took command of English, French, Latin and Spanish. He spent seven years at the university and resided at the Prinsenhof – Court of the Prince – at Delft. He had a small personal retinue including his lifelong friend, Hans Willem Bentinck, and his paternal uncle, Frederick Nassau de Zuylenstein.

When he was ten years old, his mother died of smallpox at Whitehall Palace. She was visiting her brother, the newly restored King Charles II, and in her will she asked that Charles should look after William's interests. Charles had a love-hate relationship with the Dutch and asked that the States of Holland end their interference in trade and commerce. Zuylenstein worked with Charles and asked William to write letters to his Uncle Charles asking for support in becoming Stadtholder. When the 1665 Second Anglo-Dutch War broke out due to commercial rivalries,

George Monck greets
Charles II to Dover.

Charles II.

James II.

George Monck in half armour.

Piercy Kirk – the most cruel and venal of
the army commanders.

Queen Mary.

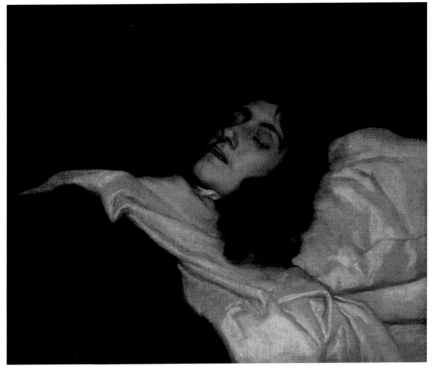

John Scott, Duke of Monmouth. Due to lack of portraits, Monmouth's head was taken and used in repose.

Sir Christopher Wren.

King William III.

Rye House – scene of the thwarted assassination attempt on the royal brothers on their return from Newmarket.

William arrives at Torbay with his invasion force.

James leaving Ireland after his defeat at the Boyne.

Judge George Jeffreys – although a Protestant, he condemned most of his prisoners to death or transportation.

Glencoe – the scene of a massacre.

Marching on Blenheim.

Marlborough leads the charge at Blenheim.

John Blackadder, leader of the Cameronian Rifles.

Daniel Defoe.

Jonathan Swift.

Samuel Pepys.

Queen Anne.

Sir Cloudsley Shovell in admiral's uniform.

England was weakened by two major disasters, the Great Plague and the Great Fire of London. One of Charles's peace conditions was the advancement of his nephew's position as the next Stadtsholder. As a countermeasure, the Dutch made William a 'Child of State', meaning that a new educational committee, chaired by Johan de Witt, was established to school William as a Hollander and spend time in instructing the youthful prince in state matters.

The Dutch referred to their country in a number of ways: the United Netherlands, the States of Holland, the Netherlands, the Dutch Republic and Holland. William I, or William the Silent (1533–84), inherited Orange from his childless cousin and founded the House of Orange-Nassau. Orange is not a town or province in the Netherlands but was in the small principality of Provencal in the south of France. For such a small province, it owned vast estates in the Low Countries (present-day Netherlands and Belgium). William I believed in the freedom of religion for all people and was shocked by the treatment of the Protestants in the Spanish Netherlands. William was one of the most prominent and popular politicians in the Netherlands and he emerged as the leader of the armed resistance against Spain. He married three times and his second wife, Anna, had previously been married to the father of the celebrated painter Peter Paul Rubens. Tragically, William was assassinated by a French Catholic who was paid by Philip II and told to destroy 'the pest on the whole of Christianity and enemy of the human race'. He fired two wheel-lock pistols at point-blank range into William, who died immediately, becoming the first head of state to be assassinated by handgun.

In 1650, William II became involved in a bitter dispute with the province of Holland and the powerful Regents of Amsterdam, Andries Bicker and his cousin, Cornelius de Graff. The Regents wanted to save money by reducing the army, which would reduce William's authority. He responded by imprisoning eight members of the States of Holland, including Bicker, de Graff and the powerful Johan de Witt. In what was a civil war, William sent his cousin, Willem Frederick of Nassau-Dietz, with an army of 10,000 to seize Amsterdam. William had served as Stadtholderl for only three years, from 1647 until his death from smallpox in 1650. It was the beginning of the First Stadtholderless Period, which lasted until 1672 when his son, the young William, was elevated to Stadtholder.

In 1654, enmity broke out from a small group that had control of Holland and the city of Amsterdam. The Republican Party excluded the House of Orange from power with the Act of Seclusion. The infant William was prevented from becoming the Prince of Orange and barred from holding the office in the state. A treaty that lasted six years was drawn up between the United Provinces and Oliver Cromwell's Commonwealth of England that recognised this exclusion.

The young, orphaned Prince William was schooled in the complexities of the Stadtholder and, from the age of eighteen, he spent his entire life struggling to defend the Netherlands against Louis XIV. In 1670, when he was twenty, he was invited by Charles II to stay for four months in England. Although James, Duke of York, had converted to Catholicism in 1668, his daughters, Mary and Anne, were brought up as Anglicans at the insistence of Charles II and it may have been during William's visit in 1670 that he first met the eight-year-old Mary. The English ambassador to the Netherlands, Sir William Temple, negotiated a treaty ending the Dutch war and, along with Thomas Osborne, Earl of Danby, arranged the marriage between William and Mary. Temple's secretary was the author and satirist Jonathan Swift, known primarily for *Gulliver's Travels*.

In 1671, the Dutch Republic, fearing an imminent attack by the Anglo-French, wanted the young William to be appointed Captain-General of the Dutch States Army. The States of Gelderland and Utrecht made this their official policy. On 19 January 1672, the States of Holland made a counterproposal to appoint William for just a single campaign. William was affronted by this and a compromise was reached; an appointment by the Staates-General for one summer, followed by a permanent appointment on his twenty-second birthday.

In October 1677, William invited himself to England. He travelled from Harwich to Newmarket, where Charles was enjoying the horse racing, and surprised the monarch with his insistence at meeting Mary before any wedding. Although he had never formally met her, this was part of the peace settlement to end the enmity between England and the Netherlands. James was set against such a marriage, as he sought Catholic husbands for both his daughters, but reluctantly accepted Charles's political manoeuvre. Mary was then fifteen and just old enough to be part of the archetypal dynastic victim of international statecraft. She grew to be 5ft 11in tall; four inches taller than her husband. When her father told her that she was to marry the twenty-seven-year-old William is a few weeks' time, she dissolved into floods of tears, which lasted for a day and a half.

William and Mary were married for reasons of state, bringing the two countries together. It was an arrangement that infuriated Louis of France, who had plans for conquering the Low Countries. The couple were wed at St James's Palace on 4 November 1677, William's birthday, during which Mary wept throughout the ceremony. William's best man was Hans Willem Bentinck, later to be ennobled Earl of Portland, and also present was Arnold Joost van Keppel, made Earl of Albemarle. The marriage was conducted in a passage close to Mary's chambers, and, as the custom of that time, few witnesses were present. The tradition was that the royal family witnessed the bedding ceremony to establish the consummation of the marriage. King Charles, drawing the curtains around their bed, declared, 'Now nephew, to your work! Hey, St George for England!'

Later that month, Mary accompanied her husband on a rough North Sea journey back to the Netherlands. They were unable to dock at Rotterdam due to the ice and were forced to disembark at the small village of Ter Heijde. From there, they walked through the frosty countryside to meet the coaches that would take them to Huis Honselaarsdijk, the palace and country residence of the Dutch Staadtholder and the Princess of Orange. On 14 December, they made their formal entry to The Hague in a grand procession. According to the author Jonathan Keates in his book, *William III and Mary II*:

> There was to be no question of an alternative attachment. The evolution, bizarre and unlikely at various stages, of their relationship into a love match has been aptly compared to the story of Beauty and the Beast.

William did have one mistress and that was Elizabeth Villiers, 'Squinting Betty', elevated to the Countess of Orkney. Despite this, the marriage turned out to be a happy one. Sadly, it was blighted by Mary suffering two miscarriages in the spring of 1678 and autumn 1679, which caused her not to have children. Mary succumbed to smallpox a few years later, which made William even more reserved. Mary's funeral procession cost £50,000, the largest and most expensive for an English monarch. It took place on 15 March 1695, four months after her death on 28 December. It was an event that expressed grief for a much-loved queen but it almost cemented William's position as the rightful king. Despite this, it was important to counter any claim to the throne by the exiled Catholic King James, who tried several times to reassert himself on the English throne.

With the Restoration in 1660, the Parliament Act declared the Long Parliament be dissolved, and the Lords and the Commons, then sitting to be the two Houses of Parliament, and not convened by the King. It was the same year that William's mother died of smallpox and William was placed under the strict guardianship of his grandmother and his uncle, Frederick William, Elector of Brandenburg. By 1666, he was made ward of the Staadten General and was educated in the post of Staadtholder.

The year 1672 was regarded by the Dutch as *rampjaar,* the disaster year, when they were involved in the Franco-Dutch War and the third Anglo-Dutch War. Besides being attacked by England and France, the German states of Galen, Bavaria and Munster also declared war. The invading armies overwhelmed the Dutch forces and occupied a large portion of the Republic. As a consequence, the Orangists seized power in the remaining provinces of Holland, Zeeland and Utrecht. William, Prince of Orange, was installed as Staadtholder, which forced his rival, Johan de Witt, to resign as Grand Pensionary. De Witt, the Dutch republican chief minister and pro-French, was vehemently opposed to the House of Orange-Nassau. He and his brother were blamed for the 1672 year of wars and paid the penalty. His brother, Cornelius, was arrested and imprisoned in The Hague for treason. On learning that his brother had been incarcerated, Johan visited him, unaware that the crowd were baying for his blood. The small contingent of soldiers guarding the prison, intimidated by the mob, left their posts. The crowd stormed the unguarded prison and dragged out the brothers, who were horribly butchered. Some say that William was responsible for inciting the mob, but no one was prosecuted for this heinous crime. William's role in the de Witt lynching has never been proved but he did reward the ringleaders Hendrik Verhoeff, Johan van Bancham and Johan Kievit.

William visited England in 1681 in an effort to persuade Charles II not to depend on France for support for James's succession. There were outbreaks of rebellion throughout the country to prevent the successive Catholic king enforcing his religion on the population. William successfully placated the Whig movement, which enabled James to succeed his brother. It was

William's intention to keep a close relationship with England to stave off Louis's aims for dominance of Europe. In 1678, the United Provinces signed a peace treaty with France at Nijmegen, with Louis being the victor who gained the provinces of Franche-Comte, Alsace, Lorraine, Freiberg and Breisach. The real gains were made by England, which now commanded the majority of seaborne trade, much to Holland's loss. In America, England also appropriated New Amsterdam, changing its name to New York, and the tiny mid-Atlantic island of St Helena, which later became Napoleon Bonaparte's prison.

William became the object of Louis's spite and, in 1683, Louis invaded the Provencal city of Orange, north of Marseilles, which was a refuge for the Huguenots. As leader of Europe's Catholics, he authorised *dragonades*, the billeting of ill-disciplined dragoons, in Protestant households to abuse the inhabitants and steal their possessions. They also desecrated Protestant churches and forced the closure of Huguenot schools. This persecution caused outrage in England and created a wave of pamphlets and books against the inhumane treatment of Huguenots, many of whom fled to England to seek asylum. This influx caused James some anxiety in his quest to turn England into a Catholic country. On 17 January 1686, Louis claimed that his draconian policy had rid France of many Huguenots but it also affected the French economy. The Huguenots possessed a work ethic that embraced textile weaving, clock-making, silver-smithing, optics and the making of musical instruments. This exodus proved beneficial to the Dutch and English and detrimental to France.

For the English exiles, the Netherlands was not a healthy place to be with Louis and his huge army making threatening movements. Some moved to Germany, Switzerland or Denmark but, somehow, the Dutch managed to hold on to their country. The English population distrusted the superstitions and cruelties of Roman Catholicism, as acted through the persecution by Mary I and, in France, the St Bartholomew Day Massacre. Also, Charles I's dedication to the Catholic faith caused the start of the English Civil War, which precipitated a decade of warfare and tore families apart for their religion.

James II was far more reckless and radical than his father and altered the Succession in favour of the Roman Catholics. As he set about filling Parliament with Catholics and importing Catholic Irish officers to fill the officer class, it seemed only a step away from having a Catholic heir.

England was predominantly Protestant and angered by James's mission to turn England into a Catholic nation, despite having only a tiny minority of Catholics. By installing Catholics to senior positions of power he only succeeded in alienating his citizens. There were those who did not want to replace James for fear of another civil war, as it was still within living memory of the chaos that the internecine conflict brought.

James began writing to William in 1686 to repeal the Succession and surprisingly inviting a Dutch invading force as early as that year. He said there would be no opposition but William replied that he would be prepared to act only if James tried to alter the Succession or if he threatened England's religion. Rebuffed by this refusal, James exploited the rumours of William's mistress, Elizabeth Villiers, in an attempt to cause a rift between his daughter and son-in-law; this was an outrageous allegation considering the number of mistresses James had. The Loyal Parliament was the only Parliament of England that sat in 1685 but it did not do so for the rest of James's reign. It was named because most of its members were loyal to the new king but, by November, they were concerned with the direction he was taking. Dismissive of Parliament, James prevented it meeting again. The Parliaments were mostly named during the Stuart period from 1660 to 1705. Long (1660), Convention (1660), Cavalier (1661), Habeas Corpus (1679), Exclusion Bill (1680), Oxford (1681), Loyal (1685), Convention (1689), 2nd Parliament of William and Mary (1690), 3rd Parliament of King William III, 4th Parliament of King William III, 5th Parliament of King William III, 6th Parliament of King William III, 1st Parliament of Queen Anne and 2nd Parliament of Queen Anne.

By June 1688, many nobles had made up their minds to send an invitation to the Prince of Orange. Some wanted Protestant William to replace Catholic James outright and others thought he could guide James in a more conciliatory manner with the threat of an invasion. The birth of a Catholic heir hastened a letter written to William that the signatories and their allies would support him. The letter included many of the grievances against the King, most prominently his determination to force the population to accept the Catholic religion. The biggest mistake was the letter William set congratulating James on the birth of his son, something that would never be acceptable to the population.

A letter sent to William was written in a secret code and signed by the following members of the nobility known as the Immortal Seven; Charles

Talbot, Earl of Shrewsbury; William Cavendish, Earl of Devonshire; Thomas Osborne, Earl of Danby; Richard Lumley, 1st Viscount Lumley; Henry Compton, Bishop of London; Edward Russell, Earl of Orford; and Henry Sidney, Earl of Romney, who wrote the letter. It was carried to The Hague by Rear Admiral Arthur Herbert, later Lord Torrington, disguised as a common sailor. The signatories were Thomas Osborne and Henry Compton of the Tories (Court Party) and the remaining were Whigs (County Party). Given their differing views, it says something for James's arrogant and biased manner that it brought the two sides together.

Chapter 12

Invasion

Louis XIV believed that William's invasion would end in disaster like the 1588 Spanish Armada. Instead of attacking the Dutch prince, Louis sent his French fleet to the Mediterranean to support his troops fighting in Italy, and his Royal army away from Holland to the Rhineland. Without the threat from France, William had already started to assemble an invasion force at the end of April 1688, and justified it with an invitation from the Immortal Seven to invade and unseat Catholic James. Gilbert Burnet noted a conversation between William and Edward Russell in which Russell asked William what he intended to do. The Prince answered:

> If he was invited by some men of the best interest, and the most valued of the nation, who should both in their own name of others who trusted them, invite him to come and rescue the nation and the religion, he believed he could be ready by the end of September to come over.

In fact, it would not be until November that he stepped on to English soil. With the marriage to Mary in 1677, William became a strong contender for the English throne. In 1680, William secretly persuaded the States General to send a message to King Charles preventing any Catholics from succeeding him. The reply from Charles and James was angry that such a request had been made and William dropped his plea. When James succeeded Charles in 1685, William urged the new king to join the 1686 League of Augsburg, an anti-French coalition of the Dutch Republic, the Holy Roman Empire, Sweden, Spain and several German states. James refused to associate with an alliance that was against France and relations worsened between William and James. Nevertheless, William, via his envoy Zuylestein, conveyed a congratulatory message to James and Mary Beatrice on the birth of their son, the spurious James Francis Edward, which did not go well with the English.

By his own stupidity, James, without the most compliant Parliament of his reign, was unable to repeal the Test Acts. By 1687, he intended to use his powers to replace the Tories who had welcomed him as king with Dissenters. His obsession with Roman Catholicism led him to alter the Succession in favour of a Catholic ruler. When Mary Beatrice announced that she was pregnant, the Catholics were jubilant, seeing that the Stuart dynasty would be extended. June seemed to be the month when momentous events took place. On 10 June 1688, Mary gave birth to a healthy boy, while on 30 June, the same day the seven bishops were acquitted, the 'Immortal Seven' nobles sent William their formal invitation to invade. Many of the aristocracy had had enough of James' tyranny and wanted William to assume the crown, while others thought that William could steer his father-in-law along a more conciliatory path.

Anne wrote to her sister, Mary:

> Whether the child be true or false. It may be it is our brother, but God only knows … one cannot help having a thousand fears and melancholy thoughts, but whatever changes may happen you shall ever find me for to my religion and faithfully yours.

In fact, William's focus was on Louis XIV's target of engulfing Continental Europe into a French-dominated Catholic state. On 25 September, France began to impose an embargo on all Dutch ships in French harbours. William had already made plans for some sort of intervention around the end of 1687 and he and his ministers had begun to earmark ships and men for an invasion in the summer of 1688. The main reasons for the Netherlands invading England was James' policy against Protestantism and the fear that he would ally himself with France. William had a pragmatic agenda as he wanted to steer England away from allying with France and hoped a free English Parliament would support this.

The invasion of England was massively expensive, with the hiring a transport fleet costing 4 million guilders. This money had been earmarked for repairing the fortresses to the east of the country, which were prone to being invaded by the French. The Dutch invasion fleet was four times the size of the 1588 Spanish Armada, which met with disaster around the British Isles. The transport fleet of 500 vessels was hired in the various Dutch ports. They were expected to carry the army, along with 11,000 horses, a supply train and 20,000 arms. The death of the Elector of Brandenburg on 29 April 1688 prompted Hans Willem Bentinck, the best man at William and Mary's wedding, to persuade the German states to supply some 13,000 troops to defend the Netherlands. The Dutch and mercenary army destined for the invasion were housed for two months in a camp near Nijmegen. When the vessels were ready, the army marched to the Zuiderzee, where they embarked for Texel and then to Hellevoetsluis.

The largest armada had been assembled at Hellevoetsluis, consisting of forty-four men of war, four light frigates, ten fire ships and about 400 tenders and flyboats chartered from the ship's owners. The latter were hired to carry some 21,000 Dutch, Danish, Anglo-Scots, Swedish and Finnish, with assorted German States soldiers. Once the soldiers and equipment was loaded, the great flotilla set sail on 19 October, and sailed north towards the coast of Essex, where the English navy was patrolling. On the second day, a ferocious storm hit the fleet, which scattered it. It looked as if the weather had wrecked the invasion plans rather in the manner of the Spanish Armada in 1588, but the damage was not as bad as predicted. Most of the ships were able to return to Hellevoetsluis, but some 500 horses suffocated in the holds as they were tossed about in the turbulent North Sea. Two men-of-war had to return to Hellevoetsluis to be rerigged and 400 soldiers were blown to Texel, but they later rejoined the fleet.

While the Dutch-friendly invasion force was under way, the English Royal Navy was in a poor condition positioned at the mouth of the Thames. Not only was the Fleet not fit to take on the Dutch invasion, it had serious problems from a lack of experienced crews and resorted to the hasty pressing of men, boys and some soldiers. The Channel Fleet commander, Admiral Richard Strickland, had complained that none of his ships were fit for him to engage with the Dutch fleet and another shortcoming was the lack of swifter, smaller vessels that could be used as scouts. Instead he had to use his heavier ships of the line to seek out the Dutch. Thirty ships were anchored at Oaze Edge off the northern end of the Thames Estuary in anticipation that many of the aristocracy had had enough of James' tyranny and wanted William to assume the crown, while others thought that William could steer his father-in-law along a more conciliatory path. The Dutch fleet's northerly passage appeared as if it would land in Essex, but the English fleet was too weak to prevent the invasion force from landing on the east coast and resorted to tracking the enemy. On 3 October, James received intelligence that the Dutch would sail further north and land, probably near Bridlington Bay in Yorkshire. The Earl of Danby anticipated that the Dutch would land at Hull, while others suggested Sole Bay in Suffolk. Strickland, a strict Catholic, attempted to have mass performed publicly on board his flagship, which almost caused a mutiny, and he was soon replaced by William Legge, Lord Dartmouth, who wrote to James:

> My old friend, Sir Roger, hath been very indiscreet, and his behaviour hath been very disobliging all this summer, which I could not at first believe, but he is sensible himself of the general dislike there is to him.

On 12 October, Dartmouth moved his fleet to the Gunfleet Buoy off the River Blackwater in Essex, and later to the Nore off the Kent coast. James ordered his numerically superior army to encamp at Hounslow Heath during the summer and autumn, and he was confident that they would see off the Dutch. It was the first time since 1640 that England faced the prospect of another civil war.

The storm had created some harm but the Dutch fleet was able to mend broken spars, rigging and the horses were replaced. The damages were minimal and within eight days the fleet was ready to sail. The storm was a blessing in disguise and William made use of it. He ordered the *Haarlem and Amsterdam Courantier* newspaper to publicise that the fleet had been miserably shattered, losing nine men-of-war and one thousand horses, and that injuries had afflicted the seamen. News reached James of the deaths of Dr Gilbert Burnet and the chief ministers under the Prince. The press circulated that the storm loss of £100,000 for damages had postponed the invasion until the spring of 1689. When James learned of this disaster, he was delighted. Mary then travelled to the town of Brielle to bid farewell to William. She later wrote:

> When he left me it was as if my heart had been torn from my body ... I stayed without moving in the room where he had left me; all that I could do was to commend him to God.

On 1 November, the Dutch fleet was prepared to set sail for the second time. Making to sail north, the wind had changed direction and blew from the east; the fortuitous Protestant Wind. The English fleet sighted some Dutch ships but were unable to move thanks to the adverse wind and tide. Dartmouth later wrote:

> Just at the break of dawn on Saturday morning [3 November], we saw 13 sail about three leagues to windward of us, I got ready to sail with the fleet on Saturday, but the sea came in so heavy, and the tide fell so cross, that we could not till yesterday [4 November] morning. Collins stated that the fleet had lifted their anchors, but the ebb being almost spent, it did not succeed in weathering the Longsand Head and the Kentish Knock.

Gilbert Burnet wrote of a single cannon fired at night:

> Upon which the Prince fired a gun, which caused a great consternation in the whole fleet; we, having a brisk easterly wind, concluded ourselves ruined; but the small advice-boats, cruising for a more certain account of the English, brought us back word, that, instead of the English fleet, which the former advice had alarmed us with, it was Admiral Herbert with part of our fleet, which had been separated some hours from the body of our fleet ...

On 2 November, the Dutch fleet entered the English Channel. Gilbert Burnet, who accompanied William, noted the fleet's progress:

> The Prince immediately thereupon gave another signal of stretching the whole fleet in a line from Dover to Calais, twenty-five deep. This sight would have ravished the most curious eyes of Europe: when our fleet was in its greatest splendour, the trumpets and drums playing various tunes to rejoice our hearts; this continued for above three hours ... By the morning we espied the Isle of Wight, and then the Prince ordered the fleet to be drawn into the same posture, as before related ... about five in the morning we made the Start, the wind chopping about to the westward; upon

which we stood fair by Dartmouth, and so made for Torbay, where the Prince again ordered the whole fleet into the same posture as at Dover and Calais.

By 5 November, the fleet found it had sailed past Torbay and on to Plymouth. The wind then turned south and the ships sorted themselves out and, in four hours, headed for Torbay. With so many ships, it took days to disembark the thousands of men, horses, weapons and even a printing press. This was used to circulate William's Declaration and the vast amounts of propaganda throughout the country; some even found its way into London. The horses were landed at a convenient place where they only had to swim for 20 yards, and after three hours all were landed. The artillery and stores were unloaded at Topsham and the Dutch army at Torbay. The army then marched 4 miles to Exeter and entered the city as if on a royal progress. With crowds lining the streets in greeting, the English troops were followed by 200 West African attendants in exotic uniforms; probably the first black men the town had ever seen. These were followed by 200 Finnish soldiers dressed in bearskins with black armour and broad swords. William rode in on a white horse clad in half-armour with forty-two footmen following behind him. Bringing up the rear were the Dutch, Swedish and Danish contingents.

As for James's fleet, they ran into a storm from the west that pushed them from the Isle of Wight back to the Downs, where they anchored. News that William's force had landed in the West Country was greeted with rapture after the appalling Bloody Assizes of 1685. News of the Protestant invasion filtered through to the towns and cities across England, and anti-Catholic riots broke out in London and Norwich. Lord Delamere, who had supported Monmouth in his rebellion, urged his supporters in Cheshire and Lancashire to take up arms, stating:

No man can love fighting for its own sake, nor find any pleasure in danger; and you may imagine I would be very glad to spend the rest of my days in peace, I having so great a share of troubles. But I see all lies at stake, I am to choose whether I will be a slave and a Papist, or Protestant and a Freeman: and the case being thus, I should think myself false to my Country, if I sat still at this time.

The Earl of Devonshire, with tenants from Chatsworth House, had entered Derby and then on to Nottingham with a sizable force of cavalry. He was joined by Lord Delamere on 21 November, who then marched south-west and released Lord Lovelace from Gloucester jail. On 22 November, the Earl of Danby occupied York and then went on to take Scarborough and Hull. On 16 November, the first officers to defect to William were Thomas Langston, the King's nephew, who commanded the Duke of St Alban's Horse, and Sir Francis Compton of the Royal Horse Guards. The latter lost his nerve and returned to the royal camp at Salisbury.

With the prospect of a pitched battle, James moved his large army further out to Salisbury to meet the threat of William's advance. James's army was not prepared to do battle but merely block William's progress to London. On 19 November, in the midst of a blizzard, James took with him the French ambassador, Paul Barillon, who commented on the lack of spirit among the officers:

> Even if they aren't capable of treason it's still obvious that they won't fight with a good heart, and the army is perfectly aware of this.

The Williamite invasion had been considered for a number of years and, with no major battle in the offing, Edward Hyde, Earl of Clarendon, was the first commander to defect to the invasion force. James began to suffer from heavy nosebleeds that incapacitated him for hours, a sure sign that he was soon to suffer from depression. James realised that his army had shrunk alarmingly. In an attempt to rally his reluctant commanders, he called a council of war. Being on the verge of a breakdown, both in health and body, on 23 November he ordered his army to retreat back to London. John Churchill thought it was madness to withdraw and calculated that he would be better off by taking his regiment over to the Prince of Orange. He was joined by Henry Fitzroy, Duke of Grafton, one of the illegitimate sons of Charles. Later that evening, Anne's husband, the Prince of Denmark, and the Duke of Ormond also joined the Dutch forces. With his army falling apart, James still believed in his absolute authority but his breakdown saw the end of his reign.

With the Prince of Orange moving ever closer to London, a brief skirmish broke out in the east Somerset town of Wincanton. An Irish officer, Patrick

Sarsfield, had returned to London in 1681 and made two separate attempts to abduct an heiress and was lucky to escape persecution. He was ordered by General Piercy Kirke to take out a patrol and scout the area around the village of Bruton. On 20 November, he rode out of the Royal camp with 120 Horse Guards and Horse Grenadier Guards including his second in command, Henry Luttrell. Finding there were no Dutch forces at Bruton, they rode into Wincanton.

William had ordered about thirty men of the Scots Brigade infantry ahead to Wincanton to find fresh horses. Under the command of Lieutenant Campbell, they were instructed to remain in the town until joined by William's main force. Receiving warning from the local inhabitants of the Royalists' approach, Campbell set an ambush for Sarsfield's cavalry just outside Wincanton. Unsure whether the approaching group were deserters or enemy, Campbell shouted out a challenge demanding to know which side they were on. Sarsfield yelled back, 'God damn you! I'll Prince you!' and both sides opened fire. In the exchange of fire, Campbell was shot dead. The rest of the Scots were in good defensive positions and managed to kill or wound several horsemen. Dismounting, the royalists fought on foot, returning the enemy fire and hurling grenades. Henry Luttrell led some men in an effort to outflank them. The skirmish abruptly ended when a local man warned Sarsfield that the Dutch reinforcements were in Wincanton. This was a false rumour and Sarsfield withdrew beyond musket range, which allowed the Scots to flee, leaving twelve of their number dead. Sarsfield then advanced into Wincanton, taking six prisoners and some of the horses the Scots had been collecting. Several of Sarsfield's men had been killed or injured, including a severely wounded Cornet John Webb, who was left behind in the village to recover. Wincanton was then occupied by the Dutch and William spent the night in the manor house known as The Dogs, because of two stone greyhounds used as finials on the gateposts.

Princess Anne, who despised the Catholics and in particular her stepmother Mary Beatrice, sought to escape from London. Henry Compton, the Bishop of London, had been in contact with Anne's closest companion, Lady Sarah Churchill, with ways of spiriting Anne from London. A secret address in Suffolk Street, just north of Whitehall, was the starting point. Anne and Sarah slipped out Whitehall Palace and met with Henry Compton and his nephew, Lord Dorset, who had a coach waiting for them. They timed their departure well, for guards had been stationed outside Sarah Churchill's house and orders came that Anne was to be placed under guard that evening. Fortunately her rooms were not checked until ten o'clock on the following morning. Sarah Churchill describes how easy it was to escape from London to Nottingham:

> The Princess went to bed at the usual time to prevent suspicion. I came to her soon after, by the backstairs which went down from her closet, her Royal Highness, my Lady Fitzharding and I, with one servant, walked to the coach where we found the Henry Compton, Bishop of London, and the Earl of Dorset. They conducted us that night to the Bishop's house in the city, and the next day to my Lord Dorset's at Copt Hall. From there we went to the Earl of Northampton's, and thence to Nottingham, where the county gathered about the Princess nor did she think herself safe till she saw that she was surrounded by the Prince of Orange's friends.

The small party headed north through Epping Forest, stopping for refreshment at Loughton, and on to Lord Dorset's mansion at Copt Hall. Leaving his nephew, the two ladies and the bishop went on through the winter countryside, noting the roads were full of bedraggled soldiers returning from Salisbury. Taking a roundabout route, they arrived at Castle Ashby, where they were joined by the Earl of Northampton and his cavalry. With this protection, they drove on to Market Harborough, where Anne was greeted by two banquets for their royal guest. On 3 December, they reached Nottingham, where Lord Danby hoped Anne would go on to York. However, Compton refused to act without William's approval. On 8 December, William instructed Compton to bring Anne south to Oxford, where she would be safe. With the disappearance of Anne, James was mortified by the news and exclaimed, 'God help me! My own children have forsaken me.'

On 6 December, William reached Hungerford on the borders of Berkshire and Wiltshire. Commissioners representing James met with William on 8 December in the Bear Inn, where they offered free elections and pardons to those who defected to the Prince of Orange. James made an exception of John Churchill, in which he said:

Churchill, whom I have raised so high, he and he alone has done all this. He has corrupted my army. He has corrupted my child (Princess Anne). He would have put me in the hands of the Prince of Orange but for God's special providence.

The only real confrontation of the Glorious Revolution was at Reading. Having retreated from Salisbury to Hounslow Heath, an advanced guard of 600 Irish Catholic soldiers under Patrick Sarsfield was sent to Reading. The remaining inhabitants, who were scared of the Irish troops, had managed to send a message to William that the royalists were drawn up facing west from where the Dutch forces would advance. Sarsfield positioned his men around the town with a troop of horse in the yard of the Bear Inn, while the walls of St Mary's churchyard were lined with musketeers. A force was posted in Broad Street and a guard was posted in St Mary's tower to watch for any advance by the Dutch. The main body of the Irish was drawn up in the Market Place.

Alerted by the Reading inhabitants that the Irish expected them to advance from the west, the Williamite army used the hedgerows to disguise their movements. Instead of marching on Reading, the troops turned left, skirted north of the town and entered from an unexpected direction. Taken by surprise, the Irishmen were thrown into confusion and had to stampede to leave Reading before they could get in a position to prevent the Dutchmen opening fire. Without stopping to fight, the Irish fled towards Twyford, where they were fired upon by the inhabitants from the upstairs windows. The Irish lost their colours and fifty men, while only five Dutch soldiers were killed.

With little option but to seek exile, on 9 December James oversaw his family moving to France. Two days later, accompanied by Sir Edward Hales, he took a small skiff down the Thames and on the way he threw the Great Seal of the Realm into the river as a means of embarrassing any future administration by destroying the laws made by Parliament. Hales, a fellow Catholic, had been made Lieutenant of the Tower of London and he was thought about to build a Catholic chapel within the Tower. When the seven bishops were discharged into Hales' custody, he demanded fees of them, but they refused on the grounds that their detention was illegal. Out of spite, Hales said if they came into his hands again they should feel his power. Gilbert Burnet later wrote:

Thus a great King, who had a good Army and a strong Fleet, did choose rather to abandon all, that either to expose himself to any danger with that part of the Army that was still firm to him, or to stay and see the issue of a Parliament ... It is not possible to put a good construction on any part of the dishonourable scene which he then acted.

The boat reached Faversham by the Thames in Kent to take on sand for ballast and the two men were brought ashore. However, Hales was recognised by some fishermen and the pair were taken to the Queen's Arms Inn, where James was recognised as an 'ugly, lean-jawed hatchet faced Popish dog' and roughly searched for valuables. Hales, as a high officer of the Tower, found himself within a short period as a prisoner in the building. After eighteen months, he was released and went into exile with James at Saint-Germain-en-Laye. He applied for a licence to return to England but died before it was granted.

The Earl of Ailesbury arrived on 14 December to take James back to Whitehall, something William did not want. The Dutch Blue Guards guarded James, while he thought of another means of escape and William held back until his father-in-law decided. James finally made up his mind and, on 22 December, he departed from Rochester with the Duke of Berwick. From the grandeur of monarchy, James ate bacon from an old frying pan on a humble merchant ship. He was greeted on Christmas Day by Louis XIV at Ambleteuse and provided with the Chateau de Saint-Germain-en-Laye to the west of Paris. He was given a pension and, apart from two attempts to retake his crown, he lived in pious luxury until his death. His wife bore him another child, Princess Louisa Mary, but she died of smallpox when she was nineteen.

While England was rioting against the Catholics, a short-lived reversal took place during December. James had increased his army with the addition of Jacobite Irish troops, which helped prop up the King's reluctant army. The Irish troops were widely detested by the predominantly Protestant population and some 2,820 had been stationed in Portsmouth for three months. The townspeople had reacted in a negative way and the local newspaper had reported that the inhabitants were making 'great complaints of the rude Irish who had caused many families to leave that place, having committed many robberies'. As William's army approached London, James ordered many of the Irish in Portsmouth to block the advance at Reading. After being trounced, the Irish retreated to Portsmouth and Uxbridge. Rumours soon spread that the Irish soldiers were preparing a campaign of massacre against the English population in revenge for James' overthrow. On 13 December, according to Gilbert Burnet:

> Country fellows, arriving about midnight at Westminster caused uproar, by reporting that the Irish, in desperate rage, were advancing to London, and putting all before them to fire and sword.

About 100,000 men were reported to have mobilised to defend their homes within half an hour. This seems unlikely, although many houses were illuminated with torches to prevent the Irish from creeping up and creating mayhem. Tuscany's ambassador wrote that he had seen the inhabitants:

> All discharging firearms, drums beating rapidly, and women, for greater noise, beating warming-pans, pots, and frying pans, and such things; which lie resulted in good against the intention of him who gave it out, because with the city so armed, and with attention to another revolt, it was a wonder the rabble did not create other disorders.

For a brief few days starting on 13 December, the Irish Fright quickly spread across England. By 14 December, Norwich, Bedford, Cambridge and Kingston-upon-Thames were all supposed to have been destroyed. The mayor of Chesterfield wrote that 7,000 Catholics and Irishmen had burned Birmingham and were advancing on Derby. A Leicestershire clergyman had heard that the Irish were slitting throats and went so far as raising a militia. After a day, he could not find one Irishmen and disbanded his briefly formed armed volunteers. On 15 December, the rumour had reached Yorkshire, where Halifax and Skipton had reportedly been burned. Lord Danby sent a troop from York to Pontefract to repel the Irish and the pro-Catholic Lancashire. Lancashire was equally alerted by the Irish Fright and took steps to defend its towns. Wakefield received warning that Doncaster had been burned, while those in Doncaster learned that Birmingham and Stafford had been sacked. In Leeds, some 7,000 agricultural workers sharpened their scythes in readiness to defend the city. Peter

Shakerley, the military governor in Chester Castle, disarmed the royalist garrison and armed the citizens. He wrote to the Secretary of War to inform him of his action:

> Ye report of a body of 8 or 9,000 bloody Irish coming this from London ... They burn all places they come at, and kill man, woman and child.

The West Country also received word of the so-called Irish massacre. At two in the morning, the Duchess of Beaufort heard that the Irish were only 5 miles from Wooten Bassett and killing all who stood in their path. Andover, Newbury, Yeovil and Marlborough were all under threat. The Irish Fright spread to even the remote parts of the country. It reached Dolgellau in Merionethshire on 18 December, where the only fatality occurred. A supposed Irishman and excise man was shot and killed by a local mob, and his passing was not particularly mourned.

At least nineteen counties had been touched by the Irish Fright. The flight of their King had created a fear of the Irish, whose numbers could not have caused so much panic. Rather than risk a terrible defeat at the hands of the Dutch army, Lord Feversham disbanded James's forces. This left the Irish soldiers poorly paid and with no way of returning home. They had little option but to break into a substantial house to keep themselves from starving and this may have led to two possibilities for the start of the mass panic. The printing press that the Dutch had brought with them was used to stir up hatred of the Irish by planting an *agent provocateur* in the main towns throughout the country. It was never determined who started the rumour but it was likely to be a follower of William. A second suggestion was that Marshal Frederick Schomberg, William's second in command, had put about talk of Irish involvement in the 'Fright' in order to blame James. Gilbert Burnet described it as 'an effectual stratagem commonly ascribed to the Duke of Schomberg'. Within a few days, the panic was over. The English Parliament passed a resolution stating:

> King James II having endeavoured to subvert the constitution of the kingdom by breaking the original contract between King and people, and by the advice of Jesuits and other wicked persons, having violated the fundamental laws, and having withdrawn himself

out of the kingdom, had abdicated the government and that the throne had thereby become vacant.

On 15 December 1687, William sent Zuylestein from Windsor with a message urging James to stay at Rochester and not to return to London. When he arrived in London, he found that James had returned to Whitehall. At their meeting, Zuylestein gave the deposed king an uncompromising response to the effect that William's royal troops were posted outside. This had the effect of removing James from his palace, leaving his short reign behind and sailing to France. Zuylestein was naturalised in England on 11 May 1689 and appointed Master of the Robes to the King until 1695, when he was created Earl of Rochford, together with subsidiary titles of Baron Enfield and Viscount Tunbridge.

The Glorious Revolution was an English bloodless tussle between the forces of liberty, as portrayed by William and the forces of tyranny enacted by James. In Ireland and Scotland it was viewed in quite a different way, with many civilians and soldiers being killed or wounded. In December 1688, the nobles appointed William as provisional governor of England until they decided whether or not to invite James back as their king. On 13 February, the Clerk of the House of Lords read the Declaration of Right and Lord Halifax asked William and Mary to accept the throne. They then went in procession to the Great Gate at Whitehall, where the Garter King at Arms proclaimed them King and Queen of England, Scotland and Ireland.

Chapter 13

Glorious Revolution

The Glorious Revolution was not recognised at that time. William had grown weary of the delaying tactics of the Tories in not offering the throne. In fact, it took two months for the Houses of Commons and peers to reach a verdict and they were pushed into making a decision by Princess Anne writing that William should receive the crown. On 22 January, the Conventional Parliament was installed by members and was the first form of a new government establishing without the consent of a new monarch, something that gave it independence. The two parties modified their positions and the Tories accepted some of the Whig proposals, including the constitutional monarchy rather that the divine right of the crown. It was written that limited power was provided for the reigning monarch and provided protection for English subjects. In the same year, the Declaration, and later, the Bill of Rights, were written into English law. A hundred years later it was adapted by the newly formed United States Constitution in 1789. The English Bill of Rights was signed by William and Mary, which limited the power of the monarchy and reaffirmed Parliament's control over taxation and legislation. These were the twelve points that made up the Bill:

The pretended power to dispense with or suspend Acts of Parliament is illegal;

The commission for ecclesiastical causes is illegal;

Levying money without consent of Parliament is illegal;

It is the right of the subject to petition the king and prosecutions for petitioning are illegal;

Maintaining a standing army in peacetime without the consent of Parliament is illegal;

Protestant subjects 'may have arms for their defence suitable to their conditions and allowed by law;

The election of members of Parliament ought to be free;

Freedom of speech and debates in Parliament 'ought not to be impeached or questioned in any court or place out of Parliament;

Excessive bail and fines not required and 'cruel and unusual punishments' not to be inflicted;

Jurors in high treason trial ought to be freeholders;

Promises of fines and forfeitures before conviction are illegal;

Parliament ought to be held frequently.

The Bill of Rights also guaranteed certain rights for all English subjects, including trial by jury and *habeas corpus*, used when lawfulness of detention was to be established.

The Whig party, once almost wiped out in previous assassination and insurrection plots, had a revival in the Commons, which had been dominated by the Tory party. To counterbalance this, the Tories had the majority in the assembly of peers. On 28 December 1688, William granted an audience at St James's Palace to one of the biggest Whigs, and one of its most notorious, Titus Oates. Incredibly, he was granted a pension but still continued to peddle fabrications of a popish plot into the 1690s. Three Whig lawyers, Sir John Maynard, George Trebly, Henry Pollexfen, and Bishop Gilbert Burnet announced that William and Mary should be crowned King and Queen. William was keen to have the monarchy bestowed on him as soon as possible, but a debate in Parliament felt that Mary should be Queen and occupy the executive office. On 29 January 1689, it was declared that England was a Protestant kingdom and only a Protestant could be ruler, thus disinheriting a Catholic claimant. On 3 February, William decided he could not tolerate the Tory objections to his becoming king, and decided to take his army back to Holland to oppose any French invasion. The threat of removing William's army and James grabbing the chance of returning to England galvanised the princesses Mary and Anne into firmly supporting William as king. It emerged that the crown would be shared by William and Mary, with the former taking the executive decisions. Gilbert Burnet later wrote about William's character in his *History of My Own Time*:

His strength lay rather in a true discerning and sound judgement than in imagination or invention: his designs were always great and good: but it was thought he trusted too much to that and that he did not descend enough to the humours of his people, to make himself and his notions more acceptable to them ... He did not like contradiction nor to have his actions censured ... yet he did not love flatterers. He knew all foreign affairs well, and understood the state of every court in Europe very particularly; he instructed his own ministers himself; but did not apply enough to affairs at home ...

He loved the Dutch, and was much beloved among them: but the ill returns he met from the English nation, their jealousies of him and their perverseness towards him, had too much soured his mind, and had a great measure alienated him from them, which he did not take care to conceal, though he saw the ill effects this had upon his business ... I consider him as a person raised up by God to resist the power of France and the progress of tyranny and persecution ... After all abatements that may be allowed for his errors and faults, he ought still to be reckoned among the greatest princes that our history, or indeed that any other, can afford.

On 13 February, William and Mary were proclaimed King and Queen of England, Scotland and Ireland. On 11 April, William III and Mary II were crowned as joint monarchs at Westminster Abbey; the first time this had happened in England. Just hours before the coronation, James sent an express letter to his daughter, Mary, warning her not to go through with the ceremony. Although it was immediately destroyed, a court attendant caught a glimpse of the letter and reportedly said:

James had hitherto been willing to make excuses for what had been done, and thought her obedience to her husband, and compliance with the nation, might have prevailed, but that her being crowned was in her own power; and if she did it, while he and the prince of Wales were living, the curses of an angry father would fall on her, as well as a God who commanded obedience to parents.

As the royal couple walked down the aisle to be crowned, Mary seemed to loom over her husband. William suffered badly from health problems, including wearing a brace to support his hunched back due to scoliosis, and chronic asthma. It had already been decided who would actually rule by the positioning of the two chairs waiting at the altar. William sat in King Edward's Chair, made about 1300, while Mary sat on facsimile chair to his side. In addition, it was the first time that a monarch took the oath to uphold the law according to the Statutes of Parliament. The ceremony was performed by the Bishop of London instead of the Archbishop of Canterbury, William Sancroft, who refused to recognise King James's removal. William was raised in the Reformed Church, which followed the teachings of John Calvin, and he did not formally convert to the Church of England. He gave assurances that he would defend the Protestant cause, although he maintained his original faith in private.

Although a neglected period of history, William and Mary's reign was one of the most important. Absolute monarchy was when the monarch held absolute power, while a constitutional monarchy exercises its powers and authority within the legal framework settled by Parliament. Laws enacted by Parliament, like the 1689 Bill of Rights and the 1701 Act of Settlement, restricted William's powers, although as a pro-Whig, he signed an agreement. Although the Bill of Rights is not a revolutionary statement of universal liberties, it dealt with the misrule of James II and is one of the landmark documents in the development of the civil liberties of England. By moderation and good faith in his exercise of the royal prerogative, he preserved the crown and gave stability to England. On 24 May 1689, there was one Parliamentary law William disagreed with and that was the Toleration Act of 1689. It allowed freedom of worship to nonconformists and dissenters, including Baptists, Congregationalists and Presbyterians, but not Roman Catholics. Dissenters were excluded from holding political office and from the universities, and had to register their preachers and their meeting houses. In 1701, Parliament passed the Act of Settlement. William and Mary were childless, and Anne's son, William, Prince of Wales, had died at the age of eleven in 1700. So, with Anne the only Stuart left, it was left for a Protestant foreigner to succeed to the English crown. That person was Electress Sophia of Hanover. As the author, Anne Somerset remarked, 'better a German prince that a French one'.

The Navigation Acts began in 1651 and were only repealed in 1849. The Acts were a long series of English laws that developed, promoted and regulated English ships, shipping, trade and commerce between other countries and with its colonies. The laws also regulated England's fisheries and restricted foreigners' participation in its colonial trade. The Acts caused

English shipping to develop in isolation and limited Dutch ships from carrying trade to Britain. The rise of English merchant shipping led to a rapid increase in the numbers of warships in the Royal Navy, which for three centuries enabled her to be a global superpower.

The revised Navigation Act of 1696 led to the suppression of piracy in 1700 and regulated semi-piratical privateers in 1702. As part of the Act, post offices with branches in England, Ireland, Scotland and the American colonies were established in 1710. These laws created a growing sense of interconnectedness between the colonies and the motherland. A new law was passed in Parliament known as the Licensing Act of 1695. With adjustments that have lasted until the present time, censorship was only used in the most momentous occasions and it was at this point that Britain gained a free political press. Before the Act, printed pamphleteers, printed news-sheets and word of mouth was the only way that news could be conveyed, albeit in a slow process. After the English government relaxed censorship in 1695, newspapers began to expand in the capital. William and James both saw the importance of winning public support in their efforts of holding on to the throne by broadcasting through the new medium of newspapers. However, it was James's pig-headed determination to wean the English public to accepting the Roman Catholic religion that ultimately caused his abdication. William, who was a Calvinist, took a more measured route and accepted the majority of the English Protestant religion. *The London Gazette* began publication twice a week and changed the look of English news printing. It printed in two columns, a clear title and date, something other newspapers started to copy, including short features, some illustrations and classified articles.

The Nine Years' War with France lasted from 1688 to 1697 and did not accomplish much. William knew constitutional disputes would focus attention away from his conflict with Louis, which had resulted in a series of crises, resulting in another English Civil War and the collapse of James II's rule. William was intelligent enough to surrender power whenever he thought by keeping it might cause trouble. He needed to convene Parliament every year in order to raise taxes for his European war and assured his ministers that he would not govern without them. In another new departure, he presented Parliament with his budget estimates and accounts. He turned his government members into public auditors, in so doing, Crown and the Constitution co-operated and instability ended.

Chapter 14

Scottish Problems

In March 1689, William and Mary were asked to formally accept the Scottish throne. Unfortunately many Scots, particularly the Highland clans, sought the reimposing of James on the throne of Scotland. William's bloodless invasion of England contrasted dramatically with the rebellion of the Scottish Jacobites, whose brief resistance ended in August 1689. The Scots had their own king (James VII and II), parliament, laws and church. The two nations were wary of the other and harboured a mutual hostility. While the English embraced the Protestant religion, the Catholics only accounted for about 1 per cent of the population. In Scotland, the Catholics, who made a tiny minority, relied on the Jacobite army to continue their opposition to England until the final battle at Dunkeld. Scottish Protestants, whether Episcopalian or Presbyterian, were outraged by James's efforts to advance the tiny minority of Catholics into positions of power. William, who knew little of Scotland and had never even set foot in it, was preoccupied with the threat from Ireland and the Nine Years' War on the Continent. He wanted to secure a settlement as soon as possible and to concentrate his aims on Ireland and the Grand Alliance he had formed to fight France. James, who had arrived in Ireland, saw Scotland as a launching pad to regain his English crown from his treacherous son-in-law, William. However, in the shifting alliances, the Pope and the Catholic Holy Roman Emperor were allied with William in the Nine Years' War and set against James's plan for an international Catholic crusade.

On 27 July 1689, the 3,500 troops under the command of Major-General Hugh MacKay led his mixture of Dutch, English and Scottish troops to take the garrison at Blair Castle, occupied by the Jacobite force of James Graham, Viscount Dundee. Negotiating a narrow track along a 2-mile pass known as Killiecrankie, MacKay's men were strung out and very vulnerable. MacKay was aware that Dundee had set a trap when he positioned his Catholic clans along the hill overlooking the track and river. MacKay recognised that he had marched into an ambush and moved his men up to a small hill to face the Highlanders. They remained on the hill with little chance of escape until eight o'clock in the evening, when Dundee ordered a charge. Donald McBane, one of MacKay's men, wrote in his book *The Expert Swordsman's Companion*, published in 1728, about the effects of the Highlanders' charge:

> At last they cast away their musquets, drew their broadswords, and advanced furiously upon us, and were in the middle of us before we could fire three shots a-piece; broke us, and obliged us to retreat. Some fled to the water, and some other way; (we were for the most part new men) I fled to the baggage, and took a horse, in order to ride the water. There followed me a Highland man with sword and targe (shield), in order to take the horse, and kill myself. You'd laugh to see how he and I scampered about. I kept always the horse between him and me; at length he drew his pistol. And I fled; he fired after me. I went above the pass, where I met another water, very deep. It was 18 foot over, betwixt two rocks. I resolved to jump it, so I laid down my gun and hat and jumped, and lost one of my shoes in the jump. Many of our men were lost in that water, and at the pass. The enemy pursuing hard, I made the best of my way to Dunkeld where I stayed until what of our men was left came up; then everyone went to his respective regiment.

On the left flank, at about 80 yards, MacKay's troops fired a volley, which killed or wounded some 600 Highlanders. Unable to rearm, the troops fitted their new plug bayonets into the muzzle of their muskets but were quickly overwhelmed by the clans. The Highlanders broke the ranks on the left and wheeled to the right to mop up the rest of MacKay's men. The regiments on the right were holding their own and were able to start a slow retreat towards the Pass of Killiecrankie. As the Highlanders engaged in hand-to-hand combat with the Williamite soldiers, a deathly hush enveloped the battle. As McBane wrote:

> Nothing was heard but the sullen and hollow clashes of broad-sword with the dismal groans and cries of dying and wounded men ... officers and soldiers cut down through the skulls and

neck, to the very breasts; others had skulls cut off above the ears. Some had both their bodies and cross belts cut through at one blow; pikes and small swords were cut like willows.

Dundee led a cavalry charge against the retreating troops but was mortally wounded by a musket shot. The whole battle had taken just thirty minutes and the mortality in that short period was immense; 1,200 of MacKay's men were killed or wounded, and more were killed in the retreat. In contrast, there were around 1,000 Jacobite casualties, most of whom had been killed, and they had lost their inspirational leader, Viscount Dundee.

The Jacobites returned to Blair Castle, where Irishman Colonel Alexander Cannon took control. It was expected that the sixty-year-old Sir Ewen Cameron of Lockiel would be in command and he was so affronted to be passed over that he took part of his clan with him and departed. On 21 August, he led some 5,000 Jacobites towards Perth and, on the way, expected to overwhelm the 1,200 troops at the small town of Dunkeld. The Scottish Privy Council ordered the newly formed Orange Covenanters, better known as the Cameronian regiment, to defend the town, which was without a surrounding wall. It should be pointed out that the Cameronians had absolutely no connection with Sir Ewan Cameron. These were the men that the Duke of Monmouth defeated at Bothwell Bridge in 1679 but were now defenders of Presbyterianism and loyal to King William.

Instead, they took up defensive position in the cathedral and at the Marquess of Athol's house. With no wall to impede the Jacobites, they made their way into the streets and occupied houses overlooking the defensive positions. They kept up a constant fire and were confident that they outnumbered the Cameronians four to one. They stormed the town from all sides, but were unable to form a charge through the narrow streets. The Highlanders took to occupying the surrounding houses, where they became bottled up.

Running short of ammunition, about a hundred Cameronians went on to the cathedral's roof and tore the lead to make musket balls. The Cameronians were driven back to the Dunkeld House, the cathedral and three other houses. A few defenders were trapped in the houses during the retreat and killed by the Highlanders. To the south by the river bank, the Highlanders bunched together and were picked off by the defenders in the cathedral. When the leader of the Cameronians, Lieutenant Colonel William Cleland, was shot and killed by bullets in the liver and head, Captain George Munro took command. He led his men to attack and burn the houses that sheltered the Jacobites. As evening turned to darkness, the Cameronians braced themselves for a final charge by the Jacobites.

In a dramatic reversal of fortunes, the 1,200 Cameronians repelled the 5,000 Jacobites. By the end of the fighting, only three houses survived unburned. In total the Jacobites torched all but three houses and departed, leaving 300 dead and dying behind. It is not clear how long the battle lasted but it appears to have lasted for sixteen hours until 11 pm, when the Jacobites withdrew, leaving the town shrouded in thick smoke from the burning buildings. A mounted messenger conveyed the news of a victory and that the Highlanders were withdrawing.

The final Jacobite battle took place at Cromdale, on 30 April and 1 May 1690. It was little more than a skirmish with a larger column of government troops from Inverness confronting the depleted ranks of 800 Highlanders. As the government troops approached the Spey River, they saw the Highlanders start to retreat from the opposite bank. The commander, Sir Thomas Livingston, led his cavalry across the river and intercepted the Jacobites at the foot of a hill. After a brief stand, a fog came rolling down the hill causing some confusion. In the retreat, some 400 Jacobites were killed or wounded with a small number of government troops killed. The following day, Livingston's men pursued a breakaway section of Highlanders on the outskirts of Aviemore, killing or capturing their prey. During the retreat, some of this band attempted to seize the castle at Lochinclan but they were driven off by the owner and his tenants.

By October 1690, the Jacobite forces were in no state to fight a major pitched battle. Due to the tardiness on the part of James, who finally got around to sending a letter on 12 December in which he gave his consent to sign the Oath of Allegiance. The letter only reached Edinburgh on 21 December, which left ten days to go before the deadline came into force. There were also problems about reaching the Highlands in the middle of winter; it was not just the MacDonalds who were late in signing the oath, other clans exceeded the deadline. It was left to John Dalrymple, the Earl of Stair, to sort out the lateness of the signatures, although he had already decided to make an example of the MacDonalds.

In June 1691, generous terms were offered at the Treaty of Achallader. The English government bribed the clans with £12,000 in exchange for the oath of allegiance to William and it was largely accepted. A Royal Proclamation offered a pardon to anyone taking the oath prior to 1 January 1692, but severe punishments to those who did not. John Dalrymple, the Secretary of State, saw an opportunity to eliminate the worst of the Highland clans, namely the MacDonalds of Glencoe. They were a small clan with few friends and powerful enemies. Having fallen on hard times, the MacDonalds had in the past been the Lords of the Isles and the predominant clan. Now they presently occupied the 8-mile deep valley of Glencoe and were ruled by their chieftain, Alastair Ruadh MacIain of the MacDonalds of Glencoe. Although they were not the only clan, they were reduced to stealing cattle mainly from their neighbours, the Campbells, who had a loathing of the thieving MacDonalds. The Glencoe MacDonalds were one of three clans living in the area of Lochaber; the others were the MacGregors and the Keppoch MacDonalds. They had a reputation for lawlessness and a fierce loyalty to their Catholic king, James VII (II). Alastair MacIain had two sons: John was married to a Glencoe Macdonald, and the younger was married to a Campbell, a distant relative of Robert Campbell of Glenlyon. It was this latter Campbell that was closely implicated in the Glencoe Massacre.

John Campbell, Earl of Breadalbane, was a member of the Scottish Privy Council and could see the wisdom of backing William as a sensible option. He also saw that James could reclaim his crown, so he sat on the sidelines. It was he who brought the clans together at Achallader Castle to pledge their support for William and Mary, who seemed to be in the ascendancy. The Highland clans were not on the list of priorities for William, who was more concerned with the French and their attempt at invading his own country, the Netherlands. In fact, he left the problem of the clans to his Scottish ministers while he prepared to confront the French at Flanders.

In 1691, the winter in the Highlands was predictably cold and snow-bound. The newly appointed Secretary of State for Scotland was John Dalrymple. He had worked with King James but when he fled to France, he quickly switched his allegiance to William and Mary. James was unable to get support from Louis XIV, so he sent his permission to the clan chief to sign the oath. The letter was opened by government spies in London and, having read it, they resealed and sent it on to Edinburgh. The deadline was fast approaching when Alastair MacIain set out through the snow for Fort William. He was told by Colonel John Hill that he was not authorised to accept the oath but he did give the chieftain a letter of protection to say he had honoured the spirit of it. It took three days of trudging through the snow to reach Inverary on 2 January 1692. By this time, he had exceeded the deadline but was confident that his signature would be accepted. The clerks at the Privy Council declared that MacIain's signature was invalid and an illegal late submission. Other clans had been held up by bad weather and exceeded the deadline, but this did not matter to Dalrymple, who wrote:

> It's an act of great charity to be exact in routing out that damnable sept (a division of a clan), the worst in all the highlands.

Still in January, Breadalbane and Stair conveyed to General Sir Thomas Livingstone orders to Lieutenant Colonel James Hamilton and Major Robert Duncanson to wipe out the MacDonald clan of Glencoe.

Quite why the MacDonalds were singled out as semi-barbarian, criminal and unpopular when other clans were just as culpable is not known. Perhaps it was because they were insignificant enough to be made an example of without reprisals from other clans. They were an ideal target, troublesome to their neighbours and known as the 'Gallows' Herd' because of their thieving abilities.

In 1689 after the Battle of Dunkeld, the MacDonalds of Glencoe, together with their Glengarry cousins, looted Captain Robert Campbell of Glenlyon, stole his cattle and burnt his remaining holdings. On 1 February 1692, Glenlyon, an alcoholic, inveterate gambler and bankrupt, was newly commissioned and given command of two companies of 120 men each of the Earl of Argyll's regiment, Chief of the Campbells. They were ordered to march into Glencoe and await further instructions. Glenlyon was fifty-nine years old, too old to be a captain, and chosen because he would be the perfect fall guy.

Breadalbane, who had financed his relative Glenlyon, gave him the choice of killing MacIain and his followers or disobeying a military order. The decision Glenlyon made ruined the rest of his life, and his clan's name was forever besmirched. It is recorded that of the 135 men thought to have participated in the slaughter, only fifteen Campbells were involved, but the name 'Campbell' would always be associated with this crime.

On 12 February, Colonel Hill ordered Hamilton to take 400 men and block the northern entrance at Kinlochleven. It was estimated that some 200 MacDonalds were living in the Glencoe at the time. Another 400 men under Major Duncanson would join Glenlyon's detachment in the south and sweep northwards up the Glen, killing anyone they found and burning their houses.

Under the protection of the Fort William garrison, the MacDonalds billeted the soldiers, three or four to a croft, and gave them food, drink and a place to sleep. Glenlyon told MacIain that he was collecting taxes from each clan and produced documents to prove it. For ten days, in the bleak weather, the soldiers enjoyed the mutual trust from their hosts. On the night before the killing, Glenlyon received a message from Major Robert Duncanson in which he wrote on 12 February from Ballachulish:

> You are hereby ordered to fall upon the Rebels, the MacDonalds of Glencoe, and put all to the sword under seventy. You are to have especial care, that the Old Fox and his Sons do upon no account escape your Hands, you are to secure all the avenues that no man can escape; this you are to put in Execution at five a Clock in the Morning precisely, and by that time or very shortly after it, I'll strive to be with you with a stronger party. If I do not come at five, you are not to tarry for me but fall on. This is by the King's Special command, for the good and safety of the country that these miscreants may be cut off root and branch. See that this be put in execution without feud or Favour, else you may expect to be treated as not true to the King or Government nor a man fit to carry Commission in the King's Service. Expecting you not to fail in the fulfilling hereof as you love yourself, I subscribe these with my hand.

Bad weather meant Duncanson arrived six hours late, by which time Glenlyon had fulfilled his orders. The MacDonalds were not the only clan to live in Glencoe. The day before the massacre, an Argyll soldier stood with one of the Henderson clan watching a game of shinty, when he suddenly struck a bolder and declared:

Great stone of the glen, great is your right to be here! But if you knew what will happen this night you would be up and away.

Around five o'clock on 13 February, at Inverriggen, Glenlyon sent Lieutenant Lindsay and a party of soldiers to kill the unsuspecting Alastair MacIain. Hearing the commotion, the elderly MacIain rose and was shot, bludgeoned and stabbed to death. His wife tried to intervene but was stripped of her clothes and the rings were pulled from her fingers. Driven out into the mountains, she died of exposure the following day. They also found in the house two men, who were hacked to death. They wounded a third, named Duncan Don, who acted as a messenger from Braemar. MacIain's two sons managed to evade being killed and made their escape into the surrounding snow-covered mountains. All along the narrow valley, crofts were set on fire as women and children ran for the mountains, where most died of exposure.

At Inverriggen, Glenlyon ordered the killing of his host. Nine men were captured, bound and then one by one, shot. A young boy grasped Glenlyon's legs, begging for mercy, but Captain Drummond killed him with his dirk. In the village of Auchnaion, a third group of soldiers under the command of Sergeant Barker saw nine men sitting around a fire. They entered the house and began shooting, killing the laird of Auchintriaten and four of his companions. The rest managed to escape through the back door, except for the brother of the laird, who was captured. With muskets trained upon him, he threw his plaid over the soldiers and managed to run off into the mountains.

Besides the killings in these three places, pockets of murder occurred along the glen. Some people were dragged out of their beds and slaughtered, while others were shot. Lieutenant Colonel James Hamilton and his 400 men were hampered by the severity of the weather and arrived too late. They fell in with Major Duncanson's group and were told that the survivors had escaped to the hills. Unable to join the slaughter, Hamilton's men began to burn the houses, collect anything of value and gather the cattle. They then withdrew to Fort William, where they divided the spoils among the officers of the garrison.

Although the massacre numbered some thirty-eight highlanders, many of the soldiers were sickened by the atrocity and refused to take part. The sound of gunfire alerted most of the MacDonalds, who left their homes to hide in the hills. The soldiers who were reluctant to take part in the killing made sure that the families were warned. Ejected from their crofts, elderly women and mothers with babes made for the hills in the hope they would find some shelter. It is not certain how many perished in these severe winter conditions, but it was probably more than the massacre.

Glenlyon was haunted by the bloodshed and he inexplicably left his orders behind in an Edinburgh coffee shop. A journalist picked them up and sold them to *The Paris Gazette*. When they were published on 12 April 1692, news of the atrocity shocked Europe.

In a pamphlet published in 1695, entitled *Gallienus Redivivus or Murther will out…*, Charles Leslie's objectives continued to shape William's reign as particularly disastrous for Scotland. Such incidents as the Glencoe Massacre, the Darien Scheme (*see* Chapter 15), the disastrous famine of the 1690s and the Union of 1707 were part of his Jacobite beliefs and put an anti-English slant on his views. He had decided to investigate the massacre, speaking with soldiers who were there and interviewed eyewitness accounts until he revealed the truth. In a rather heavy-handed style, he wrote in his pamphlet of the beginning the killings:

> I am informed that Captain Campbell [Glenlyon] inclined to spare him but one Drummond; an Officer, barbarously run his Dagger through him, whereupon he died immediately. The rehearsal of several particulars and circumstances of this tragic story, makes it appear most doleful: as that MacIain was killed as he was drawing on his breeches, standing before his bed and giving orders to his servants for the good entertainment of those who murdered him; while he was speaking the words, he was shot through the head, and fell dead in his lady's arms, who through grief of this, and other bad usages she met with, died the next day. It is not to be omitted, that most of those poor people were killed when they were asleep, and none was allowed to pray to God for Mercy. Providence ordered it so, that night was most boisterous; so a party of 400 men, who should have come to the other end of the Glen, and begun to the lie work there at the same hour, (intending that the poor inhabitants should be enclosed, and none of them escape) could not march that length, until it was nine a clock, and this afforded to many any opportunity of escaping, and none were killed but those

in whose houses Campbell of Glenlyon's men were quartered, otherwise all the males under 70 years of age, to the number of 200, had been cut off, for that was the order; and it might have easily been executed, especially considering that the inhabitants had no arms at the time; for upon the first hearing that the soldiers were coming to the Glen, they had conveyed them all out of the way: for though they relied on the promises which were made them for their safety; yet they thought it not improbable that they might be disarmed.

Parliament dismissed Leslie's findings as a Jacobite conspiracy and although William was forced into holding an official enquiry, this was never published because the King was not completely exonerated.

As anticipated, the scapegoat was the alcoholic Robert Campbell of Glenlyon, who was found guilty of 'slaughter under trust', despite acting under orders from Hamilton and Duncanson. Also his political masters, John Dalrymple and John Campbell, Earl of Breadalbane, were all culpable of the massacre but only one was removed from office; Dalrymple. Through the revolving door of politics, he was soon reinstated. Glenlyon later accompanied his regiment to Flanders, where they were defeated in the Battle of Diksmuide in 1696. After the battle, the drunken Glenlyon was found dead in a gutter in Bruges; a victim of cirrhosis. Despite criticism of the Scottish government, there was little sympathy for the MacDonalds. The military commander in Scotland, Viscount Teviot wrote that:

> It's not that anyone thinks the thieving tribe did not deserve to be destroyed but that it should have been done by those quartered amongst them makes a great noise.

William played little or no active part in the Glencoe Massacre and the English administration showed minimum interest in Scottish affairs at that time. Jonathan Keates in his book, *William III and Mary II*, states that:

> The notorious order 'to extirpate that set of thieves' was formulated by the Scottish secretary of state, John Dalrymple, Master of Stair, and countersigned by the king on the basis of false information.

Some Scots nationalists still blame William for the Glencoe Massacre, although he had more pressing things on his mind than a minor clan confrontation. He did put his signature to a document calling for an Oath of Allegiance but he was more concerned in his war with France and, within a matter of weeks he was fighting in two battles; Steenkamp and Namur. Scotland was further weakened in the 1690s by the great famine called the Seven Ill Years. It resulted in an economic slump created by failed harvests in 1695–96 and 1698–99. During this period, starvation accounted for 5 to 15 per cent of the Scottish population. In some areas such as Aberdeenshire, the death rate reached 25 per cent. It led to emigration to England, Europe and the Americas, and particularly Ireland.

The 1690s was a difficult period for Scotland, as it was for much of Europe. Poor harvests and atrocious weather caused famines in Estonia, Finland, Latvia, Norway and Sweden. In France and northern Italy, some 2 million deaths were recorded. Scotland's economy was relatively small and its exports very limited, and in an era of economic rivalry it was unable to protect itself from the expanding English export trade after 1688. During the 1690s, England boomed, becoming a rich and powerful nation, while the Netherlands was involved in the Nine Years' War, which restricted its maritime trade.

Chapter 15

The Darien Gap Project

The colony in Darien on the Isthmus of Panama was founded to boost trade between Scotland and the Far East. The Scottish traders had been excluded from the privileges enjoyed by the English merchants thanks to the English Navigation Acts. In order to expand Scotland's export trade, William Paterson, who had travelled to the Caribbean, in 1691 formulated his idea for a colony at Darien on the border with Columbia. This was a 100-mile section of impassable jungle that flooded every year. It was an impossible area to colonise as no one had been sent to access its viability. Even Spain had dismissed the area as being too forbidding in which to settle. Despite these obvious drawbacks, Paterson's plan was to facilitate trade with the Far East, so enriching Scotland, and using the Darien Gap as a gateway between the Atlantic and the Pacific. He announced his scheme in glowing terms:

> Darien would be the door of the seas, the key of the universe, reducing by half the time and expense of navigation to China and Japan, and bringing peace to both oceans without the guilt of war.

He devoted himself to the colony of Darien. He tried to get the English government interested but it turned him down. He then approached the governments of the Holy Roman Empire and the Netherlands but they would not approve of such a scheme. Paterson raised a new group named the Company of Scotland and was able to collect subscriptions in Amsterdam, Hamburg and London. King William gave only lukewarm support but was wary of giving offence to his ally, Spain, which had already claimed the territory as part of New Grenada. Paterson had made his fortune from the slave trade and moved to Edinburgh, where he was able to convince the Scottish government to fund the Darien Scheme. The Company of

Scotland raised £400,000 in a few weeks, equivalent to £53 million today. This totalled about a fifth of the wealth of Scotland and for the country it was a massive amount of capital for one project. This meant that the Darien Scheme was not only a simple threat to the English merchants but could also be a rival to their trade with the Far East. Emulating the Honourable East India Company and breaking into the lucrative trading areas of India and Africa, the Company of Scotland aimed to match or beat the English-funded company.

By 1697, with the end of the Nine Years' War, Spain and England were at peace. The Darien Company was forced to have its ships built in Hamburg and Amsterdam and large stores were accumulated in the Edinburgh warehouses. The board of directors sent William Paterson to Hamburg to pay for the five ships and their equipment. He made a grave mistake when he deposited the money with James Smyth, a merchant friend, who embezzled the deposit of £17,000. An investigation committee cleared Paterson of any wrongdoing but held him morally responsible for the loss. He managed to recover £9,000 and was told he could go on the first expedition, but only as a volunteer without official authority.

In 1698, with little knowledge of the mosquito-infested tropical jungle, Paterson led the first expedition to found a Scottish Empire. He took with him his wife and child, both of whom died of fever, and he became seriously ill. To avoid being seen by any English ships, the first expedition of five ships, *Saint Andrew*, *Caledonia*, *Unicorn*, *Dolphin* and *Endeavour*, set sail from Leith in July 1698 and headed around the north of Scotland. Many former officers and soldiers who had taken part in the Glencoe Massacre were among the colonists and were viewed with suspicion by the rest of the settlers. When the ships arrived at the Darien Gap on 2 November, the Scotsmen decreed:

> We do here settle and in the name of God establish ourselves; and in honour and for the memory of that most ancient and renowned name of our Mother Country, we do, and will from henceforward call this country by the name of Caledonia; and ourselves, successors, and associates, by the name of Caledonians.

William, whether out of spite or incurring the anger of Spain, instructed the Dutch and English colonies in America not to supply the new Scottish colony, named Caledonia. The settlers' first choice of a site was bad mistake, As Paterson wrote:

> A mere morass, neither fit to be fortified or planted, nor indeed for men to lie upon. We were clearing and making huts upon this improper place near two months, in which time experience, the schoolmaster of fools, convinced our masters that the place now called Fort St Andrew was a more proper place for us.

They soon found out that the land was unsuited for agriculture. The rainy season had arrived and, with wind-driven storms, the swamps steamed and the mosquitoes bred, leaving the settlers with little to do but keep dry. When the rains stopped, they were able to dig a ditch that divided one side of the harbour from the ocean but the high tides could easily wreck any ship trying to leave. A fort was constructed and armed with fifty cannon, and named after their patron saint, St Andrew. The settlers began to build huts in their new settlement named New Edinburgh, but one thing they had not bargained for was fresh water. Spring had brought with it torrential rain and rampant disease. It was a truly dismal setting for a new colony and with the settlers weakened by dysentery, malaria and eating rotten, worm-infested food, they lost ten settlers each day. One who survived was Roger Oswald, who wrote a harrowing account of what life was like that spring on the Darien Peninsula:

> We lived on less than a pound of mouldy flour a week. When boiled with a little water, without anything else, big maggots and worms must be skimmed off the top … In short; a man might easily have destroyed his whole week's rations in one day and have but one ordinary stomach nether. Yet for all this short allowance, every man (let him never be so weak) daily turned out to work by daylight, whether with the hatchet, or wheelbarrow, pick-axe, shovel, fore-hammer or any other instrument the case required; and so continued until 12 o'clock. And again at 2 again and stayed till night, sometimes working all day up to the headbands of the breeches in water at the trenches, My shoulders have been so wore with carrying burdens that the skin has come off them and grew full of boils. If a man were sick and obliged to stay within,

no victuals for him that day. Our Councillors all the while lying at their ease, sometimes divided into factions and, being swayed by particular interest, ruined the public. Our bodies pined away and grew so macerated with such allowance that we were like so many skeletons.

In July 1699, after eight months, the colony was abandoned. Of the 1,200 settlers who travelled to this hellhole, only 300 survived. They learned that the Spaniards were planning to attack the colony and it was with great relief that they abandoned New Edinburgh. Departing separately, the ships called in to the nearest English port for assistance. Dropping anchor in Port Royal in Jamaica, they were refused help on the orders of the English government for fear of antagonising their Spanish allies. Another ship returned directly to Scotland but was greeted with contempt by their fellow countrymen and some were disowned by their families. The *Caledonia* made its way to New York, a small town of 5,000, followed by the *Unicorn*. A letter reporting that the settlers had been struck down by tropical diseases arrived too late as two ships had already left Scotland with supplies for, what was hoped, a thriving community.

In August 1699, the *Olive Branch* and *Hopeful Beginning*, with 300 settlers, arrived at Darien to find ruined huts and 400 overgrown graves. Expecting a thriving town instead of a scene of devastation, the two ships debated their next move. A careless accident by a steward caused a fire on the *Olive Branch* that burnt all the settlers' supplies. Without provisions, it was decided to cram the *Olive Branch* settlers on board the *Hopeful Beginning* and return to Scotland. They landed at Port Royal but were not allowed ashore. In the crowded conditions, illness soon spread and over 200 souls died on the return voyage.

In this age of slow information, Captain Thomas Drummond set sail from New York in the sloop *Ann of Caledonia*, picking up a supply ship, the *Society*, en route to Darien. When they arrived, they were shocked at the scene of a ruined town and the burnt timbers of the *Olive Branch* rotting on the shore. News of the abandoned New Edinburgh did not reach Scotland before the second expedition of 1,000 settlers sailed.

A new ship, the *Rising Sun*, armed with thirty-eight cannon, led the way, supported by *The Duke of Hamilton*, *Hope of Boroughstomen* and a smaller ship, the *Hope*. The three ships received the blessing of the Church of

Scotland, who had appointed Alexander Shields as the senior of the four ministers. They reached Caledonia Bay at Darien on 30 November 1699. They found Thomas Drummond's sloops already there and some of the settlers were sent ashore to rebuild the huts. Shield, who had sailed on the *Rising Sun*, wrote to a colleague in Scotland:

> Our passage hither was very prosperous for the weather, but in other respects tedious and miserable. Our company very uncomfortable, consisting for the generality, especially the officers and volunteers of the worst of mankind, if you had scummed the Land and Raked to the borders of hell for them, men of lewd practices and venting the wickedness of principles: for these things God was provoked to smite us very signally and severely with a contagious sickness which went through the most part and cut off by death about sixty of us on our ship and near a hundred on the rest of the fleet. The most dead since our departure from Montserrat. I cannot with this send you a particular list of the dead because I have not gathered them yet but the most lamented by the better part of us were Mr Alexander Dalgleish, minister, the Laird of Dunlop, Captain Wallace engineer, and several others of the best sort. The means contributing to the increase of this sickness and mortality were our too great crowds in every ship, straightening and stifling one another, our chests of medicines ignorantly or knavishly filled and as ill-dispensed by our surgeons, our water in wooden-bound casks very unsavoury and unclean, our beef much of it rotten, many things redundant which were useless and many things needful wanting. It is a wonder that so many of us escaped and that at length we arrived at our part in safety though in great sorrow three weeks have gone by November 30. We had heard at Montserrat the colony was deserted but did not believe, though some of us feared it all along. Arriving at this bay, we found the nest was flown. The ground that was cleared was all grown up again with Mangroves. The little fortification standing was their batteries and huts all burnt down (which some said was done by a Frenchman, other by an Englishman) and nothing of shipping there but two little sloops from New England and New York ... They told us the Colony had deserted to 20 June last for sickness

(having destroyed themselves by working excessively on the fortifications) and for fear of want of provisions that the *Saint Andrew*
with her men had gone to Jamaica and the *Unicorn* to New York.

Thomas Drummond, who had served as a captain in the Duke of
Argyll's regiment at Glencoe, clashed with the merchant James Byres, who
had Drummond arrested. He outraged the minister, Alexander Shields,
by claiming it would be unlawful to resist the Spanish by force of arms,
as all war was un-Christian. One newly arrived young officer, Captain
Alexander Campbell of Fonab, persuaded his fellow settlers to launch a
pre-emptive strike against the forces gathering at the Spanish stockade
at Toubacanti in January 1700. Two days later, in the attack, Campbell
was wounded and seven Scots killed. The Caledonians were elated at
their success, although it was no more than a skirmish. Campbell had
been wounded and then caught a fever, leaving the colonists leaderless.
They returned to New Edinburgh, constructed a stockade around the
Fort St Andrews and waited for the Spaniards to attack. Shortly afterwards, in February, the Spaniards sent a small fleet under the command
of Governor-General Pimienta against the Scottish fort. The Spaniards
landed at Caret Bay, west of the settlement, and in a few skirmishes, they
advanced their line to within a mile of Fort St Andrew. The settlers held
out for a few weeks but finally surrendered in April. The Darien Project
was an abject failure and the Spanish allowed them to leave with their
guns and powder. The Scots departed after fourteen days of their brief
struggle with colonisation, although some stayed in the Caribbean, while
others travelled to New York. The survivors of this debacle chose to return
to Scotland and face criticism from their fellow Scots. Roger Oswald was
disowned by his father and wrote to a friend:

> Since it pleases God that I have preserved my life, and had not
> the good fortune to lose it in that place, and so have been happy
> by wanting the sight of so many miseries that have come upon
> myself ... I never intended , nor do intend, to trouble my father
> anymore.

The Scottish settlers lost some of their ships, including the *Hope of
Boroughstomen*, which leaked so badly that she had to be sold in Cartagena.

The Company of Scotland's *Hope* was wrecked on rocks off Cuba, while the *Rising Sun* was lost in a hurricane off Carolina, losing 112 passengers and all hands. There was a third expedition, which arrived to find that the Spanish had taken control of the Darien and had little option but to return to Scotland. The company struggled on and attempted to establish trade links with Africa and the Far East. William Paterson defended his scheme and was later awarded an indemnity of £18,000. Disillusioned, he died in 1717. He had been instrumental in establishing the Bank of England and set in motion the Union of England and Scotland.

Some Scottish nobility petitioned the English government to wipe out the Scottish national debt and stabilise the currency. The Scottish shilling was given the fixed rate of the English penny, although the question of the national debt was dealt with a later date. Many of the Scottish population had invested heavily in the Darien Project and felt they should be compensated for their losses. The 1707 Acts of Union granted £398,085 sterling to offset liability towards the English national debt.

The failure of the colonisation project provoked tremendous discontent throughout Lowland Scotland, where almost every family had been affected. Some held the English responsible, and others believed that they could and should assist in yet another effort at making the scheme work. William declined to help, saying that although he regretted the company had incurred such huge losses, reclaiming Darien would mean war with Spain. This only fuelled the bitterness the Scots felt for the English, something that still resonates today. It had bankrupted the exchequer and impoverished hundreds of Scotsmen from nobles to clerks, who had invested in a project that no one had taken the trouble to investigate. Still incensed by England's indifference, the Scots turned their attention to a minor maritime matter that soon blossomed into something that caught the population's attention.

In August 1704, some excise men, accompanied by a body of soldiers, seized one of the Scottish company's vessels, the *Annandale*, while the ship was being fitted out on the Thames. Initial efforts in the courts by the Scots to have the *Annandale* released had failed. The Company of Scotland had appealed but, by 6 August, they were still waiting for the appeal to be heard and were increasingly losing patience with what they claimed was the blatant, state-approved, English aggression.

At the same time, the *Worcester*, a whaler-merchant ship had just returned from India, carrying pepper and other East Indian cargo. She lay at anchor in the Leith Road off Edinburgh, unable to accompany the other two merchant ships, which travelled on to Newcastle. *Worcester* had a serious problem with leaks, which she tried to plug, hence she sought refuge at Leith. The English Channel was a particularly dangerous place for merchantmen, which is why *Worcester* ended up in Leigh harbour, waiting for a convoy from Newcastle to complete her journey.

In a last-ditch attempt to salvage something from a cargo lost on the Malacca coast, the Company of Scotland purchased a majority share in the *Annandale* with the intention of sending the ship east. Hence, the seizure of the *Annandale*, at the instigation of the East India Company, led to an outbreak of ill feeling in Scotland towards England. The *Worcester*, although a merchantman, was accused of piracy and murder and was said to have sunk another Scottish company ship, *Speedy Return*, in 1703. The Scottish press falsely accused the *Worcester* of piracy, while Roderick Mackenzie, the Company of Scotland's secretary and relentless enemy of the English, sold the cargo and pocketed the profits. Mackenzie was convinced the *Worcester* was an East India Company ship and he impounded the vessel by removing the sails, guns and rudder as a reprisal for the *Annandale*. He succeeded in getting legal authority, and Thomas Green, who had been given the command at the age of twenty-one, watched as his ship's cargo was impounded over the next three months and his ship stripped and all essentials removed.

After being detained for months, the crew of the English ship were freed, with the exception of three senior men; Captain Thomas Green, Chief Mate John Madder and James Simpson. It was widely believed that *Worcester* had boarded the *Speedy Return* off Madagascar and murdered the captain, Robert Drummond. In fact it was a pirate named John Bowen who took the *Speedy Return* in return for loot. Despite a total lack of evidence, Green and two of his crew, John Madden and James Simpson, were sent for trial in Edinburgh. The prosecution case, which was made in Medieval Latin, and the legalities were unintelligible to jury and accused alike. The defence advocates seem to have presented no evidence and quit after the trial. Some jurors resisted bringing in a verdict of guilty, but the men were convicted and sentenced to death by hanging.

Anne advised her thirty Privy Councillors in Edinburgh that the men should be pardoned, but the Scottish people demanded the sentence be carried out. Nineteen councillors made excuses to stay away from the deliberations of a reprieve, fearing the wrath of a huge mob that had arrived in Edinburgh to demand the sailors be put to death. Even though they had affidavits from London by the crew of the *Speedy Return*, who testified that Green and his crew had no knowledge or involvement in the fate of the ship, the remaining councillors refused to pardon the men.

On 14 March 1705, the court deliberated and Green and his crew were found guilty. A week later Green, Madder, Simpson and the crew were to be hanged over the next fortnight. Queen Anne intervened and the hangings were postponed for a week. Finally it was decided Green, Madder and Simpson would be hanged and the rest of the crew released. The three innocent men were subjected to derision and insults by the mob before they were hanged. The sentence was carried out on 11 April at Leigh to the delight of the Scottish mob, even though the men were totally innocent. It was a revenge killing for the role of England in the failure of the Scottish Darien Scheme. Queen Anne was anxious to avoid war with Scotland and wanted to prevent the Scottish Parliament from interfering with England's foreign policy. She let the matter rest.

Chapter 16

Irish Problems

The island of Ireland lay like a threat off the west coast of England. By 1687, it was ruled by Richard Talbot, the Lord Deputy, who filled the political and officer classes with Catholics, but by 1688, he was opposed by the Protestants of Ulster. The Spanish and French saw it as a way to conquer and transform the Protestant English to the Catholic religion, but neither wanted to send more than a token force. The deposed King James II saw it as a means to regain his throne. The English government intended to develop Ireland as a reliable possession, without the risk of a foreign invasion. The reign of Charles I saw Ireland as a relatively peaceful country, but after the brutal conquest by the hated Cromwell in the 1650s the country was in turmoil. England saw impoverished Ireland as land that had great farming potential with its mild weather and plentiful rainfall. This plan was thwarted by the many Gaelic clans that carved areas for themselves. The Irish Catholics constituted about 75 per cent of the population of 2.2 million and were supportive of King James and the French army. During the wars fought in Ireland from Oliver Cromwell's Interregnum to the Williamite War it was estimated that 20,000 were battlefield casualties and about 200,000 civilians died of war-related famine and disease. A further 50,000 were sent into indentured servitude in the West Indies to work in the sugar cane fields. This form of slavery was often brutal and many died before the expiration of their indentures.

The Williamite War fought from 1688 to 1691 was an Irish conflict between Catholic Jacobite supporters of James II and the Protestant followers of William III. In 1689, James landed at Kinsale on 12 March to reclaim his crown, counting on strong support from the Catholic Irish. He took with him 7,000 French troops, who linked up with his military commander in Ireland, Richard Talbot, later the Earl of Tyrconnel. The lyrics of 'Lillibulero' were used as a satire on Talbot's appointment as Lord Deputy of Ireland, who began appointing Catholics to the army and public offices. The melody of

'Lillibulero' became popular during the Golden Revolution, when James began transferring Irish troops to bolster his shrinking English army in late summer of 1688. It was also used as a political tune by supporters of the Prince of Orange during the invasion.

Tyrconnel was only eleven when he was the standard bearer in Thomas Dongan, 2nd Earl of Limerick's regiment in the English Civil War and remained a military figure for the rest of his life. He twice escaped imprisonment and fled to the Continent. He plotted to kill Oliver Cromwell during the Interregnum but was arrested; it was rumoured that he bribed Cromwell into letting him go. He later was involved in an infamous scandal to ruin the character of Anne Hyde, James's wife to be. Despite this, he remained a loyal supporter of the exiled king. He married Francis Jenyns, the elder sister of Sarah Churchill, whose husband was the Duke of Marlborough. In this tangled family conspiracy, Talbot ended up in opposition to John Churchill at the Battle of the Boyne. Thomas Sheridan, Tyrconnel's secretary, described his master as, over the next three months:

> A tall handsome man, but publicly known to be most insolent in prosperity and most abject in adversity, a cunning dissembling courtier of mean judgement and small understanding, uncertain and unsteady in his resolutions, turning with every wind to bring about his ambitious ends and purposes, on which he was intent that to compass them he would stick at nothing and so false that a most impudent notorious lie was called at Whitehall and St James's on of Dick Talbot's ordinary truths.

One of the Irish professional officers captured during William's advance on London was Richard Hamilton. He was imprisoned in the Tower after James's flight in December. In January, William paroled Hamilton to go to Ireland and negotiate with Tyrconnel. Once there, he abandoned his mission and boasted that he had fooled William. The following year he was wounded at the Boyne and captured. He was interrogated by William, who muttered 'Your Honour!' to remind Hamilton of his broken parole. He was imprisoned in Dublin and Chester Castle and finally the Tower. In April 1692, he was exchanged for Lord Mountjoy. In 1688, he was appointed Jacobite commander of the Catholic English, Scottish and Irish volunteers. He then served the exiled James as a lieutenant general with the intention of landing in the south of England and marching on London. The French fleet was intercepted by the English and Dutch ships at Barfleur and La Hogue in May 1692 and the invasion was cancelled. While the Williamite War diverted England's attention away from the Nine Years' War, which was what Louis had wanted, William viewed Ireland as a French proxy invasion. He reluctantly accepted that the abandonment of Irish Protestants would not be accepted by his English subjects. Although Louis sent an additional 3,000 troops, he regarded Ireland merely as a diversion to his Continental aspirations. William was still wary of the French involvement and decided to join England with the Grand Alliance, which then comprised of the Dutch Republic, England, Scotland, Holy Roman Empire, Spanish Empire, Duchy of Savoy, Sweden, and the Portuguese Empire.

The second attempt to take Londonderry was on 18 April 1689, when James appeared before the walls and demanded that the city should surrender. Refusing the terms, the city fought off the besiegers as they tried to storm the walls. With the death of the Comte de Maumont, the command devolved to Richard Hamilton. The Jacobites resorted to starving the citizens until they surrendered. The Londonderry defenders resorted to eating dogs, cats and finally, rats. Four battalions under Peircy Kirke landed on the Foyle and broke the Jacobite blockade on 28 July. After 105 days, the siege was finally lifted when, four ships carrying food entered the River Foyle. HMS *Dartmouth* gave covering fire on the shore batteries, while the three merchant ships, the *Mountjoy*, the *Phoenix* and the *Jerusalem*, rammed the boom and sailed up the river to relieve Londonderry. Some 4,000 out of 8,000 Londonderry citizens died during the siege. The besieging Jacobite army, which also suffered during the attacks on Londonderry, gave up and departed.

On the same day, a 3,000-strong Jacobite army led by Viscount Mountcashel, camped near Enniskillen and bombarded a Williamite outpost at Crom Castle, which stood about 5 miles from the village of Newtownbutler. Two days later the camp was confronted with about 2,000 Enniskillen volunteers. Led by Colonel Berry, they laid an ambush into which the Jacobite dragoons had entered and suffered 230 casualties. Mountcashel managed to drive off Berry's men with his main force, but then faced the Enniskillen volunteers. With poorly equipped troops, Mountcashel decided to draw up his men for battle near Newtownbutler. When the first shots were fired, about 1,500 Jacobite soldiers fled to the only place to escape; Upper Lough

Erne. Pursued by Berry's cavalry, about 500 men attempted to swim across the Erne but only one managed to reach the other side. Mountcashel was wounded and, along with 400 troops, was captured and later exchanged for Williamite prisoners.

On 13 August, Marshal Hermann Schomberg landed at Belfast Lough with the main Williamite army and by the end of the month he had more than 20,000 men. Ireland was an impoverished country and both sides relied on external supplies. Schomberg's men lacked tents, food and clothing. Their officers chose a low and boggy campsite where their soldiers suffered badly from rain, cold and poor sanitation; around 6,000 men were to die from disease and poor food. The commissariat in Chester could not get hold of enough ships to carry these necessary supplies to Ireland. Finally they were moved to more suitable winter quarters in November. An English Catholic, John Stevens, serving with the Jacobites, noted that:

> Besides the infinite number of graves a vast number of dead bodies were found there unburied, and not a few yet breathing but almost devoured with lice and other vermin. The spectacle not a little astonished such of our men as ventured in amongst them.

In March 1690, about 6,200 experienced Danish soldiers arrived from Hull to help William stamp out the Jacobite army before returning to take part in the war in Flanders. The Danes were supported by 3,000 ox carts, which stretched for 18 miles, supplying tents, ammunition, food and other supplies. William's army consisted of 2,300 Dutch troops, 2,600 Huguenots and over 3,000 horses. In total the army amounted to 25,000 men, including all the camp followers. At the same time, Louis sent some of his troops to help James establish himself in Ireland and also to keep William's attention diverted away from the increasing conflict in Flanders. On 21 June, William embarked his troops at Chester, arriving at Carrickfergus. From there he marched his army south towards Dublin. James led his mixture of French and poorly armed Irish troops north to the River Boyne, just to the west of Drogheda.

Chapter 17

The Battle of the Boyne

By January 1690, James had virtually taken control of Ireland, except for Londonderry and Enniskillen. It was clear that William would have to sail to Ireland with a large force to expel James and his Catholic army. To the Catholics' dismay and disgust, the Battle of the Boyne is the only conflict that is annually celebrated by the Protestants in Northern Ireland. It is arguably the most famous event in Irish history due to the symbolic Catholic–Protestant confrontation, yet it is barely acknowledged in England. In fact, the battle was fought mainly by Dutch, French Huguenots, Germans, Danes and men of the Ulster Enniskillen. The English regiments were raw recruits who had never fought before and kept in reserve. These new enlisted soldiers were clothed in long red coats, yellow breeches and a sash on which they hung their cartridges. The best infantry were the Danes and Dutch soldiers armed with the latest flintlock muskets. The Danish infantry was commanded by General Julius Ernst von Tettau, a Prussian who had served with several countries, including France and Flanders. William did not have a high opinion of the English and Scottish troops, who he felt were politically unreliable since King James had been their legitimate monarch a year before. In total, William's army amounted to 36,000, while the Jacobites' strength was 23,500.

On 12 March, James landed at Kinsale accompanied by a French fleet of thirty men-of-war and his many supporters. He also brought with him money and equipment but few French troops, who were needed in Flanders. His Lord Deputy, Richard Talbot, had already raised a large Irish army, albeit lacking in equipment and money to pay them. The French troops were led by Compte de Lauzun, who offered advice to James. The Jacobite army marched out of Dublin and they reached Oldbridge on the River Boyne. It was a good position as they commanded the bridge and the river; they had a day to prepare for the advance of William's army. The Jacobites' strength consisted of several regiments of French troops but the majority was made up of Irish Catholics. The cavalry were made up of disposed Irish gentry well versed in riding to hounds, while the infantry consisted of Irish peasants, poorly armed with scythes and other farm implements. Those that had matchlocks were equipped with the obsolete musket, which was outdated. To differentiate between the two sides, the Jacobite army wore a white cockade to distinguish themselves from the Williamites, who wore a sprig of green leaves in their hats.

William had marched 15 miles from Ardee on 31 June and arrived at Tullyallen Hill, about a mile from the Boyne. He ordered his artillery to set up facing the Jacobites and they began a barrage, which did little damage. William decided to move closer to the river bank to observe the Jacobite positions. Dismounting, he sat in the grass noting the fords that crossed the river. He spotted a group of Jacobite horse, who moved closer to the bank, so William mounted up and prepared to ride away. William's padre, George Story, witnessed the following event:

> This small party (of Jacobites) brought two field pieces with them, dropping them by a hedge, in the ploughed land undiscovered, they did not offer to fire them until His Majesty was mounted and then, he and the rest riding back softly the same way, their gunner fired a piece which killed us two horses and a man, about a hundred yards above where the King was, but immediately came a second which had almost been a fatal one, for it grazed upon the bank of the river, and in the rising slanted upon the King's right shoulder, took out a piece of coat, and tore the skin and flesh and afterwards broke the head of the gentleman's pistol.

Fortunately, William was wearing a thick coat, which protected him, although he did tumble from his horse. Another ecclesiastical witness was the Reverend Rowland Davies, chaplain of one of the English regiments:

> At two in the morning we decamped again, and marched towards Drogheda, where we found King James encamped on the other side of the Boyne; we drew up all our horse in a line opposite him within cannon-shot, and as his Majesty passed out line they fired six shots at him, one whereof fell and struck of the top of the Duke of Wurttemberg's pistol, and the whiskers off his horse, and another

tore the King's coat on the shoulder. We stood open during at least twenty shot, until a man and two horses being killed among the Dutch Guards, we all retired into a trench behind us, where we lay safe while much mischief was done to other regiments, and in the evening drew off and encamped behind the hill.

The Jacobites cheered for they thought they had killed or wounded the King and sent a despatch to France telling of the monarch's death. William quickly mounted his horse and rode around his men to show that he was well and truly alive. That night, at the ruined Mellifont Abbey, he held a conference to decide on how to cross the river and defeat the Jacobite army. The Dutch Count Solms, a man disliked by the English officers, put forward a frontal attack on Oldbridge, but this was rejected. Marshal Frederick Schomberg suggested a right-wing crossing by his son, Meinhard, and hitting the enemy on their flank. William proposed a compromise in that the artillery would pound the Jacobite positions at Oldbridge, so diverting attention away from the right flank. The King's wound was not serious but it was painful, and he resorted to pointing a stick rather than a heavy sword. The images seen on the buildings in Northern Ireland show a more mobile King Billy on a prancing horse and pointing his sword towards the enemy.

At five o'clock on the morning of 1 July, a third of his army, including artillery, would march to the village of Slane, some 4 miles to the west. The bridge was damaged so the troops would have to cross in single file over one of the fords. As the river was tidal, they would only be able to cross in the two hours at low tide. James was unable to see Meinhard's men make their way to Slane due to the early morning mist. He was advised by the Comte de Lauzun that a detachment of dragoons under Sir Neil O'Neill should be sent to Rosnaree to watch the ford about a mile from Slane. This was shrewd advice, as they managed to delay Meinhard's men until midday, when the tide was at its lowest. Then the Dutch Guards waded over, followed by the Huguenots under Lord Caillemote and the Enniskilleners. Caillemote led the Huguenots until he was mortally wounded. Marshal Schomberg saw this and eased his horse across the river to take command. The seventy-five-year-old soldier soon ran into trouble and was hacked by a Jacobite officer and shot in the back of the head, probably accidentally by a Huguenot soldier. George Walker, the Governor of Londonderry, rushed to help Schomberg but was cut down. For half an hour, the Jacobites seemed to be winning. The Reverend Rowland Davies wrote of the advance on the right flank as they waded through the river:

> About six in the morning the Earl of Portland (Hans Willem Bentinck) marched up the river almost to the bridge at Slane, with the right wing, consisting of 24 squadrons of horse and dragoons and six regiments of foot, and at two fords we passed the river where there were six squadrons of the enemy to guard the pass; but, at the first firing of our dragoons and three pieces of cannon that marched with us, they all ran away killing nothing but one of our dragoon's horses.

This left William with the Danes, the Dutch Cavalry and the English regiments further downstream on the north bank. He ordered his men to open fire on the Jacobite horses on the other bank. These were Dungan's Dragoons, whose leader was killed by a cannon shot. Not waiting to return fire, the dragoons mounted their horses and retreated. The river was at least 30 yards wide and as William's force crossed, his horse floundered on the muddy bottom and threw him into the river. Quickly, two Danish infantry soldiers grabbed him and put him back on his horse to complete his crossing. All around were the crack of muskets and the groans of wounded soldiers. The Irish had used all their ammunition and had swiftly withdrawn. What neither side realised at Rosnaree was that there was a deep ravine running away from the river, covered with trees, with a bog at the bottom, which kept the two sides apart. Many of the infantry on either side did not get to fire their weapons. Reverend Davies again:

> As soon as we passed (crossed) the river, we saw the enemy marching towards us, and that they drew up on the side of a hill in two lines; the river on their right, and all their horse on the left wing; their foot appeared very numerous but in horse we far exceeded. Whereupon the Earl of Portland drew us up also in two lines, intermixing the horse and foot by squadron and battalion, and sent away for more foot to enforce us; and thus the armies stood for a considerable time, an impossible bog being between them.

The right wing of William's force, which included the cavalry, marched around the bog and engaged the enemy, who slowly retreated towards the village of Duleek, south-west of Drogheda. Meanwhile, at the main ford at Oldbridge, Count Solms led the Dutch Blue Guards as they forced their way over the river, climbed a hill and drove back the Jacobite infantry. The Jacobite cavalry counter attacked until the Williamite cavalry managed to cross the river and force the Jacobites to withdraw. The Jacobite army began to retreat, most going west towards Limerick, while James and his Frenchmen withdrew to Duncannon. The Irish soldiers were disillusioned by James's lack of fight. He deserted his Irish army and was rewarded with the epithet, 'James the Shit'. William was loath to capture his father-in-law, as he was when he approached London during the Glorious Revolution. By the end of the battle, the Williamites lost 400 men through death or wounds, while James' casualties amounted to 1,300.

On 3 July, the exiled James sailed for France, where he supported the Jacobite plots to either assassinate or kidnap King William. On March 1701, while he was hearing mass, he suffered a stroke that left him partially paralysed. He died on 16 September of a seizure and was buried at St Germaine. Later, William was annoyed when Louis XIV named James's son as the next King of England, Scotland and Ireland. On her husband's death, Mary Beatrice entered a Convent of Visitations at Chaillot and stayed there with her daughter, twenty-year-old Louisa Maria. In 1712, Louisa Maria died of smallpox and, with the death of Louis, James Francis Edward was forced to find another refuge abroad.

In another confrontation on 10 July, fifty-six ships of the Anglo-Dutch fleet took on the seventy-five vessels of the French at the Battle of Beachy Head, off Eastbourne. The eight-hour battle was a victory for the French, who lost no ships, but did not take advantage of it. On the other hand, the Anglo-Dutch fleet, which initially had the wind advantage, lost several ships. One was captured and two were sunk, while eight were burnt to avoid capture by the French. The Dutch were furious as they had borne the brunt of the battle with little help from the English. It was barely an epic battle but it did give the French supremacy of the Channel, which they chose to ignore.

On 1 July, another major Continental battle took place on the same day as the Battle of the Boyne, fought at Fleurus in present-day Belgium. Commanded by the Duc de Luxembourge, 35,000 French troops overcame

Prince Waldeck's command of 38,000 Allies comprising of Dutch, German and Spaniards. The Battle of Fleurus was a complete French victory but devoid of result. Compared with the casualties sustained on the Boyne, the Fleurus battle saw the Allies lose 6,000 dead and 8,000 captured while the French lost 3,000 dead and 3,000 wounded. Louis XVI then ordered Luxembourg to send part of his army to assist the Dauphin's army on the Rhine, so negating the great victory the French had won. Prince Waldeck retreated to Brussels to rebuild his army but was astonished that the French did not follow up their victory battle and the Flanders campaign petered out.

Chapter 18

The Ousting of the Jacobites

William followed up his victory at the Boyne by pursuing the 17,000 Jacobites westward to the fortified town of Limerick on the River Shannon. They reached the walls of Limerick on 7 August with 25,000 men. Lacking in siege guns, he had only had his field artillery, and had to wait for the arrival of the large cannon from Dublin. The Williamites quickly occupied two forts outside the town, Ireton and Cromwell, and settled down for the arrival of his siege pieces.

A Huguenot artillery man defected to the Jacobites and informed them that the siege train was on its way from Dublin. It was a laborious task transporting such heavy ordnance over the rough country roads and it took no fewer than 9,900 horses to convey the artillery pieces. In a 2-mile procession, some 200 wagoners, wheelwrights, smithies and gunners were employed moving these huge objects. They were escorted by a small detachment of cavalry commanded by Captain Poultney. Patrick Sarsfield, later Earl of Lucan, obtained permission from Tyrconnel to attack and destroy the siege artillery. On the night of 11 August, the siege train camped for the night at the ruins of Ballyneety Castle near Tipperary. A *rapparee*, or guerrilla, Michael 'Galloping' Hogan, led Sarsfield and his 600 men to the camp. With the light of a full moon, Sarsfield decided to attack and charged into the slumbering camp. The civilians, including women and children, were cut down and the wagons overturned. The large herd of horses were rounded up and taken away. Unfortunately the guns were a problem for they were dislodged from the carriages and left. All the powder barrels were emptied and the food stocks raided. The only piece of good news was that the wagon containing money was left undisturbed. When the site was reached and examined, the Williamites found the money wagon and six cannon had been left intact, but the cannon balls and power had been scattered.

For the Irish, it was total victory. Their only drawback was that ordnance soon arrived from Waterford and the bombardment began on the Limerick fortifications. By 27 August, a breach was made and was stormed by the Danish Grenadiers. Alexandre de Rainier de Droue, a French officer, had built an earthwork inside the walls, which held up the Danish advance. Overcoming this barrier, the Grenadiers were joined by eight regiments as they fought their way through the barricaded streets, taking heavy casualties. A regiment of Jacobite dragoons attacked the Williamites outside the breach and, after over three hours of fighting, William called off the assault. The weather was cold and wet with the trenches filling with water and the loss of the Danes decided William to move his army to winter quarters at Mullingar. Realising that his troops were unable to take Limerick, he was anxious to join the fighting in Flanders. Leaving his force, William returned to England in late August, leaving his close friend, General Godert de Ginkel, to command the King's forces in Ireland. Once again William showed his preference for Dutch leaders than English, although he did recognise the success of John Churchill at Cork and Kinsale and later appointed him commander of the Anglo-Dutch army. George Macaulay later wrote about the French soldiers, who were heartedly sick of Ireland and could not wait to get back to France:

> The climate affected their health and spirits. In that unhappy country, wasted by years of predatory war, hospitality could afford little more than a couch of straw, a trencher of meat, half raw and half burned, and a draught of sour milk. A crust of bread, a pint of wine, could hardly be purchased for money … better to be a prisoner in the Bastille, better to be a recluse in La Trappe, than to be generalissimo of the half naked savages who burrowed in the dreary swamps of Munster.

There followed the Siege of Athlone on 19 June, which the Williamites took with few casualties. On 12 July 1691, just before the Second Battle of Limerick, the Battle of Aughrim was the bloodiest battle ever fought on Irish soil. Over 7,000 men were killed, which saw the effective end of the Jacobites' cause in Ireland for several years. General Ginkel marched down the Ballinasloe track to the Galway road, when he came upon the extremely strong Jacobite defensive position along the 2-mile ridge known as Kilcommadan Hill. A large morass lay at the foot of the hill, while the flanks were protected by marshy ground. Along the slopes of the hill and parallel with its base ran two or three hedgerows giving protection to the musketeers. The long ridge was manned by the majority of the Jacobite army, with Charles Chalmot de Saint-Ruhe in command. The balance of the two sides was nearly equal with a strength of 20,000 each, although the Williamites had an advantage in artillery. Ginkel and his deputy, the Duke of Württemburg, stood on the Urraghy Hill, where they had a good view of their troops. At about five o'clock in the afternoon, an attack was launched on the Jacobite right flank against the Irish cavalry but to little effect. At half past six, Ginkel, having investigated the morass to his front, decided to order his infantry to advance. The first four regiments waded through mud and water before they reached the first of the hedgerows. Then the Irish retreated up the slope to the second row of hedges. The gates had been left open, which enabled the Jacobite cavalry to ride down and cut the retreating infantry. Saint-Ruhe was convinced that he had victory in his hands, having nature's morass to aid him.

Unable to overrun the men of Kilcommadan Hill, Ginkel withdrew. He then sent his cavalry on his right flank under the Marquis de Ruvigny and Compton's Blues, who had not yet seen action. They were opposed by Henry Luttrell and Dominic Sheldon. The former was later accused of treason when correspondence with the besiegers was discovered and he scarcely escaped hanging. After the surrender of Limerick, he brought his regiment of horse over to the Williamite side. As a reward, he received the forfeited estates of his elder brother and was made a general in the Dutch army. When he was sixty-three, he was shot and mortally wounded in his sedan chair on the night of 22 October 1717, on the Blind Quay in Dublin. The killers were never found.

De Ruvigny and Compton's Blues had to ride two abreast over the causeway to Aughrim Castle. This was defended by Colonel Burke's men, who were running short of ammunition. By mischance, they were issued with the French firelock, and the ammunition they were sent was the ball for the English muskets, which were larger and consequently useless. As a last resort, they cut the buttons from their jackets and used them as bullets, which were ineffective. The two Williamite cavalry regiments managed to overwhelm Burke's men and drive off the Jacobite horse.

At the same moment, Saint-Ruhe placed himself at the head of the cavalry and charged down the slope to confront the Williamite infantry, who were struggling in the bog. Halfway down the slope he halted a moment to give the cavalry time to catch up. Then, drawing his sword, he pointed at the enemy exclaiming, 'They are beaten, gentlemen; let us drive them back to the gates of Dublin.' At that instant, an English cannon ball decapitated him, much to the shock of his staff. From then on the Williamite army was in the ascendancy. The Jacobite army disintegrated, with the cavalry retreating down the Loughrea road and the poor infantry throwing away their weapons and fleeing into the bog as the misty rain broke over the battlefield. The casualties in this messy and muddy battle were between 1,000 to 2,000 Williamite dead and over 4,000 Jacobites slain.

Tyrconnel returned from France in January 1691 appointing Sarsfield as Earl of Lucan in an attempt to placate an 'increasingly influential and troublesome figure'. The second siege on Limerick happened on 26 September 1691, and in a surprise attack, the Williamites drove out the Irish from the town. In October the Treaty of Limerick was signed, permitting Catholics to retain their right to practice their religion but forfeit their land. Along with Sarsfield, 14,000 soldiers and 4,000 women and children sailed in English ships for France, an exodus known as 'the Flight of the Wild Geese'. On 29 July 1693, Sarsfield was wounded fighting the English at Neerwinden and died a few days later.

Michael 'Galloping' Hogan was one of the exiles. He was appointed a general in the French army, but he killed a fellow officer in a duel in Flanders in 1706. He left the French army and joined the Portuguese army, where he remained until his death. Over 14,000 Irish joined mercenary armies in Spain, France, Sweden, Poland, Austria, and Italy. They formed regiments that fought in the early 1700s in such faraway countries as Cuba, Honduras and Mexico.

Chapter 19

William's Mid-Reign

William and Mary's mid-reign was full of both innovation and disappointments. From 1690, William was away fighting the Jacobites in Ireland until 1692. With his deep obsession with Louis XIV's determination to expand his borders, including taking over the Netherlands, he travelled to Flanders and took part in the sieges that marked the Nine Years' War rather than the few battles that were fought. It was while he was away that Mary took the reins and proved to be a firm ruler. One of her acts was ordering her uncle, Henry Hyde, 2nd Earl of Claredon to imprisoned in the Tower for trying to get James II back on the throne.

Mary had some inkling that the self-serving John Churchill, the Earl of Marlborough, was writing to James. The persistent charges of Jacobinism led to Churchill being stripped of all his appointments. Mary had him sent to the Tower on suspicion that he was implicated in restoring James II to the throne. Mary was strongly suspicious and said; 'I will say nothing, because it is he I could say the most of and will never trust or esteem.' He was released soon after, but remained out of favour at court for three years and unemployed during the remainder of the Nine Years' War. In May 1694, Churchill was driven by jealousy of the appointment of General Thomas Tollemache, who received the command of a seaborne attack on Brest. In a fit of pique, he disclosed the planned raid to the French, something that would have resulted in a treasonable act resulting in an execution. Tollemache was badly wounded in the attack and succumbed to his wounds in Plymouth.

Churchill's dismay at being passed over as senior officer was in some way due to William favouring Dutch associates and officers over their English counterparts. Mary supported her husband and damaged her relationship with her sister, Anne, who had a close relationship with Churchill's wife, Sarah. Mary knew that Anne was under the influence of Sarah and she should be dismissed. When Mary visited her sister after her baby was born, she spent the time attacking Sarah. The relationship between the two sisters remained frosty and they never saw each other again.

When William returned from a pause in the Williamite Wars, he took over the mantle of politics, leaving Mary to the matter of the Church, something she relished. She was a staunch Anglican, which appealed to the Tories, who were sceptical of William's Calvinism. Mary was determined to defend the Church of England, and her chaplain, William Payne, said she wanted her religion to bring joy to the whole world. She was generous in her relations with dissenters and fostered co-operation between the different Protestant denominations. When it came to choosing appointments to the Church, she spread her net wide to include conformity and non-conformity.

During the Nine Years' War, William took time to pardon John Blackadder for the duel he fought in 1691 at Maastricht. Blackadder had fought at Bothwell Bridge against Monmouth and now he allied this Cameronian regiment to William's Anglo-Scottish brigade. By 1709, he was promoted to lieutenant colonel of the same regiment and wrote of the duel, an event that troubled him for the rest of his life. Taken from his diary, it was introduced into a book written in 1824, and it expresses the regret he had until his death:

> This refers to a duel which he fought with a brother officer, the son of a noble family in this country, and in which he was unhappily instrumental in depriving him of his life. The affair took place in 1691, when he was a very young man. It is said that to have originated in some trifling verbal dispute with a Captain (Robert Murray of the Royal Scots), while over their wine, in a company after dinner. Captain (Murray) it appears, had taken offence at some expressions dropped by his friend in conversations, as if intended to call in question his veracity. Meeting him some time afterwards, he reminded him of the alleged insult, and insisted upon immediate satisfaction. His friend, astonished and unconscious of giving offence, asserted his innocence, as he could not recollect of nothing he had said that could have the least tendency to asperse or injure his character. In vain, however, did he attempt to justify himself, and to show him that the words were on a trifling occasion, and not capable of the construction he put

upon them? In vain did he assure him, that if he had given him just provocation, he was ready to make any proper apology, or any concession or reparation he had a right to demand?

In a paroxysm of rage, and incapable of listening to reason, Captain Murray drew his sword and rushed on Lieutenant Blackadder, who for some time kept retreating and expostulating; willing to terminate the dispute in some more amicable way. At length, finding all his remonstrance's ineffectual, and perceiving his own life in danger, he was himself obliged, in self defence to close with his antagonist. An unfortunate thrust soon laid the Captain lifeless at his feet.

The duel had been witnessed by men on the ramparts of Maastricht and at the regimental trial Blackadder was acquitted. The duel made too deep an impression on his mind ever to be forgotten and he observed the anniversary in penitence and prayer.

William was beaten at the battle of Landen, or Neerwinden, in 29 July 1693, when the French overwhelmed the Allies in the Spanish Netherlands. For four years both sides had struggled with the financial and material costs of this protracted war, which failed to reach a decisive result. One battle that saw the Jacobite intention of invading England was fought off the Cotentin, or Cherbourg Peninsula, between 29 May and 4 June 1692. Louis XIV and his naval minister, Louis Phelypeaux, planned landing an invasion force on England's south coast to restore James to his throne. Louis wanted James back on the English throne to be the French ally in his plan for an expanded French nation. The Battles of Barfleur and La Hogue soon put pay to the French monarch's plans. It was planned that Admiral de Tourville would protect the invasion with his forty-four warships before the Anglo-Dutch fleets emerged from their respective winter ports. The French admiral was instructed to intercept them before they could combine into an organised fleet. Unfortunately, by 21 May he was forced by delays in intercepting the Allied fleet, which numbered eighty-two vessels.

Victor-Marie d'Estrees was to join de Tourville from Toulon but was beaten back by a fierce storm in the Strait of Gibraltar that sank two ships. Also, the Rochefort squadron was delayed. De Tourville's Brest fleet was undermanned and he was forced to leave twenty ships behind as he battled adverse winds up the Cotentin Peninsula. His plan was to collect the infantry, cavalry and artillery from La Hogue and Le Havre and then sail for the English coast. Although he was in charge of the fleet, the strategic decisions were made by James, Francois d'Usson de Bonrepaus and Bernardin Gigault de Bellefonds. This trio failed to put up any resistance and the battle was a purely maritime conflict.

Tourville entered the English Channel with thirty-seven ships, accompanied by seven fire ships, frigates, scouts and transports. He was later joined by Villette's squadron of seven ships from Rochefort, giving Tourville a combined fleet of forty-four ships, plus the attendant vessels numbering eighty sail. Meanwhile, the Anglo-Dutch fleet assembled off the Isle of Wight before sailing across the Channel to confront the French fleet. On 19 May off Cap Barfleur, the two sides met. Admiral Russell arrived from the north-west but Tourville had the weather gage from the south. The conditions were calm and it took some time to manoeuvre into position. In slow motion, the two fleets finally clashed. Russell held his fire until the French came closer and then ordered a bombardment. Both fleets pummelled each other, causing considerable damage. The battle lasted the rest of the day and into the night. A change of wind direction gave Sir Cloudsley Shovell the chance to break the French line and in the process received a wound. At around 1800 hours a flat calm descended, enveloping both fleets in a fog.

Although both sides had sustained damage, Tourville took advantage, cut the anchor cables and used the ebb tide to sail away from the scene of the battle. Russell realised what had happened and gave chase. At dawn the next day, Tourville's ships were scattered over a wide area. To the south, six ships led by Andre, Marquis of Nesmond, a formidable seaman, was forced to abandon some of his ships. Two were beached at Saint-Vaast-la-Hougue, while one was wrecked as it entered Le Havre. Nesmond managed to sail around England and Scotland before returning to Brest. This part of the extended battle was an English victory but it was the second part, which was carried out by small ships and longboats, that gave the Anglo-Dutch fleet complete control.

Much of the invasion fleet was made up of Irish Catholic soldiers who had gone into exile in the Flight of the Wild Geese. James was on hand to view his invasion fleet at Morsalines near the tip of the Cotentin Peninsula. The artillery and cavalry were to be loaded on transports at La Havre and the invasion force would combine to retake England. In charge of the ground troops was Sir John Fenwick, who later helped hatch a Jacobite plot in 1696. The infantry were covered by the sixty-eight guns of Fort St Vaast, and also the cannon on gun platforms along the shore. In addition there were forty-four guns on the island of Tatihou offshore. The invasion fleet consisted of 200 boats and three-oared galleys each mounting twelve cannon, ready to cross the Channel.

Admiral of the Fleet, Edward Russell had lost Rear Admiral Sir Cloudesley Shovell, who received a wound in the thigh during action off Cap Barfleur, and gave the command to Rear Admiral George Rooke, who led the attack the following day. Peregrine Osborne, Earl of Danby, was a politician who favoured the Royal Navy. He pleaded to command the boat parties that went in close to the shore. One small ship, the *Eagle*, sailed too close in and was grounded. In an unusual encounter, a group of the French cavalry attacked the stranded ship. One of the troopers was unsaddled by a boat hook wielded by a sailor before the ship was refloated. The French ships, having beached and with the French crews onshore, gave the English sailors free rein to board the ships and set them alight. The next day on the south shore, six ships at anchor were boarded and then burnt, supported by gunfire from two warships. This destruction was observed by James II, who said tactlessly, 'Only my English tars could have done such a deed.' The following day, Rooke sent in his boats into La Hogue harbour to destroy the invasion craft. They were only partially successful but caused enough damage to prevent any invasion of England. Some 5,000 English seamen were killed or wounded against 1,700 French. The French lost fifteen ships and two frigates destroyed compared with the English loss of two ships sunk.

The curious feature of this period was that many leading men, including Admiral Edward Russell and General John Churchill, still corresponded with James. Churchill was in secret and treacherous correspondence over the Dutch favourites of William. In particular, Churchill was opposed to Bentinck and had asked for James to somehow intercede. This gave James the illusion that the English were in favour of restoring him to his throne, something that only some Tories wanted. James issued a proclamation stating that he would issue a general pardon to those who supported him but excluded those who endorsed William. The English government used this Jacobite correspondence in broadsheets and pamphlets to their citizens to bring the nation into line. With his support stranded onshore, the impotent James saw his restoration to the throne destroyed. This great victory gave England the maritime ascendency she needed, coming two years after the humiliating defeat by the French at Beachy Head. William's primary achievement was to contain France when it was in a position to impose its will across much of Europe and also to kill off any attempt to reinstate James to the throne of England.

In the spring of 1693, a large convoy of Anglo-Dutch merchant ships known as the Smyrna Convoy was bound for the Mediterranean when it was attacked by Admiral de Tourville and his seventy ships of the line, coupled with an additional thirty auxiliary vessels. The French had made good their losses after the la Hougue fiasco and decided to attack the Allies' trade and commercial interests rather than its maritime strength. Having left the Channel under protection of many men-of-war, which turned back to cover the Channel, the convoy continued south protected by eight English and five Dutch warships. On 17 June, as they approached Lagos Bay in the Algarve, they spotted the French ships approaching. Admiral George Rooke ordered the merchant ships to scatter while his squadron took up battle positions.

Two Dutch ships, the *Zeeland* and *Wapen van Meemblik*, sacrificed themselves by taking on the French fleet. After some hours they surrendered, which gave Rooke time to collect the remaining fifty-four of his merchantmen. Four French warships went in pursuit but Rooke's flagship, the *Royal Oak*, laid down a bombardment that forced the French to withdraw. The convoy was able to reach Madeira, where they found an English and Dutch warship and fifty merchant ships. Admitting defeat, Rooke guided the convoy back to Ireland. Half the convoy was saved, although ninety ships were lost. The French had achieved a notable victory with a huge gain in prizes. London calculated that it was the worst financial disaster since the Great Fire.

After four years of war, both sets of combatants were struggling with financial and material costs. William's expensive wars had left the country in a mess. The demand for a bank whose sole purpose was to raise funds to allow the Allies to continue fighting the French in the Nine Years' War seemed to be the only way out. It was William Paterson, a Scottish trader and banker, who noticed that the nation's finances were in disarray with no real system of money or credit, and a central bank was what was needed. Paterson's project originated in 1691, and three years later the Bank of England was established. Paterson proclaimed in the introduction to his pamphlet, *A Brief Account of the Intended Bank of England*:

> The want of a Bank or Public Fund, for the convenience and secu-
> rity of great payments, and the better to facilitate the circulation of
> money, in and about this great and opulent City, hath in our time,
> among other inconveniences, occasioned much unnecessary credit,
> to the loss of several millions, by which Trade hath been exceed-
> ingly discouraged and obstructed. This together with the height of
> Interest or Forbearance of Money, which for some time past hath
> born no manner of proportion – to that of our rival neighbours,
> and for which no tolerable reason could ever be given either in
> notion or practice, considering the Effects of the Nation, in some
> sort, might be disposed to answer the use, and do the Office of
> Money, and become more useful to the Trade and Improvements
> thereof.

Paterson became a co-director but, in a disagreement in 1695, he withdrew and concentrated his efforts on the disastrous Darien Scheme. The Bank of England Act of 1694, which is sometimes referred to as the Tonnage Act 1694, was passed by Parliament. Subscriptions of £1.2 million were raised, worth considerably more today. A royal charter allowed the bank to operate as a joint stock bank with limited liability, which continued until 1826. It was referred to as the government's banker, and this gave it a considerable competitive advantage. It was the second oldest central bank in the world after the Swedish Riksbank, which was founded in 1668. At the end of 1694, it moved to Mercer's Hall, where it had more room, but in the 1730s it moved to its current home and became known as the 'Old Lady of Threadneedle Street'.

During this period of the late 1690s and early 1700s, England succeeded Holland as Europe's premier trader, something the Dutch resented, despite having a Dutchman as the King of England. William returned from Holland on 9 November 1694 and was met by Mary at Rochester. They were cheered all the way to London by enthusiastic crowds, bonfires and bell-ringing. On 19 December, Mary noticed that rashes had broken out on her arms and shoulders, and knew at once that it was smallpox. William disclosed to Gilbert Burnet:

There is no hope for the Queen. From being the happiest he was now going to be the miserablest creature on earth. I have never known one single fault in here.

Mary was 5ft 11in tall and in robust good health – she was fit enough to walk regularly between the palaces of Whitehall and Kensington – so to be struck down by a common disease when she was so hale was a disaster. When she caught smallpox, her sister, Anne, wrote to her saying she would run any risk to see her sister again. Sadly death came quite swiftly and at midnight on 28 December 1694, she died at the young age of thirty-two. William had grown to depend on his wife and was heartbroken when she died. At her lavish funeral in Westminster Abbey, Henry Purcell wrote 'Music for the Funeral of Queen Mary', the coffin cost a staggering £850 and there was a lying in state at the Banqueting Hall in Whitehall. The catafalque, or raised platform, was designed by Christopher Wren and was accompanied by 400 poor women dressed in black, each with a boy train-bearer. This was to pay respect to Mary's charity to the poor. Despite the war, France was saddened by Mary's death, but James forbade mourning at Saint-Germain and prompted comments from two women. William's cousin, Liselotte, Duchess d'Orleans, expressed the boredom at James's palace. 'The more one sees of this King, the more favourably one feels towards the Prince of Orange.' Madame de Sevigne was equally scathing. 'Listening to him talk, you realise why he is here.' She also declared:

To tell the truth, our good King James is a brave and honest man, but the silliest I have ever seen in my life; a child of seven would not make such crass mistakes as he does. Piety makes people outrageously stupid.

By 1694, the Nine Years' War was running out of steam. A French soldier admitted that France was suffering from the most severe famine in living memory. Food shortages were so acute that the French army was unable to mount offensive assaults during the whole of 1694. The following year, the Duke of Luxembourg, France's best military leader, died, which left William able to take Namur. In July 1695, Admiral Russell was able to lift the blockade on Barcelona, which sent the French navy sailing back to Toulon, so leaving the English navy in control of the western Mediterranean.

Chapter 20

The Fenwick Plot 1696

Jacobite plots to replace James on the throne haunted William's reign. Most were hatched in France, so they were protected and that made them more dangerous. Over the next decade, English politics was overshadowed by James's efforts, supported by those of Louis XIV, of retrieving his crown. There was even another invasion plan in 1695, which was to be led by James Fitzjames, the Duke of Berwick, the illegitimate son of James II and his mistress, Arabella Churchill. It was rejected as hopeless and there were no more attempts. There was, however, another plot to assassinate William, one of several attempts since the Glorious Revolution.

James Fitzjames travelled to London with a commission from James 'requiring our loving subjects to rise in arms and make war upon the Prince of Orange, the usurper of our throne'. According to Fitzjames, he hoped to raise some 2,000 horse to augment James's invasion, and to be greeted by Sir John Fenwick as major general and Sir George Barclay as brigadier. William was also conversant with the plot to kidnap and kill as he returned from his hunt at Richmond Park. It also implicated James, who was kept abreast of the machinations of the plot. Over the following decade, English politics was blighted by James's attempts to retrieve his throne. He was supported by many Tories whose religious and political attitudes meant they wished to see James back on the throne. It took a long while to reconcile the broad gulf between those who believed the Glorious Revolution was to be celebrated as a means of preserving the constitution and religion of England, and those who thought it might threaten the survival of the Church of England and the integrity of the English monarchy.

The man behind the plot to assassinate William was Sir John Fenwick, from an old Northumberland family. He entered the army and fought in the Flanders campaigns of the 1670s. With the death of his father, Fenwick succeeded him as one of the Members of Parliament for Northumberland. He was a prominent advocate of James and one of the principal supporters of the Act of Attainder against the Duke of Monmouth and his rebellion. He ran into financial difficulties and in 1688 sold his home, Wallington Hall near Morpeth, and a large part of his estates. With James exiling himself to France, Fenwick began a series of plots to remove William and Mary, resulting in imprisonment for a short time in 1689. Along with Sir George Barclay, a plot to assassinate William was hatched, although it took some years before it came to fruition. Macaulay wrote that John Fenwick was the only one to whom William felt an intense personal aversion. The dislike of each other stemmed from William's reprimand when they were serving in Holland.

The principal agent of the Fenwick Plot was Sir George Barclay, a sixty-year-old Scotsman. After fighting in Ireland, he returned with a warrant from King James to urge the Highlanders to rise against the English and the Scottish Protestants. As there was little appetite to fight, Barclay rejoined James in France. Although commissioned in the Jacobite army, he was mostly engaged in the plots of the English Jacobites. In 1696, he landed at Romney with a message from James 'requiring our loving subjects to rise in arms and make war upon the Prince of Orange, the usurper of our throne'. He correctly ascertained that there was negligible inclination to start a serious rebellion. Barclay and his co-conspirators, known as the 'Select Number', a secret Jacobite club, already had the idea of assassinating William when he returned from his hunting trip at Richmond Park. Barclay gathered around him some forty men to his headquarters in Covent Garden and explained the conspiracy,

Fenwick had become alarmed at the amount of information that George Porter, one of the conspirators, possessed, so he arranged for Porter to leave England and receive a free pardon from James. He promised Porter a large sum of money and the transaction was carried out by a middleman, a barber named Clancy, at a tavern in Covent Garden. However, the plot was already discovered and Clancy was arrested. He was convicted and suffered being pilloried. Porter, a Catholic, a scoundrel and 'haunter of Jacobite taverns', was rogue and, in October 1684, he had been accused of murder. According to the Middlesex Sessions Rolls of 1684:

On the said day, on view of the body of Sir James Halkett there lying dead and slain: With verdict of Jurors saying that on 11th day of October aforesaid at St Bride's within Farringdon Ward without London, George Porter last of the last-named parish esquire, assaulted the said Sir James Halkett and slew and murdered him, by then and there, giving him a rapier thrust a mortal wound in the left thigh.

This was before Halkett could draw his sword. For some unknown reason, the jury acquitted Porter of all charges. Porter took the opportunity of joining the army as a captain in Colonel Slingsby's regiment of horse. By May 1692, he was noted as a dangerous Jacobite and, by 1695, had returned to his old haunts. He was arrested in June for causing a disturbance in a Drury Lane tavern and drinking King James's health, but was soon released. He associated with George Barclay's 'Select Number' and brought his servant, Thomas Keyes, into the plot.

Robert Charnock was for a while vice-president of the Magdalen College, Oxford, and a confirmed Catholic. He was elected fellow of his college and, at the death of the president of Magdalen, strenuously supported James in the appointment of Anthony Farmer. A college meeting was convened and they rejected Farmer, whose scandalous life disqualified him from the post, and they voted instead for John Hough. An all-Catholic authority expelled the fellows for voting against their man and replaced them with Catholics. Charnock was installed as Dean and took part in the arguments that saw off the remaining fellows. On 1687–88, a royal mandate appointed him as vice-president of Magdalen College, a post he held for six months until he was expelled. He travelled to France and joined the Jacobites at the palace of St Germain. After 1692, he frequently crossed to England and joined in the plans to restore James to the throne. In 1695, he took lodging with Porter, an unlikely companion, and became heavily implicated in the assassination of William.

An English soldier, Major John Bernardi, another Jacobite plotter, was born in Evesham to a wealthy Genoese family. His father, Francis, had treated Bernardi harshly and he left home at the young age of thirteen and stayed with Sir Clement Fisher at Packington Old Hall, Warwickshire. When he was old enough, he enlisted in the army and rose to the rank of captain. In 1674, he was wounded at the Siege of Grave, losing an eye, and was shot in the arm at Maastricht. He was recalled from Holland in 1687 and served James loyally. When James left for France, Bernardi followed. He was given a Jacobite division, which he commanded at the Battle of Killiecrankie and the Irish battles. After James bolted from Ireland, Bernardi managed to escape to southern England but was captured attempting to board a ship to Holland. He was released on parole to Holland but shortly returned to London and began meeting other Jacobites, including his former commanding officer, Sir John Fenwick, and his brigadier, Ambrose Rookwood. In 1696, he was arrested in a tavern along with Rookwood and charged with being one of the plotters. He protested, but his name appeared among the conspirators.

Robert Blackbourn was the eldest son of Richard Blackbourn of Thistleton, and was considerably influential in Lancashire. Along with Bernardi, he was arrested on the discovery of the plot to kill William. Blackbourn had been part of James's troop of Guards in London and had travelled to the Chateau de Saint Germain in 1695. He was one of the group led by Rookwood who intended to murder William but the evidence was not compelling enough and was discharged from court. He then attempted to reach France but was again arrested at the Nore in December travelling without a pass.

Sir John Friend was the son of a brewer in St Katherine's near the Tower of London. He had built up the business and amassed a fortune. He was appointed a Commissioner of Excise and also a colonel in the Honourable Artillery Company (HAC). He was honoured when James, Duke of York, and his son-in-law, Prince George of Denmark, attended a banquet at the Artillery Ground. He was also knighted by James on 3 August 1685. When William came to the throne in February 1689, Friend lost his position at the Board of Excise. As one of the plotters, he was set against any assassination of William, although he kept the secret.

The son of a clergyman, Cardell Goodman was known to his enemies as 'Scum'. He attended St John's College, Cambridge, and, according to his own account, he cut and defaced a painting of the Duke of Monmouth and was expelled. He then became a page to Charles II but, after five years, was dismissed for negligence. He took up acting and for ten years acted on the London stage. He quickly frittered away the £2,000 inheritance from his father's estate, and to supplement his income he took to highway robbery. He was captured but was speedily pardoned by James and returned to the stage. In his later years he became the lover of Barbara Palmer (Villiers), the Duchess of Cleveland. He was detected trying to poison her two sons, not with murder in mind, but to keep them quiet. For this, he was fined heavily. In 1688, he became a gamester and an exponent of the card game *ombre*. Goodman became a Jacobite and was connected with the Fenwick–Charnock Plot.

William was fond of hunting and would frequently drive to and fro to Richmond Park for a day's hunting. The Jacobite gang assembled on the north bank of the Thames near Turnham Green on 15 February, but the King did not appear. A week later they waited on 22 February 1696, hoping that William would return from Richmond Park to catch a ferry across the Thames, which would funnel his party in a narrow lane that ran from Turnham Green to Brentford. Unable to cross with the entire escort on the ferry, the coach and escort would be temporarily separated. It was arranged that Porter should be one of the three leaders to attack the escort.

On the eve of the intended attack, the conspirators assembled in the lodgings that Porter shared with Charnock in Norfolk Street off the Strand. The plot was exposed and Porter and his servant, Keyes, were chased. They were finally captured at Leatherhead in Surrey. Porter confessed and gave up the names of his fellow plotters. Shamefully, he also betrayed Keyes. In June 1697, a woman was bribed to bring a scandalous charge against Porter but he managed to make his way across the Channel to France.

The plot was carefully thought out by Sir George Barclay, so that there were three parties of armed men, forty in number; one to capture the King and the others to deal with the reduced armed escort. A point was chosen on the lane that was narrow enough so the royal coach and six horses would not be able to turn. However, before this assassination attempt could be put in motion, the Jacobites' attempt at secrecy had collapsed.

William Turnbull, who was Secretary of State for the Northern Department, heard rumours of an assassination plot as early as August 1695. He gathered intelligence through his informers, which he later handed over to John Vernon. One of his informants was Sir Thomas Prendergast, an Irish politician and soldier. He was rewarded with a baronetage from William. Porter, the man who had received so much information, according to George Barclay, approached Prendergast on 13 February 1696 and together they went to William Bentinck, Earl of Portland, to reveal the conspiracy. Some 300 suspects were rounded up but the majority were soon released. All Roman Catholics were expelled from London for a distance of 20 miles until the culprits were caught.

Fenwick actively implicated fellow peers Lord Godolphin, Marlborough, Shrewsbury and Edward Russell, Earl of Orford. This led to awkward questions as these gentlemen had been in correspondence with James at St Germain. A number of Jacobites who had been connected to Fenwick but not involved in the plot included James Grahame and Thomas and Bevil Higgons, who were all later released. Thomas Bruce, Earl of Ailesbury, was not involved in the plot but was kept in the Tower of London until February 1697. Likewise, Viscount Montgomery went into hiding but gave himself up and was held in Newgate Prison for about seven months before being released.

A long sequence of trials began in March 1696. The 1695 Act made the date crucial for the defence counsel but this was denied to Friend, Parkyns and Charnock. Friend's companions searched for him around Covent Garden, where he frequented his favourite taverns. He was a Protestant and Tory, and protested that the witnesses against him 'were Papists, and not to be believed against Protestants'.

Sir William Parkyns was tried on 24 March and he defended himself. The testimony of the villainous George Porter, who had turned king's evidence, was explicit and Parkyns was condemned. Although he suffered from gout, he had provided horses, saddles and weapons for the forty horsemen. His Covent Garden house was searched but nothing was found. An examination of his house in Warwickshire revealed all the equipment needed for William's assassination. He was visited by a deputation of nine Members of Parliament and confessed that he was involved in the assassination plot, but would not disclose the names of those whom he had nominated to commissions in his regiment.

Sentenced to death, Friend and Parkyns were attended by three non-juror priests, who absolved them of their sins but declared the conspirators to be correct in their actions. This caused a considerable storm and the three priests were outlawed and later released.

On 13 April 1696, Parkyns and Friend were executed on Tower Hill and their heads were stuck on spikes on Temple Bar.

The actor Cardell Goodman was offered a free pardon if he would inform against Sir John Fenwick, which he gladly did. Goodman accepted £500 a year with exile abroad and escaped to France, dying of fever at the age of fifty in 1699.

After the arrest of his co-conspirators, Fenwick remained hidden until June, when he was apprehended. To save himself, he revealed the leading Whig nobles as part of the plot. By the time his friends removed one of the two witnesses, he felt he was in the clear. The government overcame this difficulty by introducing a Bill of Attainder, which after a lengthy process, was passed. William allowed Sir John Fenwick to be beheaded rather than suffer the ignominy of being hanged. He was taken to Tower Hill on 28 January and executed.

Sir George Barclay was one of the few who made his escape to France, and he went to pains to exonerate James from all knowledge of the plot. During negotiations with France in 1698, Bentinck demanded that Barclay should be returned to England to face trial. Louis responded by saying that the regiment that Barclay had commanded had been disbanded and his whereabouts were unknown.

On 16 February, Robert Charnock and several conspirators were arrested. He stood trial at the Old Bailey on 11 March along with Edward King and Thomas Keyes, the unfortunate servant who Porter implicated in the plot. Charnock faced a capital sentence and was hanged, drawn and quartered at Tyburn on 18 March. On the scaffold he handed a paper to the sheriff acknowledging his guilt but excused James and his Catholic comrades from blame. Charnock also denied:

> that the killing of a monster of iniquity like William is otherwise than an honourable act which would merit the approval of James II and all right-minded men.

Ambrose Rookwood was the grandson of the like-named Ambrose Rookwood, one of the Gunpowder Plot conspirators. On 27 March, the younger Ambrose Rookwood was found in bed in a Jacobite alehouse and taken to Newgate Prison. At his trial he was found guilty of treason along with Robert Lowick and Charles Cranburn, who was the gang's quartermaster. On 7 April a true bill of High Treason was found against Rookwood at the Middlesex County Sessions. The principal witness was George Porter, who gave compelling evidence against the three men. They were taken to Tyburn on 29 April and faced the dreadful process of being hanged, drawn and quartered.

Seven plotters were executed and a further five were imprisoned without coming to trial. The latter were John Bernardi, Robert Blackbourn, Robert Cassels, James Counter, Robert Meldrum and James Chambers. Counter was released by Queen Anne but by 1727, Bernardi, Cassels and Blackbourn submitted a petition for release, while Meldrum and Chambers had died in prison. In one of the longest incarcerations, Bernardi died in prison in 1736 at the age of eighty. In 1712, he got married for a second time at the age of sixty-eight to a woman named Abigail, who was around forty-eight years younger, and they went on to produce ten children. In 1729, he wrote his autobiography, *A Short History of the Life of Major Bernardi by Himself*, regarded as accurate but very boastful.

Bernardi and Blackbourn were the two final survivors who were detained in Newgate Prison indefinitely. An Irish mercenary soldier named Captain Peter Drake met Blackbourn in the pressyard at Newgate. He writes in his memoirs that, 'Blackbourn I last saw in April, 1745. He was then in the pressyard and well and as hearty as ever.' It appears that Blackbourn did not die until 1748, by which time he had been imprisoned for over fifty years without trial.

The Signing of the Association Act of 1696 was created after the failed Jacobite plot to murder William and to pledge loyalty to him. This gave towns and cities a chance to commit their devotion to the King and his popularity increased.

Chapter 21

William's Last Days

The Nine Years' War was one of the least great wars of the seventeenth century. From William's enthronement in 1689, his diplomatic skill over the next eighteen months brought together an alliance of Holland, Brandenburg, Hanover, Saxony, Bavaria, Savoy, Spain and England, which became the mainstay of the federation. Although France seemed to always win, she did little to press home her advantage, while William, although a shrewd general, contributed little in the way of victories.

King Louis had emerged from the Franco-Dutch War of 1678 as the most powerful ruler in Europe. Although victorious, he was not satisfied and used a mixture of aggression and annexation to expand France's frontier. The Truce of Ratisbon, or Regensburg, was signed between Spain, the Holy Roman Empire, and France. Louis retained Strasbourg and the Duchy of Luxembourg, but had to submit Courtrai and Dixmude. The truce was aimed at lasting for twenty years, but Louis ended it by declaring war on the Dutch, so starting the Nine Years' War. With William monarch of Great Britain, he used his new kingdom to fund the war against the French. By 1697, Britain was financing the Alliance to the sum of 45 per cent of the costs.

The war was financially crippling, especially to France. The armies had grown in size from 25,000 in 1648 to 100,000 by 1697, which was unsustainable for the pre-industrial economies. For the English State Revenue, the war took 80 per cent, which badly affected the economy. The main fighting was around France's borders in the Spanish Netherlands, the Rhineland, Savoy and Catalonia. William was obsessed with France dominating Europe and for six months each year during the Nine Years' War, he was away fighting in the Spanish Netherlands, where the main fighting took place. Next in line was the Rhineland, and France managed to cross the River Rhine and take the towns of Mannheim, Frankenthal, Oppenheim, Worms, Bingen, Kaiserslauten, Heidelberg, Speyer and the key fortress at Mainz.

Louis XIV now controlled the Rhine south of Mainz to the Swiss border. There were minor confrontations in Catalonia and Piedmont-Savoy, as well as the Caribbean and Canada. England had to send large amounts of money to supply her allies in the Low Countries and grant subsidies to her minor associates.

The campaigns were less about open warfare as with the battles of Fleurus and Marsaglia, and more to do with siege operations at Mons, Namur and Charleroi. The imminent death of the Spanish king, Charles II, heralded another lengthy war with France as the protagonist for the inheritance of the Spanish Empire. The French wars of 1689–97 and the Spanish Succession of 1702–13 became a matter of survival. These were wars on a scale that England had never experienced before and she set about recruiting soldiers and building warships. Thanks to an exceptional general, John Churchill, Duke of Marlborough, they won a string of exceptional victories in Europe, notably Blenheim, after which he named his palace in Oxfordshire.

The Maritime Powers of England and the Dutch Republic were financially exhausted. When Savoy defected from the Alliance, all parties were keen for a negotiated settlement, which was thrashed out at the Treaty of Ryswick (1697). The negotiations were handled by the signatories of Hans William Bentinck, the Earl of Portland, and Marshal Louis-Francois de Boufflers. The terms were protracted but did bring a brief respite. Within three years, the death of Charles II of Spain brought a new war over the inheritance of the Spanish crown; the most important unsolved question of European politics. Charles was mentally and physically incapable of governing Spain; he was known as *El Hechizado*, or the Bewitched, and was the last Spanish Habsburg ruler. Although he was a Habsburg, he chose Philip of Anjou, a Bourbon and grandson of Louis, as his heir; this would inevitably lead to the War of Spanish Succession.

With the final throes of the Nine Years' War, in 1696 William addressed his Parliament and appointed a Ministry known as the 'Junto'. He selected it from the political party with the greatest majority, which happened to be the Whigs. This was regarded with suspicion by the Members of Parliament but it became the forerunner of the modern Cabinet of Ministers. In 1697, Parliament granted William £700,000 for life, which included the upkeep of the civil government as well as royal household expenses.

On 2 December 1697, the newly built St Paul's Cathedral was opened, thirty-one years after the old one burnt down in the Great Fire of 1666. It was Sir Christopher Wren's crowning masterpiece. The first service to be held there was to celebrate the Treaty of Ryswick. Wren had plans for the grand-scale reconstruction of the City, and although some of his ideas were too far-fetched, he nevertheless played a major part in the City's rebirth.

Also in 1697, the French author Charles Perrault collected folk tales and wove them into such favourites in his book, *Histoires ou contes du temps passé*. He started a new literary genre known as the fairy tale and some of his best-known stories include *Little Red Riding Hood, Cinderella, Puss in Boots* and *Sleeping Beauty.*

On 4 January 1698, the rambling Palace of Whitehall was destroyed by fire, with only the Banqueting Hall left standing. Several works of art were destroyed, including Michelangelo's *Cupid*, Hans Holbein's *Portrait of Henry VIII* and Benini's marble bust of *King Charles I.* The choice of the royal palace lay between St James's Palace and Kensington Palace. William and Mary favoured Kensington Palace, but on her death William preferred Hampton Court, which was situated further up the Thames away from London.

On 19 January 1699, a Parliament dominated by the Tories sought to limit the size of the country's standing army to 7,000 'native-born men'. This meant that William's favourite Dutch Blue Guards were forced to leave England as they could not serve in the line. Another Parliamentary Act of 1 February also required the disbandment of foreign troops in Ireland.

In 1700 another war was set to break out. With Charles II, the last Spanish king of the House of Habsburg, dying of insanity at the age of thirty-eight, Louis XIV accepted the Spanish crown on behalf of his grandson, Philip of Anjou, who became Philip V. This was rejected by William, who recalled John Churchill to lead his army as his deputy in Flanders just before the War of Spanish Succession of 1701–14.

On 24 June 1701, the Act of Settlement was passed by Parliament to exclude the Catholic Stuarts from claiming the British throne. The child-less William would be succeeded by his sister-in-law, Princess Anne. If she could not produce an heir and died, then the sixty-year-old Sophie of Hanover would be in line to become the queen. She was the daughter of Elizabeth, Electress of the Palatinate, James I's second child and eldest daughter. This would herald the Hanoverians, who would rule from 1714 to 1837.

When William was fifty-one he had a bad fall from his horse, named White Sorrel, which had a reddish coat with some white hairs. The horse was formally owned by Sir John Fenwick, one of the executed scheming plotters in the 1696 Jacobite Plot. Fenwick had his estate confiscated, including the horse, which was partly responsible for William's death. On 21 February, despite his deteriorating health, William went for a ride in Home Park at Hampton Court Palace when his horse stumbled upon a molehill. The King was thrown from the saddle and broke his collarbone. Many Catholics toasted the mole as 'the gentleman in the black velvet waistcoat' but it was not the fall that led to William's death. It could have been much worse and, after the doctors set the bone, he asked to be taken to Kensington Palace, about 12 miles away. Riding in a bone-jolting carriage ride, he suffered badly and the bone had to be set again when he arrived.

It was a cold February day as he paced up and down the King's Gallery before taking a nap. When he awoke, he was feverish and feeling ill from falling asleep by an open window. The next few days saw his condition deteriorate, but he continued to attend to his paperwork and hold meetings with his advisors. Finally, on 5 March, he collapsed while walking in the King's Gallery and confined to bed. He was attended by Archbishop Thomas Tenison, Bishop Gilbert Burnet and his closest friends, Arnold van Keppel and Hans Bentinck. On the morning of 8 March he expired, muttering his last recognisable words 'Je tire vers man fin' (I draw towards my end). He died, not from the fall from his horse, but pulmonary fever brought on by his accident and the long-term respiratory problems he had suffered from all his life. A post-mortem examination was performed and the surgeon wrote:

> The Thorax or Chest we observed that the Right side of the Lungs adhered to the Pleura: and the Left, much more. From which upon separation, there issued forth a quantity of purulent or frothy serum. The upper lobe on the Left side of the Lungs and the part of the Pleura next to it were inflamed to a degree of mortification. And this we look upon as the Immediate Cause of

the King's death. From the ventricles of the heart and the greater blood vessels arising out of them were taken several large tough flesh-like substances of the kind called Polypus. The Heart itself was of the smaller size: but firm and strong.

In keeping with his stand-offish manner, William was given a private funeral on 12 April and was buried alongside his wife in Westminster Abbey. The Privy Council made plans for monuments to be erected but these never came to fruition. Although William had changed the way kingship was enacted in contrast to Charles and James, he was soon for-gotten. In his place, Anne ascended the throne and England became a world leader as Spain, Holland and France declined. Albion's brilliant age had begun.

Chapter 22

Marlborough's Victories at Schellenberg and Blenheim

William's last year on the throne in 1701 was the start of the War of the Spanish Succession, which would last most of Queen Anne's reign. The fifty-one year-old Marlborough was the commander of the Second Grand Alliance (the First was in the Nine Years' War), and this was made up of England, the United Provinces (Holland) and Austria. Marlborough was prepared to fight Louis XIV and Bourbon Spain with the addition of Dutch-paid 12,000 Danish soldiers, made available through a treaty with England and the United Provinces. The Spanish successor was triggered by the death of the childless King Charles II of Spain. This set in motion the dynastic rights of the Habsburgs and the Bourbons. Who should reign over Spain was disputed by the Habsburg Archduke Charles of Austria and the Bourbon Duke of Anjou. In Charles's will, he named Phillip of Anjou, the grandson of Louis XIV, as his heir and if he refused then the title would fall to his younger brother, the Duke of Berry. The third option was Archduke Charles, the son of Leopold the First, the Holy Roman Emperor of Austria. Charles' candidature was supported by England, Scotland, Ireland, Portugal, Sardinia and the majority of the Holy Roman Empire. This convoluted line led to the start of the thirteen-year-long wars against Louis XIV, 'Sun King'. Louis had approved of William ruling England but then later annoyed him by recognising the son of the deposed James II as the rightful king. This was part of William's never-ending war against France, a conflict that William sought and one that Queen Anne continued under the guidance of her ministers, Godolphin and Marlborough.

William's increasing asthma attacks and his fall from his horse led to his death on 8 March 1702. Before that, he had appointed Marlborough as Ambassador-Extraordinary and commander of the English forces for the conference at The Hague. When Anne succeeded William, she made

Marlborough Master-General of the Ordnance, a Knight of the Garter and Captain-General of the Alliance forces. The campaign began in the Low Countries and, after outmanoeuvring the French, Marlborough captured Venlo, Roermond, Stevensweert and Liège. The last mentioned was on 10 May 1703, when the Queen's Regiment and a Dutch Regiment were quartered in the small town of Tongres, near Liège. They were attacked by an army of 40,000 French, who were intent on destroying Marlborough's ally, the Dutch Marshal Overkirke. The French Marshal Bouflers decided to deal with the lightly defended Tongres first, but the fighting continued for twenty-eight hours before the Queen's and van Elst's regiments surrendered. This gave ample time for Overkirke and Marlborough to concentrate their defensive positions. Unable to take the Allies by surprise, Bouflers had abandoned his plan. These were outstanding victories and Anne rewarded John Churchill with the Dukedom of Marlborough and the estate at Woodstock in Oxfordshire.

As the war entered its third year, Marlborough met the Imperial War Council and decided to extend his scope of fighting in order to secure Vienna, as its loss would reverse all his Low Countries victories. In early 1704, he learned that the combined French, Spanish and Bavarian forces were intent on absorbing Vienna, which was already under threat from a serious Hungarian uprising. The French leader, the Duc de Vendome, was poised to cross the Alps from Savoy, while the Elector of Bavaria and Marshal Marsin were camped around Ulm waiting for the Duc de Tallard to arrive from Strasbourg. In February 1704, Marlborough gloomily wrote, 'For this campaign I see so very ill a prospect that I am extremely out of heart.'

He realised that he had to march 250 miles along part of the route dominated by French troops. He secretly detached part of his Netherlands army and, on 20 May 1704, he departed the town of Bedburg, near Cologne, with 21,000 troops. It took just thirty-five days to reach Southern Germany, but Marlborough had organised the epic march so his men were in a fit condition to fight. He spread the word that he intended to campaign along the Moselle River using Koblenz as his base. Instead, he crossed the Moselle and took with him 5,000 Hanoverian soldiers before passing on to Mainz, where he picked up 14,000 Danish and German troops. He had ordered that his force should march 10 to 12 miles each day, with a full rest day every four marches. The weather was terrible and the crude roads were soon turned into quagmires, but Marlborough had the foresight to have replacement shoes and saddles ready at Heidelberg in early June. Captain Robert Parker of the 18th Foot wrote of the march:

> We frequently marched three, sometimes for day, successively, and halted a day. We generally began our march about three in the morning, proceeded for about four leagues (1 league equalled 3 miles), or four and a half each day, and reached our ground about nine. As we marched through the countries of our Allies, commissaries were appointed to furnish us with all manner of necessaries for man and horse; these were brought to the ground before we arrived, and the soldiers had nothing to do, but to pitch their tents, boil their kettles, and lie down to rest. Surely never was such a march carried on with more order and regularity, and with less fatigue both to man and horse.

The following British regiments took part in Marlborough's march to Southern Germany: Dragoon Guards, 1st, 3rd, 5th, 6th, 7th, 2nd Dragoons, 1st Guards, 1st Foot, 3rd, 8th, 10th, 15th, 16th, 18th, 21st, 23rd, 24th, 26th, 37th, plus part of the Flanders artillery. By now Marlborough was in Baden and linked up with Prince Louis and his Hessians, Hanoverians and Prussians. Now that Marlborough had diverted away from the French-dominated Rhine, he had been assured by the Austrians that heavy guns would be provided; a promise that was soon broken. By 13 June his Allied force now numbered 40,000 strong.

On 28 June, he linked up with Prince Eugene of Savoy with his Imperial troops at Launsheim. Like William III, Prince Eugene was in poor health but turned out to be one of the most successful military commanders of his time. Marlborough sent the Savoy army to block any attempt by Duc de Tallard to cross the Rhine, while he took the rest of the troops in a move against the Elector of Bavaria.

On 1 July, Marlborough neared the village of Donauwörth, when he was approached by a corporal from the Bavarian army with information about the Franco-Bavarian position on the steep hill of Schellenberg. Several French regiments had been sent to prevent the English and Baden troops taking this important hill, which overlooked the Danube. Lieutenant Colonel

Jean-Martin de la Colonie later wrote of his experience as a French officer in the Battle of Schellenberg:

> Scouting parties were sent out all over the country to discover their movements (Marlborough), and on their report that an advance had been made, which threatened the safety of Augsburg and Donauwört, a Bavarian infantry corps, with several squadrons of dragoons was detached under Marechal d'Archo to occupy the heights of Schellenberg and several French regiments were sent to garrison (the village) of Donauwört.

Marlborough ordered a night march with the pace forced, which would bring the Allies to the steep north side of the Schellenberg. The early morning sight of the Allies unnerved the defenders, who hurriedly attempted to construct a palisade on the defenceless flank. The Allied army split into two to the east of hamlet of Berg; Marlborough's 10,000 troops taking the north side and Baden's 50,000 troops the south-west flank. De la Colonie explained the enemy's rush to take the Schellenberg:

> The Imperialists (Allies), whose first object was to lose no time, formed their army as fast as its units arrived at the points along the edge of the wood where they were sheltering from the fire from the fortress. Having planted a battery of ten guns, they began cannonading us high and low, with the idea of smashing our feeble parapet, shaking the courage of our troops …
>
> Marachal d'Archo who had flattered himself when they first appeared that they would hardly be in condition to attack us that very day and that the army from Augsburg would have time to send us reinforcements, now realised from the prompt action of this battery that they had resolved to make short work of us before this could happen, and that it was upon the defenceless flank that the enemy were about to deliver their assault …
>
> I had hardly finished speaking when the enemy's battery opened fire upon us, and raked us through and through. They concentrated their fire upon us, and with their first discharge carried off Count de la Bastide, the lieutenant of my own company, with whom when at the moment of speaking, and twelve grenadiers,

who fell side by side in the ranks, so my coat was covered with brains and blood ... At last the enemy's army began to move to the assault, and still it was necessary for me to suffer this sacrifice to avoid a still greater misfortune, though I had five officers and eighty grenadiers killed on the spot before we fired a single shot.

The first assault took over an hour and left a terrible carnage along the parapet. De la Colonie wrote:

So steep was the slope in front of us that as soon almost as the enemy's column began its advance it was lost to view, and it came into sight only two hundred paces from our entrenchments. I noticed that it kept as far as possible from the glacis of the town and close alongside of the wood, but I could not make out whether a portion might not also be marching within the latter, with the purpose of attacking that part of our entrenchments facing it, and the uncertainty caused me to delay movement ...

The English infantry led the attack with the greatest intrepidity, right up to our parapet, but there were opposed with a courage at least equal to their own. Rage, fury, and desperation were manifested by both sides, with the more obstinacy as the assailants and assailed were perhaps the bravest soldiers in the world. The little parapet which separated the two forces became a scene of the bloodiest struggle that could be conceived. Thirteen hundred grenadiers, of whom seven hundred belonged to the Elector's Guards, and six hundred who were left under my command, bore the brunt of the enemy's attack at the forefront of the Bavarian infantry ...

We were fighting hand to hand, hurling them back as they clutched at the parapet; men were slaying, or tearing at the muzzles of guns and the bayonets which pierced their entrails; crushing under their feet their wounded comrades, and even gouging out their opponents' eyes with their nails, when the grip was so close that neither could make use of their weapons. I verily believe that it would have been quite impossible to find a more terrible representation of Hell itself than was shown in the savagery of both sides on this occasion ... The ground around our parapet was covered with dead and dying, in heaps almost as high as our fascines, but our whole attention was fixed on the enemy and his movements …

There were three assaults, in the last of which the English managed to force the Franco-Bavarians from the hill by appearing on the flank. This precipitated a mass retreat, which the English rolled up, sending the enemy towards the Danube. The troops in Donauwörth also vacated the village, thanks to the men of Baden's army who attacked the south of the hill and the village. The weight of so many escaping soldiers in the rush to cross the Danube via the pontoon bridge caused it to collapse, and many were drowned in the fast-flowing river. The cavalry then chased the enemy soldiers and cut them down among the corn and reeds that bordered the river. Although the battle was quite a minor affair, its casualty rate was very high. Marlborough lost 1,342, while the wounded amounted to 3,700. The Franco-Bavarians came off worst, having over 5,000 killed or drowned.

Lieutenant Colonel de la Colonie found he was alone on the parapet. He was unable to find his horse and, despite his heavy thigh boots, he managed to evade the enemy troops and escaped through the corn fields until he came to the banks of the Danube. He spotted the wife of a Bavarian soldier and persuaded her to help remove his heavy riding boots. He then disrobed and, now unencumbered, he plunged into the Danube:

> Before taking to the water I took the precaution of leaving on the bank my richly embroidered uniform, rather spoiled as it was by the events of the late action. I scattered in a similar manner my hat, wig, pistols, and sword, at one point and another, so that if the troopers came before I had got away, they would devote their attention to collecting articles instead of looking in the water, and it turned out just as I thought. I kept my stockings, vest, and breeches simply buttoning the sleeves of the vest and tucking the pockets within my breeches for safety; this done, I threw myself upon the mercy of the stream … Finally, after a very long and hard swim, I was lucky enough to each the other bank …

Marlborough used his time to lay waste to some 300 to 400 villages, farmhouses and mills in the Bavarian area to demonstrate to the Elector that he should sever his association with the French. This was something Maximilian, the Elector of Bavaria, refused to comply with and he stayed with Marechal Count Camille de Tallard. Major Blackadder wrote in his diary:

> Finding it impossible to dislodge him from this strong position, the Duke of Marlborough, eager to profit by his recent victory, resolved to cut him off from all supplies. He entered the Bavarian territory and took several places by storm. He ravaged the whole country, as far as Munich, with fire and sword, in order to compel the Elector to sue for peace or relinquish his connections with France. A negotiation was begun, without sincerity on the part of the Elector.

On 29 July, Prince Eugene received news that the Franco-Bavarian armies were crossing the Danube about 3 miles from his position. He quickly put some distance between his army and the enemy's by moving east of the Kessel River, a tributary of the Danube. He sent an urgent message to Marlborough, who was marching east of Donauwörth on the south side of the Danube. He made his crossing at Donauwörth and turned west to join up with Prince Eugene, who was then about 5 miles away from the French and Bavarians. By this time, the Bavarians were aware that the Allies were running short of supplies and were confident that they would not have to face an imminent attack.

Tallard took up a position at Blenheim (then named Blindheim) with its garrison of twenty-six battalions and twelve squadrons. Marshal Marsin and the Elector concentrated the strength of their separate army protecting the villages of Lutzingen and Oberglau; twenty-two battalions and thirty-six squadrons masking Lutzingen on the far left. Positioned forward of the line, the hamlet of Oberglau was held by fourteen battalions, including the three Irish regiments in the French service. Between Oberglau and Blenheim, where the division fell between Tallard's army and the army of Marsin and the Elector, lay eighty squadrons of horse and seven battalions of foot.

The Allies sent some 'deserters' to the French lines to spread the rumour that Marlborough's army was about to retreat to Nördlingen to protect their communications. On the evening of 12 August, Marlborough and Eugene climbed the church steeple at Merxheim and saw enemy dispositions. They saw that the ground was cut by a number of tributary streams flowing north-west to south-east into the Danube and that the village of Blenheim lay beyond the point where one of the streams, the Nebel, joined the main river. Although the opposing armies were almost equal in numbers, Tallard's forces appeared to hold the stronger position. Their right flank was anchored to the Danube, while their left was protected by woodland, with the Nebel stream running to their front. Too late, Tallard realised that a full-scale army was approaching. In the early hours of 13 August, Marlborough and Eugene ordered their lumbering 52,000 troops forward. Prince Eugene approached the right flank at Lutzingen with his Savoy troops to cause enough problems that more Bavarian troops were sent to prop up the flank. On the French side, the Comte de Mèdrode-Westerloo, declared:

> It would be impossible to imagine a more magnificent specta-
> cle. Two armies in full battle array were so close to one another
> that they exchanged fanfares of trumpet-calls and rolls of kettle
> drums. When our music stopped, their music struck up again.
> This went on until the deployment of their right flank was com-
> pleted, their left preparing to attack the village. The brightest
> imaginable sun shone down on the two armies drawn up in the
> plain. You could even distinguish the uniforms of each successive
> unit; a number of generals and aides-de-camp galloped here and
> there all in all, it was an almost indescribably stirring sight.

Marlborough took command of the centre in order to launch two simultaneous attacks, which would, when working in conjunction with one another, weaken the French centre. On Marlborough's left flank was his third in command, General Lord Cutts, known as 'the Salamander', who was ordered to attack the village of Blenheim with nineteen battalions. John Blackadder noted in his diary:

> About noon, orders were given for a general attack, which was
> begun on the left, at the village of Blenheim, by the British infan-
> try and four battalions of Hessians, who boldly advanced to the

muzzels of the enemy's muskets, some of the officers exchanging sword-thrusts with the French through the palisades. But the tremendous fire made such havoc among them, that they were forced to retreat, leaving nearly one third of their number dead on the spot.

A second assault, in which John Blackadder was wounded, was made by Brigadier Ferguson, who took three or four attempts before being forced to retreat. In this action the Cameronians suffered severely, having about twenty officers either killed or wounded. The head of the British Guards was Brigadier Rowe, who led his men in a full-scale charge. Many were killed but with the rest of the foot battalions coming up, they managed to drive the enemy from the outskirts of the village into the heart of it. The mistake of the defence of Blenheim was due to Marquis de Clèrembault, who had decided to pack the village with at least twenty-seven battalions, some of whom were unable to fire upon Marlborough's men.

John Blackadder had joined the fiercely religious regiment, the 26th Foot, known as the Cameronians. They had reformed as a regiment in William's army and fought in Flanders under the command of the Earl of Angus. Each Cameronian company had a Presbyterian elder, the regimental chaplain and a Bible, which was issued to every new recruit in recognition of these religious origins. Blackadder fought at Schellenberg and Blenheim, where he was wounded. He was promoted to major and went on to serve at Ramillies in 1706, and Oudenarde and Wynendaele in 1708. In the same year, during which the regiment besieged Lille, he was wounded twice. At Malplaquet in 1709, the regiment's colonel, Cranston, was wounded and Blackadder took his place. He went on to fight through the sieges of Douai and Bouchain before selling his commission in 1711.

Captain Parker was with the 18th Foot and later wrote:

Here they threw up an entrenchment, within which they were pent up in so narrow a compass, that they had not room to draw up in any manner of order, or even to make use of their arms. Thereupon we drew up in great order about 80 paces from them, from whence we made several vain attempts to break in upon them, in which many brave men were lost to no purpose; and after all, we were obliged to remain where we first drew up. The enemy also made several attempts to come out upon us; but as they were necessarily thrown into confusion in getting over their trenches, so before they could form into any order for attacking us, we mowed them down with our platoons in such numbers, that they were always obliged to retire with great loss; and it was not possible for them to rush out upon us in a disorderly manner, without running upon the very points of our bayonets. This great body of troops therefore was of no further use to Tallard ...

De Mèrode-Westerloo commented about the conduct of his ally, the French:

Whilst the French, following their usual deplorable custom, set fire to all the villages, mills, and hamlets to our front, and flames and smoke billowed up to the clouds.

Marlborough also ordered Prince Holstein-Beck's six battalions to attack Oberglau and two battalions to attack the mills. He was unable to force the enemy from the village but did manage to set the mills on fire. Marachal Marsin, who was under fire from Prince Eugene's troops, was taken by surprise as Danish troops had stumbled through the thick woods and outflanked the Lutzingen. Prince Eugene led a second frontal attack, which was resisted. Thanks to Marlborough's quick thinking, he ordered his cavalry to attack. They rode uphill at a fast trot and, after a fierce struggle, the French resistance broke and they fled. Some escaped upstream to Höchstadt on the river, including de Mèrode-Westerloo, and others to the Danube, where they drowned.

In the centre, Marlborough unleashed Colonel Francis Palmes's cavalry the moment the villages were attacked. They had to negotiate the boggy ground made by the Nebel using straw but reached the other side without mishap. Tallard saw Palmes had advanced his squadrons some distance from the French line and ordered five squadrons to attack and then retire. He ordered the squadron on his right and the left to edge outward so they could wheel inward and fall on Palmes's flanks, while he charged them from the front. Palmes anticipated this and ordered both flanks to turn and charge the French flanks. He then ordered his centre to meet the French centre head on and cause such a surprise that the French folded. Tallard was mortified that three squadrons of British cavalry could easily beat five French of horse. It was something that played on his mind for the rest of the battle.

As the lines of the foot regiments reached the slope, they received a charge by the Gendarmerie under Count Zurlauben, a Swiss-born officer. The British were pushed back towards the Nebel marshes. Marlborough saw the French lines advance in a charge, which broke the first line. As they confronted the second line, they were rebuffed and were forced to retire back up the hill. Colonel Blood managed to manhandle his nine cannon over the Nebel and the artillery provided close support to the regiments of foot as they faced Obergau. Lord Orkney of the 1st Foot recalled:

> I marched with my battalion to sustain the Horse, and found them repulsed, crying out for Foot, being pressed by the Gendarmerie. Went to the head of several squadrons and got them to rally on my right and left, and brought up four pieces of cannon, and then charged ... Without vanity, I think we all did our parts.

After several hours of hand-to-hand fighting, the French were forced back. Marlborough called a halt and Tallard called for assistance from Blenheim but they were under pressure and unable to help. De Mèrode-Westerloo wrote of his narrow escape:

> When I was riding past Forsac's regiment a shot carried away the head of my horse and killed two troopers; another of my Spanish mounts was killed behind one of the Orlèans squadrons, whilst yet a third received a hit which carried away the buts of my pistols, the pommel of the saddle and a piece of flesh as the crown of a hat. He recovered his wound, however, without disfigurement, and years later I gave him to the Duke of Wolfenbüttel ...
>
> To make things worse, the village had been set on fire by the French troops, and our poor fellows were grilled amidst the continually collapsing roofs and beams of the blazing houses, and thus were burnt alive amidst the ashes of this smaller Troy of their own making.

Tallard's centre was effectively doomed and it gave way. For Tallard, it was a disastrous day, for he not only lost the battle, he also lost his son, who had been killed by his side. The commander, Marquis de Clèrambault, managed to escape from the village and rode down into the Danube, where he drowned. As Tallard retreated to the river, he was captured and later taken back to England. He was kept at Newdigate House in Nottingham and made the best of his captivity. He even taught the local housewives how to make French rolls and salads. He was a keen gardener and introduced celery, which he cultivated from the wild celery he found on the banks of the Trent. Portions of his garden still exist behind the high brick walls. He was released in 1711 and returned to France.

Twenty-eight battalions and twelve squadrons of cavalry surrendered to the British, who had little idea what to do with them. In the end, they were herded into a lane on the outskirts of Blenheim. The Allies had no depot in which to house or feed them. In the end, Marlborough decided to take a proportion of them by river down the Rhine to Mentz, where the prisoners were to disembark.

Colonel Parke brought the momentous despatch from the Duke of Marlborough to the Queen. She was playing dominoes at Windsor Castle and on 21 August, just eight days' ride from the battlefield, she held Marlborough's message, written on the back of a tavern bill, which read:

> I have not time to say more but I beg you will give my duty to the Queen and let her know that her army has had a glorious victory. Monsieur Tallard and two other generals are in my coach, and I am following the rest. The bearer, my Aide-de-Camp, Colonel Parke, will give her an account of what has passed. I shall do it in a day or two by another more at large.

With tears running down her face, Anne gave Parke a miniature painting of herself and a thousand guineas in reward.

Chapter 23

Marlborough's Later Victories

The focus returned to Flanders, the 'Cockpit of Europe'. The Duke of Marlborough returned in spring 1705 to The Hague and from there to Maastricht. The campaign of 1705–06 had been particularly good for King Louis for he had won victories in Italy and Germany. He turned his attention to Flanders, where he sent his brave, but undistinguished, Marshal Duc de Villeroi off from Leuven on 18 May 1706 with 60,000 troops with the expected ability to outmanoeuvre Marlborough. Meanwhile, Marlborough had assembled his Anglo-Dutch army of 62,000 men with the intention of encountering Villeroi's troops. Marlborough wrote on 15 May to his friend, Sydney Godolphin:

> God knows I go with a heavy heart for I have no hope of doing anything considerable, unless the French do what I am very confident they will not court battle.

On 23 May 1706, they met on the dry ground between the Mehaigne and Petite Gheete rivers, close to the village of Ramillies. The Hanoverians, Hessians and the Danes found reasons for withholding support. Marlborough wrote to the Duke of Württemberg, commander of the Danish army, pleading for his Danish cavalry in the battle that was to follow. Captain Robert Parker wrote:

> The nature of the ground and disposition of their army was as follows. They had the (river) Mehaigne on their right, with the village of Franquenay on the bank of it; in this village they had place a good body of foot and dragoons, and had also thrown up such an entrenchment as the time would admit of. From hence to the village of Ramillies, which was a little to the left of their centre, was a fine plain of near half a league in length, where

they knew the main stress of the battle must fall. On this plain, therefore, they drew up the choicest, and the greatest number of their cavalry, interlined with their best infantry. In the village of Ramillies, they placed twenty battalions with ten pieces of cannon. From Ramillies runs the River Gheete, which makes the ground on both sides marshy, and not passable, especially for horse. Along this river to the villages of Offus and Autre Eglise, which covered their left flank, was posted a thin line of the worst of their infantry, with squadrons after a scattering manner posted in their rear. This was the dispositions of the enemy, when we came up to them.

Marlborough, whose military intelligence was superior to his opposite commander, had outthought his opponent. He sent his troops with pontoons to lay bridges across the marshy ground on his right flank to attack the enemy at their weakest part. Villeroi spotted this and sent large bodies of horse and foot that should have been taking part in the decisive struggle south of Ramillies. Robert Parker again wrote:

When the Duke observed that these had arrived there, he sent orders to our right wing to retire easily up the hill, without altering their aspect. This we did, until our rear line had got on the back of the rising ground, out of sight of the enemy. But the front line halted on the summit of the hill in full view of them, and there stood, ready to march down and attack them. As soon as our rear line had retired out of sight of the enemy, they immediately faced to the left, and both horse and foot, with a good many squadrons, that slunk out of the front line, marched down the plain, as fast as they could, by this time the greater part of our horse of the left wing had arrived there also, and we were now superior in numbers to them in that quarter. The Duke soon put them in order for attacking the enemy on the plain.

Marlborough had two narrow escapes. A French cavalry unit came close when an Irishman, Patrick O'Meighan, shot the Duke's horse dead. Now unhorsed, Marlborough was defenceless when Captain Richard Molesworth, newly appointed aide-de-camp, rushed to his general's rescue.

He lifted him into his saddle and made their escape. An hour later Robert Parker recalled:

> His Grace had another narrow escape; when in shifting back from Captain Molesworth's horse to his own, Colonel (James) Bringfield holding the stirrup, was killed by a cannon shot from the village of Ramillies.

At the last moment, the Duke of Württemberg arrived with his Danish cavalry and immediately charged through the gap that opened up at the village of Franquenay on the French left flank. The centre had been reduced of men sent to prop up the left flank, which was a Marlborough feint. De la Colonie with his Grenadiers Rouge regiment and the Cologne Guards were ordered forward from his post south of Ramillies to support the faltering counterattack on the village. When he arrived, all was chaos. De la Colonie wrote:

> Scarcely had my troops got over when the dragoons and Swiss, who had preceded us, came tumbling down upon my battalions in full flight ... My own fellows turned about and fled along with them.

He did manage to rally a few of his men but could only offer a fragile support for the right wing. Compte de Mèrode-Westerloo also wrote of the Danish attack:

> The French army protected its left, behind some inaccessible places, and through overconfidence placed only the Maison de Roi on their right, believing the formation to be more valiant that Alexander the Great's phalanx. In fact this formation was soon broken up by a newly raised regiment of Danish dragoons as the French failed to support it ...

The Franco-Bavarian army fought on but they were staring at another defeat. The French lost 6,759 killed with 5,328 wounded and 5,729 prisoners. Marlborough pursued the enemy, never giving them a chance to reorganise, and they fled to Lille, having lost many to desertions. The

Anglo-Dutch army seized sixty cannon, about 2,000 wagons, but their loss was put at just over 4,000.

Having suffered a defeat at Ramillies, the following year the French had considerable success by preventing Marlborough and his Allies achieving anything notable in the Low Countries. In July 1708, the Duc de Bourgogne (Louis XIV's grandson) and the Duc de Vendôme led their armies to Oudenarde but Marlborough learned of this and force-marched his troops during the night. On 11 July the two forces met north of Oudenarde. The Allied army numbered 80,000 and the Franco-Bavarian about 85,000. The French were preparing to besiege Oudenarde but were caught unawares by the arrival of Marlborough's army, who appeared on the other side of the Scheldt. The Allied army had marched 50 miles in sixty-five hours, and immediately went on the attack. To add to the confusion, the two French Dukes had quarrelled previously; one wanted to retreat, while the other wanted to fight. In the end, they remained to fight.

Vendôme received the intelligence that the Anglo-Dutch were still crossing the Scheldt and ordered his army to take up a position along the heights above Oudenarde on the eastern side of the Norken River. He then ordered seven French regiments forward to occupy and hold the village of Heurne. Bourgogne again disagreed with Vendôme's dispositions and directed that the army take up positions on the heights to the west of the Norken River. Vendôme mistook the village of Heurne and sent his troops to occupy Eine, which was in a more exposed position. Around the village was marshy ground, which is where he placed the greater part of his infantry. They cut down trees and laid them in a way that would prevent Marlborough's troops advancing. This did not stop the Dutch troops, who encountered little resistance. Led by General William Cadogan, the regiments moved towards Eine, whereupon the cavalry encircled the village and annihilated the French defenders. The cavalry was led by the future British King George II, who attacked the few French squadrons and had his horse killed under him. He rather bored his listeners by relating his part in the Ramillies battle. By 4 pm, the absence of an Allied assault prompted Bourgogne to launch a French attack. This was countered by the English foot that had crossed the Scheldt and were ready to face the French.

Unnoticed by the French, Marlborough sent a Dutch and Danish force on a long detour to the west hidden by higher ground. When it emerged, it struck the French right flank in the rear. The Dutch cavalry under General d'Auverquerque moved even wider and caught the French cavalry standing in the rear of their line. With the French right surrounded, it began to collapse. On the other flank, Prince Eugene took eighteen battalions in support of General Cadogan pressed against the French.

To relieve the centre and right, Vendôme and Bourgogne attempted to bring the French left across the Norken into the battle but they were unable to cross the river. Vendôme had long since lost control of the battle and decided to lead his troops in a charge, which was soon surrounded. With dusk falling over the battleground, Marlborough ordered a ceasefire. The French streamed away in disorder, saved by the onset of darkness. The Allies captured parties of stragglers amounting to 9,000. The French had lost about 6,000 casualties, with the Allies suffering about 3,000. The next day, Vendôme managed to rally his defeated army and take the town of Ghent. In January 1709, Marlborough recaptured Ghent and Bruges and the French withdrew to their own border.

The Battle of Malplaquet was fought near the border of France and Spanish Netherlands on 11 September 1709. It was the last battle that the Duke of Marlborough was involved in as he was roundly criticised for the loss of so many men. His opponents were Marshals Villars and Boufflers, who settled on a defence embedded in the Forest of Lagnières. Their dispositions stretched for some 3 miles into the Forest of Taisnières. Their defence lines were covered by log *abattis*, fronted with redoubts, and at the left end of the line a fortification jutted forward from the main line on to a hill in the forest. As one witness explained, 'Our position was a peculiar one but advantageous withal.'

Marlborough and Prince Eugene of Savoy decided on a feint on the French right by edge of the Forest of Lagnières, which would threaten the French centre. The true attack through the Forest of Taisnières was to be on the French left flank. General Henry Withers would take another strong force and assault the village of La Folie. Once this was done, the cavalry would sweep through and break up the Franco-Bavarian horse, which stood behind the infantry.

A thick mist lay over the battlefield but by eight o'clock it had cleared. The Allies had brought up their heavy guns to bombard the flanks, with the lighter guns firing at the centre. Generals Lottum, Schulenburg and

Lord Orkney commanded a substantial force of German and British foot opposing the French fortified left wing. Captain Robert Parker wrote of the battle as the 18th Foot was the last to join the army, having marched from Tournai and were ordered to draw up on the right of the whole army by the Forest of Taisnières:

> ... when also advanced unto that part of the wood which was in our front. We continued marching slowly on, till we came to an opening in the wood. It was a small plain, on the opposite side of which we perceived a battalion of the enemy drawn up, a skirt of the wood being in the rear of them. Upon this Colonel Kane, who was then head of the regiment, having drawn us up, and formed our platoons, advanced gently towards them, with the six platoons of our first fire made ready. When we had advanced within a hundred paces of them, they gave us a fire of one of their ranks: whereupon we halted, and returned them the fire of our six platoons at once; and immediately made ready the six platoons of our second fire, and advanced upon them again. They then gave us the fire of another rank, and we returned them a second fire, which made them shrink; however, they gave us the fire of a third rank after a scattering manner, and then retired into the great wood in great disorder: on which we sent our third fire after them, and saw them no more. We advanced cautiously up to the ground which they had quitted, and found several of them killed and wounded; among the latter was one Lieutenant O'Sullivan, who told us the battalion we had engaged was the Royal Regiment of Ireland ... We had but four men killed and six wounded: and found near forty of them on the spot killed and wounded.

Off to their right was General Henry Withers, who was to take the fortified village of La Folie. Ahead of the 18th Foot were Generals Luttum, Schulenburg and Lord Orkney, later to be the first Field Marshal, commanding a considerable force to attack the fortifications within the forest. It took much bitter fighting to force the French back from their first line. The British regiment, the Buffs, was held up by struggling through a marsh to deliver their attack. Fighting within a wood made things far from clear, especially as they had to contend with freshly cut timber *abattis*, behind which stood the enemy.

At this point, Villars called for reinforcements from the right flank, but Boufflers was unable to oblige as he was under heavy attack. The Prince of Orange failed to carry out his orders and launched his men in an all-out assault on the French positions in and around the Forest of Lagnières. The initial attack included the Scottish regiments as part of the Dutch army along with regiments of Tullibardines, Hepburns, the Dutch Blue Guards and the Hanover regiments, pressed forward and was met with a fearful cannonade. The attack broke down with some 6,000 casualties. Despite his failure to obey orders, Boufflers was unable to release reinforcements to Villars' left flank.

On the French left, Schulenburg's attack with his Prussian, Austrian, and British foot was forcing the French out of their fortifications, while General Withers had attacked La Folie. Villars had called up the Irish Brigade from the centre and sent them to fight the Prussians. The confusion in the woods, in which the Irish became dispersed, allowed the Allies to resume their advance. Villars received a serious leg wound and had to leave the fighting. The Allied artillery advanced and began to pummel the *abattis* until the Allied cavalry were able to pour through the broken French line and meet the French horse comprising of the Mousquetaires, the Gens d'Armes and the Garde de Corps. It was during this fighting that the Old Pretender, James Stuart, was wounded.

Lord Orkney's foot managed to fight off the Gens d'Armes while Marlborough brought up the Prussian cavalry from the right flank to enter the fighting. In the fearful carnage that went on until Boufflers ordered a withdrawal, the French claimed they had won even when they withdrew. The Allies were in no position to follow up their victory and the French exited the battlefield in good order. The casualty rate was appalling. Some put the Franco-Bavarian casualties as 15,000 and the Allied at 17,000. Others record that the Allies suffered 10,500 killed, 14,000 wounded, a total of about 24,000. The Franco-Bavarians had 4,500 killed and 10,500 wounded. One soldier who survived was Ambrose Tennant, who served at Malplaquet and died in Tetbury in 1800 at the age of 106, having served in the army for sixty years.

The Duke of Marlborough's return to England was greeted, not with acclaim, but with criticism. The cost of the war, its mounting casualty roll and the French attempts at a peace settlement in 1709 and 1710 led to a new Tory government taking office. Determined to make peace with France, the Tories persuaded the Queen to dismiss Marlborough, which she did at the end of 1711. The excuse was one of corruption. He had taken a commission from the suppliers of bread for the army and deducted pay from the wages of foreign soldiers. He defended himself vigorously, but Parliament condemned him and he decided to leave the country for a few months. Marlborough's three-year exile to the Continent was elevated with his gaining the command of the British army from the new monarch, George I.

In December 1711, Marlborough crossed to Ostend, where he was greeted by large crowds and a special salute by the artillery. He visited Antwerp, Aachen and Maastricht, where he was hailed as the victor of the Spanish Succession. Sarah joined him in February, bringing with her several servants and a chaplain. Together they went on to Frankfurt in May, where they settled down. Sarah was forthright and critical of Marlborough, who she considered lazy, although he had been in command of an army for ten years. Word reached the Marlboroughs that Queen Anne was seriously ill in the summer of 1714. They moved back to Antwerp to be informed of any news. Britain and the Dutch had made peace with France with the Treaty of Utrecht in 1713, by which time the Tory administration had begun to collapse. It was time to return home and they reached Dover on the day that Anne died. The Elector, George, was crowned king, although he preferred to remain in Hanover. He restored Marlborough to the office of captain-general in 1714, but by that time the Duke's health began to fail and after a series of strokes, he died in 1722.

The string of defeats prompted Louis to start talks, but the Allies were in no mood to begin negotiations. They presented some humiliating terms, which Louis could not accept. The Grand Alliance's outstanding victories at Blenheim and Ramillies pushed the French out of Germany and the Netherlands. The pyrrhic victory at Malplaquet, which cost so many lives, was considered a win for both the British and the French. By 1712, it was time for a peace treaty to be negotiated.

Chapter 24

The Maritime War of Spanish Succession

The battles at sea happened principally around Spain, while the majority of conflicts were fought in Flanders, Germany and Italy. On June 1702, soon after Queen Anne's accession, an English and Dutch fleet carrying a strong body of troops sailed to Cadiz in an attempt to capture and occupy the port. At the start of the War of the Spanish Succession, it was hoped that the Allies would persuade King Peter II of Portugal to join them by capturing a Spanish port to bottle up the French Mediterranean fleet in Toulon. The landing took place on 26 August 1702, on the other side of the bay at Rota. From there, they marched to Port St Mary, where they found the town deserted. The warehouses were filled with wine and brandy, and the troops became unmanageable. As one merchant remarked, 'Our fleet had left such a filthy stench among the Spaniards that a whole age will hardly blot it out.' The immediate effects of the looting and drunkenness by the troops proved an own goal for the expedition as they had no chance of taking Cadiz. Bad weather and a lack of fight led to the Allies withdrawing. On 26 September, the attempt to capture Cadiz ended in an abject failure.

Unable to land, they turned their attention to Vigo on the north-west coast of Spain, where they learned that the Spanish treasure galleons were due to arrive from the West Indies. The entrance to Vigo was only ¾ mile wide and defended by batteries and forts on both sides. It was also protected by a boom that stretched across the entrance. Inside the harbour were five Franco-Spanish ships with sixty or seventy guns commanding the passage, which was too shallow for the first-rate ships, so the leaders transferred their colours to smaller vessels. They landed the troops on the south side of the harbour and carried Fort Rande at the entrance. Vice-Admiral Thomas Hopson in *Torbay*, with a good following wind, rammed the boom, which parted. The following ships were unable to follow due to a lull in the wind and Hopson found himself temporarily outnumbered. A fire ship grappled with *Torbay* and set her on fire. About one hundred and fifteen men were killed or drowned and the ship was so badly shattered that Hopson left her and joined the *Monmouth*.

The forts were taken by the troops or destroyed by the ships. Vigo was a major disaster for the French, with all ships captured by the English and Dutch. The Spanish suffered as badly, losing three galleons and thirteen trading vessels. By 24 October 1702, the damage was complete and, on the 27th, Admiral Shovell's squadron destroyed the fortifications. Unfortunately, the vast wealth of silver had already been unloaded and deposited in the castle at Segovia. What was left belonged, ironically, to the merchants of Amsterdam and London and consisted of pepper, cochineal, cocoa, indigo and hides. The naval victory at Vigo made an indirect and powerful contribution to Britain's prosperity.

Vigo was not even considered by the Anglo-Dutch fleet. Instead, they sailed to Barcelona but it was a fruitless expedition and they sailed south to the Strait of Gibraltar. On 28 July, it was Prince George of Hesse-Darmstadt who suggested that they should take Gibraltar to make up for the loss of Cadiz. This persuaded the Portuguese King to join the Allies. The Twelfth Siege of Gibraltar was fought between September 1704 and May 1705 and followed the capture, in August 1704, of the fortified town, at the southern tip of Spain. Gibraltar was selected for its strategic value but had a weak garrison and an anchorage that was unprotected. The purely maritime campaign was orchestrated by an Anglo-Dutch naval force led by Sir George Rooke and Prince George of Hesse-Darmstadt. The war that began in northern Europe was largely contained there until 1703. From then on, English naval attentions were focused on mounting a campaign in the Mediterranean to distract the French navy, disrupt French and Bourbon Spanish shipping and capture a port for use as a naval base. Since the beginning of the war the Alliance had been looking for a suitable harbour to keep the French fleet in the western Mediterranean Sea.

The Grand Alliance fleet crossed from Tetuan, off North Africa, to Gibraltar, with Prince George prepared to land 1,900 English and 400 Dutch Marines on the night of 3 August. They were covered by the fleet pounding the small town at the foot of the Rock. The defenders were able to hold off the numerically superior besieging force through exploiting Gibraltar's geography and the small town's fortifications, though they were frequently short of manpower and ammunition. The Marines, who served on board the

ships of the Royal and Dutch Navies, played a heroic part in the capture of
Gibraltar. The bombardment and the Marine assault proved too much for
the defenders and they eventually surrendered to Prince George. By his own
account, the governor, Don Diego de Salinas, had no more than fifty-six
men and a few hundred civilian militia of such bad quality that they ran away
as soon as they saw the Allied fleet. The Rock was defended by about 100
cannon scattered about but had few gunners to fire them. They left the Rock
and camped on the spit of land that connected Gibraltar with the mainland,
and eventually established a town they named San Roque after the Chapel
of San Roque.

The Marines made up the garrison of British, Dutch, Austrian and
pro-Habsburg troops, who now faced a besieging force of up to 8,000
pro-Bourbon Spanish and Irish troops. Admiral Sir George Rooke, commanding the Royal Navy, stepped ashore, ordered the British flag to be
hoisted and declared that he was taking the Rock in the name of Queen
Anne. Rooke's claim of English sovereignty was ultimately accepted but
over the centuries it has been challenged by Spain. To safeguard the
Rock, the fleet left six months' provisions before returning to England
for the winter.

The 2,000-odd Marines left were confronted by a combined force of
French and Spanish ships, which landed 4,500 troops on the spit of land.
An additional 400 Marines were landed to help defend the Rock. On 11
November, 500 Franco-Spanish Grenadiers attempted a surprise attack
at dawn on the Round Tower, a fortification at Gibraltar's main land
entrance. They succeeded in breaching the defences but were thrown
back by the defenders. Captain Fisher, with just seventeen Marines,
managed to hold off the Grenadiers until reinforcements arrived to bolster the defences in the Tower. The French moved more reinforcements
to break the stubborn defence by the Marines. With the numbers unable
to cover the weak points, the Marines were reduced to fewer than 1,000
men who were short of supplies. Fortunately, supply ships arrived with
ammunition and rations, and a few months later, 2,000 troops arrived to
boost the numbers.

The besiegers were undermined by disputes between the French
and Spanish officers, and the troops faced terrible conditions in their
trenches and bastions that led to outbreaks of epidemic disease, which
undermined morale. Sea power proved crucial, as the French navy

sought unsuccessfully to prevent the Grand Alliance shipping in fresh troops, ammunition and food. Three naval battles were fought during the siege, two of which were clear defeats for the French and the last of which resulted in the siege being abandoned as hopeless after nine months of fruitless shelling. The outcome was disastrous for the French and Bourbon Spanish side, which was said to have lost 10,000 men against only 400 for the Grand Alliance. The siege dragged on until 1705, by which time the Franco-Spanish attacks petered out and they gave up on 31 March 1705. By the end of the war, Spain formally ceded the territory to the British.

Less than a week after the capture of Gibraltar, Admiral George Rooke received information that a French fleet under the dual command of Louis Alexandre, Count de Toulon and the Duc d'Estrees was approaching Gibraltar. What was to prove to be the biggest naval battle fought during the War of the Spanish Succession was fought on 26 August off the coast of Malaga. Neither fleet was in good condition: the French were low on ammunition and the English ships had received a battering at Gibraltar that had reduced their crews and damaged their masts. Admiral Byng's squadron had expended so much ammunition during the Gibraltar battle that they were forced to withdraw. The French claimed they had won the skirmish, in which no ship was sunk. As it was not really a battle, both sides withdrew, having battered each other without causing much damage.

In 1707, the Allied fleet attacked and then broke off its attack on Toulon to return home. Sir Cloudesley Shovell, who had been given control of the Mediterranean Fleet, had managed to bottle up the French Fleet in Toulon. Having failed to capture the port, the bombardment had panicked the French into scuttling their own fleet. Returning to Gibraltar for supplies, Shovell's fleet departed on 29 September 1707, plagued by bad weather and strong gales. Thinking they were off Ushant, they entered the English Channel, and encountered murky and stormy conditions not helped by the navigator's inability to calculate longitude. On the morning of 22 October, Sir Cloudesley called a council of his senior officers. Only one officer, Captain Sir William Jumper of the *Lenox*, disagreed with the others, having calculated that they were near the Scilly Isles. His was one of three ships that shepherded the merchant ships into Falmouth.

Having little knowledge of the navigation in the stormy conditions, the fleet drifted close to the Scilly Islands. Thinking they were mid-Channel, disaster struck the remainder of the fleet. The *Association* was the first ship to be holed by the Outer Gilstone rocks and sank immediately. The *St George* struck the same rocks but a strong wave lifted her and she landed in deep water with minimal damage. The *Swiftsure* heard the warning gun from the *Association* but then vanished from sight. The *Eagle* hit Crim Rock and sank with all hands. The westernmost part of the Isles of Scilly is the Bishop's Rock, about 28 miles from Land's End, and it was here that the smaller ship, the *Rumney*, collided and sank. One man survived: George Lawrence, quartermaster, the only man to escape out of the 1,900 drowning men. The fire ship *Firebrand* struck the Gilstone Ledge but was lifted clear by a wave and found refuge in Smith Sound, where she sank. One who kept a record was Captain Redell of the *Isabella*, who wrote in quaint manner:

> We perceived ye rocks on both sides of us, we being very near to them, we immediately wore our yacht [?] and layed our head to westward, crowding all ye sail we could to weather ye rocks under our lee, we filled full and full, and by God's mercy we got clear of them all, for which deliverance God's holy name be blest and praised. Which caused a great separation of the fleet, for happy was he that could shift for himself, some steering with their heads to ye southward, and others to ye northward, and those that lay with their heads to ye southward were most of them lost.

There was a large monetary reward that was offered to expert mathematicians and horologists who could come up with a reliable longitudinal calculator. Parliament passed the Longitude Act on 1714, following the Scilly Isles disaster in 1707. It took decades before a reliable longitude device was devised. It was John Harrison who dedicated his work for another sixty years before the marine chronometer was accepted by the Board of Longitude. The system used for calculating longitude (east and west position) was dead reckoning, which was looking at the speed of the ship, its direction and hazarding an educated guess. The problem of determining latitude was reliant on taking readings off the horizon and fixed points in the night sky. Unfortunately the terrible weather rendered this inaccurate, too. Instead, the ships were pushed off course and became tangled among the rocks around the Isles of Scilly. Sir Cloudesley Shovell was hailed as a popular hero and was the only victim who was not buried on the Isles of Scilly. Instead his body was taken to Westminster Abbey to be interred and a monument erected by Grinling Gibbons.

Chapter 25

Mrs Freeman and Mrs Morley

How quickly the reign of William and Mary receded. It should be recognised that, although William was Dutch and consorted with his Dutch friends, he did change the way Britain was ruled. His sister-in-law, Anne, had fallen out with her sister, Mary, but still acknowledged William's right to the throne. When Anne was a child she suffered from an eye infection known as defluxion. For medical treatment, she was sent to France, where she lived with her paternal grandmother, Henrietta Maria. When her grandmother died in 1669, Anne lived with her aunt, Henrietta Anne, Duchess of Orleans, who died suddenly in 1670. Anne was only eight when she returned to England, only for her mother (Anne Hyde) to die the following year. Losing three members of her family in quick succession, Anne formed an attachment to Sarah Jennings, a girl five years older than herself, who had a strong will and a violent temper; something that appealed to her. Anne was placed in the care of Colonel Edward and Lady Frances Villiers and educated in the teachings of the Anglican Church. As with many of the population, Anne caught smallpox, which she passed on to Lady Villiers and she died soon after.

As Princess Anne grew older, she was expected to marry George, Elector of Hanover, but this did not happen. In 1682, John Sheffield, Earl of Mulgrave, was dismissed from the court for submitting himself as suitor for the hand of Anne, who was seventeen while he was thirty-five. When James came to the throne, he reinstated Sheffield, who received a seat on the Privy Council and was made Lord Chamberlain. Instead, on 28 July 1683, Anne married the Danish Prince George, the brother of King Christian V, in the Chapel Royal. They were given some buildings in Whitehall called the Cockpit on the site of Downing Street.

Anne went through a series of miscarriages. By early 1687, her husband caught smallpox and her two infant young daughters died of the same infection. Thankfully, her husband recovered. Anne's medical condition was painfully dire and based on her foetal losses and physical symptoms, she may have had systemic lupus erthematosus or antiphospholipid syndrome. Her miscarriages can be put down to pelvic inflammatory disease due to listeriosis, diabetes, intrauterine growth retardation and rhesus incompatibility.

Life for Anne's friend Sarah and her husband during the reign of William and Mary was difficult and they enjoyed considerably less favour than they had during the reign of James II. The new Earl of Marlborough had supported the now exiled James and by this time Sarah's dominance of Anne and her involvement in the Whig party led to a serious falling out between the two sisters. Mary demanded that Anne dismiss Sarah, something that Anne refused to do, and the rift grew wider.

When Anne came to the throne, two men and a woman would dominate her reign; John Churchill, Earl of Marlborough; Sidney Godolphin, Earl of Godolphin, and Sarah Churchill. Godolphin was a leading politician who served on the Privy Council before being appointed as First Lord of the Treasury. He was instrumental in negotiating and passing the Acts of Union 1707 with Scotland, which created the Kingdom of Great Britain. He was present at the birth of the James's only son, James Francis Edward Stuart, the Old Pretender. He diplomatically said he was too far from the bed to see anything. When the Tories came to power in 1700, he was appointed Lord Treasurer after Anne ascended the throne. In 1704 he was made a Knight of the Garter and two years later made Viscount Rialton and Earl of Godolphin.

Disliking the radical Whigs, Anne refused to appoint Charles Spencer, the 3rd Earl of Sunderland, who was Sarah's son-in-law, who she perceived as a threat to her royal prerogative. Sarah used her close friendship with Sydney Godolphin, a Tory, to send reading matters to Anne in the hope that she would come over to the Whig party. Sarah's intelligence – she could have become a Member of Parliament – was so admired by Anne. She had a close relationship with her husband and Sydney Godolphin; the latter considered refusing high office after Anne's succession. Although he liked Sarah, he found her too overpowering and interfering, telling him what to do when her husband was away on the Continent. On the other hand, she did have charm and wit that was admired by many of her followers. Although Anne admired Sarah, there were political differences between them: Anne was religious and a High Church Tory and Sarah was a Whig who supported

Marlborough in his wars. Sarah did not share the Queen's deep interest in religion as it was a subject she rarely mentioned, but she pointed out that Anne risked God's vengeance for her seeming cruelty to her.

After a bumpy ride during the 1680s–90s, during which John Churchill divulged the naval raid on Brest to James, who ignored it, he was deprived of his position and put for a short time in the Tower. He was appointed the title of the Earl of Marlborough, something he felt was beneath his dignity. Later, William came around to acknowledging that he was the best commander of the army. Although he was suspicious of Churchill, he did promote him to lead the Allied army at the beginning of the War of Spanish Succession.

With Anne on the throne, Churchill's reputation was entwined with his queen. He was elevated to the first Duke of Marlborough and granted the subsidiary title Marquess of Blandford. His four great victories against the French from 1704 to 1709 had him regarded as having elevated Great Britain to a front-runner in European affairs. A grateful nation led by Queen Anne intended to grant their national hero a suitable home. After the Battle of Blenheim, a large amount of money was allocated for the building at Woodstock. The parliamentary treasurer, Sidney Godolphin, on Churchill's recommendation, appointed Sir John Vanbrugh as architect.

Vanbrugh, untrained as an architect, was a popular dramatist who met Churchill at a playhouse. He worked with Nicholas Hawksmoor, famous for his London churches, and together they had successfully completed Castle Howard in Yorkshire. Although Vanbrugh is credited with the building of Blenheim, it was at the time not well-regarded and lacked the architectural plaudits he hoped it would receive. In a disagreement over the funding of this project and its over-ostentation, he ran into difficulties with Sarah, who still wished Sir Christopher Wren to design the house. She criticised Vanbrugh's design and taste and wanted a comfortable home, whereas the architect wanted a monument to the outstanding victories Marlborough had achieved on the Continent. With the early days of the building, the Duke was frequently away on his military campaigns, and it was left to the Duchess to negotiate with Vanbrugh. More aware than her husband of the precarious state of the financial aid they were receiving, she criticised Vanbrugh's grandiose ideas for their extravagance. In their final altercation, Vanbrugh was banned from the site, but did view the palace in secret while Sarah was away. When Blenheim Palace was completed in 1725, the widowed Sarah refused Vanbrugh's wife permission to enter the park. The Baroque style that Vanbrugh favoured found little acceptance with the public and was soon changed to a less fussy Palladian style. Finding little acceptance from the public, Vanbrugh's reputation was damaged irreparably and he received no further public commissions.

When George died on 28 October 1708 at Kensington Palace, the Queen was devastated. James Brydges wrote:

> His death has flung the Queen into an unspeakable grief. She never left him till he was dead, but continued kissing him the very moment his breath went out of his body, and 'twas with a great deal of difficulty my Lady Marlborough prevailed upon her to leave him.

Sarah Jennings was born on 5 June 1660 at Hollywell House near St Albans. Her father, Richard, first met James, Duke of York, and the two became friendly to the extent that Sarah was appointed maid of honour to Anne Hyde, Duchess of York. In 1675, she established a lasting friendship with the younger Princess Anne, which came to an end in 1710, a few years before Anne's death.

When she was only fifteen, Sarah met John Churchill, ten years her senior. Despite objections from both sides of the family, they married in secret during the winter of 1677. Anne and Sarah invented pet names for themselves, Mrs Freeman (Sarah) and Mrs Morley (Anne), which enabled them to converse on terms of equality and which they continued to use after Anne became Queen. Sarah was good with money and controlled the Queen's purse. She also manipulated who would be admitted to Anne's presence. As the author, Herbert Paul wrote:

> Although she chose to call herself a Whig, Sarah's real politics were avarice, pride, and the advancement of her own family at public expense.

Sarah's dominant role eventually led to a split when, in 1708, Abigail Hill took over as Anne's best friend. Jonathan Swift observed that Anne 'had not a store of amity by her for more than one friend at a time'.

After the seventeen pregnancies that Anne went through, she became subject to perpetual pain, probably caused by gout. By 1702, she was already so lame she had to be carried to her coronation in a sedan chair. She became increasingly overweight and had to be moved around in chairs and even pullies. She was aware that she had abandoned her father, who had exiled himself in France, and attempted reconciliation, but nothing came of it. Although she was unhappy and depressed, she was devoted to the Church of England. She even started a charity referred to as Queen Anne's Bounty to assist impoverished ministers of the clergy. Sir John Clerk of Penicuik was admitted to the private apartments of the Queen and later wrote:

> One day I had occasion to observe the calamities which attend human nature, even in the greatest dignities of life. Her Majesty was labouring under a fit of gout, and in extreme pain and agony, and on this occasion everything about her was much in the same disorder as about the meanest of her subjects. Her face, which was red and spotted, was rendered something frightful by her negligent dress, and the foot affected was tied up with a poultice and some nasty bandages.

From about 1698, Anne began to seriously suffer from gout, which spread to her limbs, stomach and head. This caused her lameness and she had to be carried around in a sedan chair or wheelchair. In the fresh air, which she did not particularly like, she used a one-horse chaise, which she drove at high speed with her scarves flying behind her.

She fell out with her sister, which lasted for five years. Sadly, Mary died in December 1694, so the women were never reconciled. They rowed over Anne's choice of acquaintances, namely the Churchills. One of the reasons for the rift was John Churchill's feeling that he had not been adequately rewarded for his service. Also, Mary disapproved of the friendship between Anne and Sarah. Anne requested the use of Richmond Palace and a parliamentary allowance of £50,000. She later took up residence at Syon House and then Berkeley House in Piccadilly. Three months later, William restored Marlborough's titles and Berkeley House became a social centre for courtiers who had avoided contact with Anne and the Marlboroughs. In her first speech to Parliament on 11 March 1702, she put some distance between herself and William, saying:

As I know my heart to be entirely English, I can very sincerely assure you there is not anything you can expect or desire from me which I shall not be ready to do for the happiness and prosperity of England.

Anne was crowned at Westminster Abbey on St George's Day. She was suffering from gout and had to be carried in an open sedan chair with a low back, which allowed her train to flow out behind her. She took a lively interest in state affairs and was a patron of the theatre, poetry and music. She also knighted Isaac Newton during a royal visit to Trinity College, Cambridge in April 1705. The knighthood was timed for the parliamentary election in May rather that for Newton's scientific work or as Master of the Mint. He was only the second scientist to be knighted after Sir Francis Bacon.

In her first speech to Parliament she brought up the union of England and Scotland. A joint Anglo-Scots commission met at her former residence, the Cockpit in October 1702, but it broke up in February 1703 having failed to reach an agreement. Scotland's problem was the failure of the Darien Scheme and the series of crop failures during the 1690s, resulting in a total economic failure. The Company of Scotland, who founded the Darien Scheme lost over £232,884, leaving the country incapable of recovering. In the discussions that followed, and part of the deal, England paid off £398,000. A bank was formed to administer this money, which later became the Royal Bank of Scotland. Scotland believed that England had deliberately sabotaged its chance of independence and over the next fifty years supported the Jacobite rebellions that plagued the Union.

During the last year of William's reign an Act of Settlement was passed that applied to the kingdoms of England and Ireland but not Scotland. This gave Scotland the right to choose a Stuart monarch in an Act of Security, but failing that, it would chose a Scottish Protestant from the royal line of Scotland. The person chosen would not be the same person chosen to rule the English throne. Anne withheld the Royal Assent until the following year, when the Scottish merchants threatened to withhold Scottish support for England's wars.

In response, England enforced the Alien Act of 1705, which threatened economic sanctions and declare Scottish subjects aliens of England. If Scotland repealed the Act of Security she could unite with England, which she reluctantly did. The English Parliament repealed the Alien Act and a new body of commissioners were appointed by Queen Anne to negotiate the terms of a Union. In what was the most important act of her reign, Anne gave her blessing to the Act of Union in 1707.

Under the Acts of Union, England and Scotland were united under a single kingdom called Great Britain, with one parliament. Despite opposition from both sides of the border, Anne celebrated the Act by attending a thanksgiving service at St Paul's Cathedral. Sir John Clerk was one of the congregation and wrote:

> Nobody on this occasion appeared more sincerely devout and thankful than the Queen herself.

The historian Simon Schama wrote:

> What began as a hostile merger, would end in a full partnership in the most powerful going concern in the world ... it was one of the most astonishing transformations in European history.

Scottish politicians were divided about the Union and one who was outspoken was Andrew Fletcher. He was an opponent of the 1707 Act of Union and became an exile after being accused of promoting insurrection. He had been appointed commander of the Duke of Monmouth's cavalry in the invasion of the West Country. He had become embroiled in an argument with Thomas Dare, a local sympathiser, over who should own a horse that Dare had appropriated. In the dispute, Fletcher killed Dare and was withdrawn from Monmouth's army. He then went into exile and forfeited his estates. Later, he went to Spain and was imprisoned before escaping. He then travelled to Hungary to join the Duc d'Lorraine's fight against the Turks. He then joined William of Orange's Glorious Revolution and returned to Scotland as Commissioner for East Lothian and head of the nationalist party. It became apparent that William's priority was fighting the French on the Continent. Fletcher's estates were restored to him and he became increasingly nationalistic over England's increasing wealth.

Fletcher was also a supporter of the Darien Scheme and subscribed £1,000 of his own money. He deplored London's relative size, which attracted a greater proportion of wealth and decision, making it into an expanding capital. When the Act of Union of 1707 was signed, he left politics and set about improving his agricultural methods at his estate at Saltoun. Scotland was a poor county, having been devastated by years of poor harvests, bad weather and impoverished farming methods. Fletcher saw a way to improve Scottish agriculture by establishing the Saltoun mill in 1712. With some financial backing, Fletcher was able to introduce modern machinery he had seen in Holland. He was helped by James Meikles, a mill-right, at Saltoun, who replaced the old method with a new machine. His sister, Margaret, went to Amsterdam and through industrial espionage acquired the method for weaving fine linen. Fletcher died in London, a city he abhorred, in September 1716 and his body was taken back to Saltoun to be buried in the family vault.

On 26 November 1703, the Great Storm was one of the most destructive cyclones to hit central and southern England. This was not just a passing storm, for weeks of wind and rain blew through the country. The storm wreaked havoc in Europe, causing severe damage to the Netherlands, Denmark and Germany. High winds caused 2,000 chimney stacks to collapse in London, some 4,000 oaks in the New Forest were blown down, over 1,000 seamen lost their lives on the Goodwin Sands and the lead roofing was blown off Westminster Abbey. In the Pool of London, over 700 ships were destroyed. HMS *Association* was blown from Harwich to Gothenburg before it could make its way back to England. Queen Anne had to take shelter in the cellar at St James's Palace and described the storm as:

> a Calamity so Dreadful and Astonishing, that the like hath not been Seen or Felt, in the Memory of any Person Living in this Our Kingdom.

She went on to describe the storm as:

> Just before the 1703 storm struck, the novelist Daniel Defoe noticed the Mercury had 'sunk lower that ever I had observed it' and assumed the instrument had been meddled with by his children.

Defoe went on a tour of Kent and stopped counting fallen trees when he reached 17,000. Orchards were flattened and one witness declared that,

'Our loss in the apple-trees is the greatest, because we shall want liquor to make our hearts merry.' Over 100 churches across the south of England had their roofs ripped off and the spires were either damaged or completely destroyed. Windmills bore the brunt and many were destroyed by fire thanks to the friction generated by their spinning sails. The Eddystone lighthouse was swept away, taking with it six keepers including the designer, Henry Winstanley. John Evelyn wrote in an apocalyptic manner in his diary of the destruction of his estate in Surrey:

> The dismal effects of the hurricane and tempest of wind, rain and lightening through all the nation, especially London, many houses demolished, many people killed. As to my own loss, the subversion of woods and timber both left for ornament, and valuable material through the whole of my Estate, and about my house, the woods crowning the Garden Mount, and growing along the Park meadow; the damage to my own dwelling, and tenants' farms and outhouses, is most tragically: not to be paralleled with anything happening in our age or in any history almost, I am not able to describe, but submit to the Almighty pleasure of God, with acknowledgement of his justice for our national sins and my own, who yet have not suffered as I deserve to: every moment like Job's Messengers, bring the sad tidings of this universal Judgement.

At sea, the ships were at the mercy of high winds and stormy seas. One seaman described the horror:

> By two o'clock we could hear guns firing in several parts of this road [anchorage], as signals of distress, and though the noise was very great with sea and wind, yet we could distinguish plainly, in some short intervals, the cries of poor souls in extremities. I was a full sight full of terrible particulars, to see a ship of eighty guns and about six hundred men in that dismal case; she had cut away all her masts, the men were all in the confusions of death and despair; she had neither anchor, nor cable, nor boat to help her; the sea breaking over her in a terrible manner, that sometimes she seemed all under water; and they knew, as well as we that saw her, that they drove by the tempest directly for the Goodwin, where

they could expect nothing but destruction. The cries of the men, and the firing their guns, one by one, every half minute for help, terrified us in such a manner, that I think we were half dead with the horror of it.

Many of the Royal Navy ships anchored at the Downs off the Kentish coast were ready for action in the War of Spanish Succession when the Great Storm hit them. They were driven on to the Goodwin Sands, which was above the water at low tide. Miles Nobcliffe wrote from HMS *Shrewsbury*:

These lines I hope in God will find you in good health; we are left here in a dismal condition, expecting every moment to be all drowned: for here is a great storm, and is very likely to continue; we have here the rear admiral of the blew in the ship called the *Mary*, a third rate, the very next ships to ours, sunk, with Admiral Beaumont. And above 500 men drowned: the ship called the *Northumberland*, a third rate, about 500 men all sunk and drowned: the ship called the *Sterling Castle*, a third rate, all sunk and drowned above 500 souls: and the ship called the *Restoration*, a third rate, all sunk and drowned: these ships were all close by us which I saw; these ships fire their guns all night and day long, poor souls, for help, but the storm being so fierce and raging, could have none to save them: the ships called the *Shrewsbury*, that we are in, broke two anchors, and did run mighty fierce backwards, with 60 or 80 yards of the Sands, and as God Almighty would have it, we flung our sheet anchor down, which is the biggest, and so stopped: here we all prayed to God to forgive our sins, and to save us, or else to receive us into his heavenly kingdom. If our sheet anchor had given way, we had been all drowned: but I humbly thank God, it was his gracious mercy that saved us. There's one, Captain Fanel's ship, three hospital ships, all split, some sunk, and most of the men drowned.

There were above 40 merchant ships cast away and sunk: to see Admiral Beaumont, that was next to us, and all the rest of his men, how they climbed up the main mast, hundreds at a time crying out for help, and thinking to save their lives and in a twinkling of an eye, were drowned: I can give you no account, but of those four men-of-war aforesaid, which I saw with my own eyes, and those hospital ships, at present, by reason the storm hath drove us far from one another: Captain Crow, of our ship, believes we have lost several more ships of war, by reason we see so few; we lie here in great danger, and waiting for a north-easterly wind to bring us back to Portsmouth, and it is our great prayers to God for it ...

On 5 December, after the Great Storm, Anne declared a general fast to implore God 'to pardon the crying sins of this nation which had drawn down this sad judgement'. The Great Storm coincided with the increase in English journalism. Daniel Defoe was moved to write about the Great Storm and requested witnesses who had experienced its impact. The following year he published his book, *The Storm: or, a Collection of the most Remarkable Casualties and Disasters which happened in the late Dreadful Tempest, both by Sea and Land*. This volume has been called the first substantial work of modern journalism. Although his book veers towards exaggeration, it is gripping and well-researched. In the introduction, he writes:

The main inference I shall pretend to make or at least venture the exposing to public view, in this case, is, the strong evidence God has been pleased to give in this terrible manner to His own being, which mankind began more than ever to affront and despise.

Abigail Hill was the daughter of Francis Hill, a London merchant who lost most of his money in speculation. Her mother was Elizabeth Jennings, aunt to Sarah Jennings, who befriended her. Sarah may have felt some compassion for her cousin rather than genuine affection, for she took Abigail into her household at St Albans. When Anne ascended to the throne on 1702, Abigail managed to procure an appointment in the Queen's Household in 1704. Sarah thought that she had risen above her station, writing:

I never thought her education was such as to make her fit company for a great queen. Many people have liked the humour of their chambermaids and have been very kind to them, but 'tis very uncommon to hold a private correspondence with them and put them upon the foot of a friend.

Sarah Churchill was often absent for months and Abigail began to take over as a close friend of Anne. She had a gentler manner than the imperious style of Sarah and gradually she was accepted into the Queen's friendship. It was not until 1707 that Sarah learned of Abigail's secret marriage to Samuel Masham, one of the Queen's courtiers, and that Anne had been present at the marriage. The ceremony was the first overt sign of Anne's displeasure with Sarah's overbearing manner and took place in the apartments of the Queen's doctor, John Arbuthnot, at St James's Palace. Arbuthnot was made a Physician in Ordinary to the Queen, which made him part of the Royal Household. Sarah was further angered when she discovered that Abigail had moved into the apartments in Kensington Palace, which she considered her own, although she rarely used them. The relationship between the Queen and the Duchess became evermore strained and in their final quarrel in 1711, the money for the grand house at Woodstock ceased.

Abigail, now Lady Masham, was appointed Keeper of the Privy Purse, while Elizabeth Seymour, Duchess of Somerset, replaced her as Mistress of the Robes and Groom of the Stole. Elizabeth married three times: at the age of twelve in 1679 to Henry Cavendish, who died the following year. A year later at the age of fourteen, she married Thomas Thynne of Longleat, a relative of Viscount Weymouth. In February 1682, Thynne was murdered by a gang on the order of the Swedish Count Karl von Konigsmark, who had been captivated by Elizabeth. He had heard a rumour that the marriage was unhappy and that gossip had spread to implicate Elizabeth in the murder. The gang were rounded up, tried and hanged, while von Konigsmark was acquitted and banished from England. Her last husband, who she married at the age of fifteen, was Charles Seymour, Duke of Somerset; it was not a happy marriage, yet she managed to produce seven children. She showed great skill in dealing with the ailing Anne in that she never pressed the Queen to do anything for her. In contrast, Abigail Masham was constantly asking for favours. Anne, who was fond of Elizabeth's gossip, called her 'one of the most observing, prying ladies in England'.

In 1707, John Hill, Abigail's brother, commanded a brigade at the Battle of Almansa in Spain. It was a rather one-sided encounter but was praised by many, including Frederick the Great, who described it as the most impressive battle of the century. Hill managed to hold off the French while the rest of the army retreated and his brigade was captured. He was paroled and returned to England to reform his regiment, which was sent to the Netherlands in 1708. On 26 September 1709, Hill's regiment was sent to advance on the siege line at Mons, which resulted in 150 casualties including Hill, who was wounded. In 1710, Anne persuaded John Churchill to grant an important command to Hill. This rapid rise owed little to any military talent but was due to the patronage of the Duke of Marlborough and Abigail's replacement of Sarah at court.

The planned French Invasion of Britain in 1708, also known as the 'Entreprise d'Ecosse', took place during the War of the Spanish Succession. The French planned to land 5,000 to 6,000 troops in north-east Scotland to link up with the local Jacobites and restore James, the Old Pretender, to the throne of Great Britain. Thanks to the efforts of the Royal Navy and the weather, the French were forced to return to their home ports. Despite their defeat, the French managed to achieve a short-term result when the pro-war Whigs won the 1708 election.

Abigail was related to Robert Harley, who later became the Speaker, Chancellor of the Exchequer and Lord Treasurer. He promoted the careers of Jonathan Swift, Alexander Pope and John Gay, as well as writing some decent poetry. Abigail acted as an intermediary between the Queen and Harley, who attempted to foster business without his former colleagues. On 8 March 1711, a French refugee and double agent known as the Marquis de Guiscard, was arrested having made a feeble attempt of killing Harley as he stood before the Privy Council. Wearing fine clothes and thick brocaded waistcoat, Harley was stabbed by de Guiscard with a penknife that struck one of the bejewelled objects sewn into his waistcoat. In the following fracas, de Guiscard was attacked by several members of the Council and fatally wounded. James Butler, the Duke of Ormond, refused to kill him, saying that 'it was not for him to cheat the hangman'. It was hoped to question the would-be killer, but he died of his wounds a week later in Newgate Prison.

Another attempt to kill Harley took place in November 1712, when the Whigs attempted to assassinate Harley in what has become known as the Bandbox Plot. A hat box was sent to Harley, who had his friend Jonathan

Swift with him. They noticed the attached string, which they cut, and opened the box to find three pistols tied to the lid that were primed to kill the politician. Although the Whigs denied any attempt to kill what became known as the prime minister, no charge was ever made. The unsuccessful attempt to murder Harley had major political consequences. Harley's popularity, which had been on the decline, recovered at once as a wave of rejoicing at his survival swept the country, and even his enemies praised his courage in the face of danger.

Anne's fragile health grew worse by Christmas 1713. She recovered slightly in January 1714, but her death was expected sometime during the year. She rejected the eighty-four-year-old Sophie of Hanover and also refused any visits from the Hanoverians while her ministers were in contact with James, her half-brother. Through her chief minister, Robert Harley, now Earl of Oxford, and Secretary of State, Lord Bolingbroke, they wrote to James Francis Edward, the Old Pretender, offering the crown if he would reject the Catholic religion. James, a devout Catholic, replied, 'I have chosen my own curse, therefore it is for others to change their sentiments.' Harley and Bolingbroke concluded that James's refusal to change his religion was insurmountable, but they did continue their correspondence with him.

Following the death of her only surviving son, Prince William, Duke of Gloucester (1689–1700), Queen Anne had decided in favour of the Protestant succession of the House of Hanover. On the death of Queen Anne in 1714, her second cousin, the German George I, was duly accepted as King of England and Scotland. James had entered into correspondence with John, Earl of Mar, known as 'Bobbing John' for the amount of times he had changed his allegiance from one side to the other. Mar gathered the Scottish clans in rebellion. The Jacobite standard was hoisted on 6 September, 1715 and Mar managed to occupy Perth by the end of the month. He met the government forces at the indecisive battle of Sheriffmuir on 13 November, which both sides strongly claimed to have won.

On 22 December, James at last set foot in Scotland. After a few skirmishes with the enemy, his Highland army dispersed and James returned to the safety of France. His patron, Louis XIV, had died the previous year, depriving him of his most staunch supporter. By this time the French were negotiating with the English government and the Old Pretender was abruptly ordered to leave France along with his Jacobite friends. They ended up in Rome, too far from England to be invaded.

The strain of ill health told on Anne. She suffered a stroke on 30 July 1714, and on 1 August she died. Her doctor, John Arbuthnot, wrote to Jonathan Swift, saying that her death was a release of ill health and tragedy, 'I believe sleep was never more welcome to a weary traveller that death was to her.' Arbuthnot was a mathematician and writer who invented the character 'John Bull', an enduring symbol for Great Britain. On 24 August, Anne was buried beside her husband and children in the Henry VII Chapel at Westminster Abbey. The Electress Sophia died on 28 May 1714, two months before Anne, so the Electress's son, George, succeeded to Great Britain's throne. The Elector's accession was relatively stable, although for the next century, the Britons would be ruled by Germans, having had a Dutchman rule them for twelve years.

Bibliography

Bishop Burnet's History of His Own Time, Vol. 1, London, 1724.

The Glorious Revolution – 1688 – Britain's Fight for Liberty, Edward Valland, 2006.

William III, S. Baxter, 1966.

Revolution: The Great Crisis of the British Monarchy 1685–1720, Tim Harris, 2007.

Bloody Assizes, Ed. G. Muddiman, 1928.

The Glorious Revolution, John Miller, 1997.

The Army, James II and the Glorious Revolution, J. Childs, 1980.

The Life of General Monck, Duke of Albemarle, Thomas Gubbins, 1671.

Brief Relation of the Famous Siege of Breda, Quartermaster Henry Hexham, 1637.

The Boyne and Aughrim – The War of Two Kings, John Kinross, 1998.

The Kings and Queens of England, Antonia Fraser, 1975.

The First Modern Revolution, Steve Pincus, 2009.

The Secret History of the Rye House Plot and Monmouth's Rebellion, Forde Grey, Earl of Tankerville, 1685.

The Dreadful Judgement – The True Story of the Great Fire of London, Neil Hanson, 2001.

Annals of Cambridge, Charles Henry Cooper, 1845.

The Indomitable John Scott – Citizen of Long Island, Lillian Mower, 1960.

The Journal of the Great Plague, Daniel Defoe, 1715.

The Expert Swordsman's Companion, Donald McBane, 1728.

The Williamite Wars in Ireland, John Childs, 2007.

A Chronology of the Bloody Assizes, Donald E. Wilkes, 1991.

Short History of the Life of Major Bernardi by Himself, John Bernardi, Paperback. 2012.

Queen Anne, Herbert W. Paul, 2019.

1688: The First Modern Revolution, Steve Pincus, 2009.

Life and Diary of Lt. Col. J. Blackadder of the Cameronian Regt, 1824.

Military Memoirs of Marlborough's Campaigns 1700–1713, Captain Robert Parker, 1968.

Mèmoires de Feld-Marèchal Comte de Merode-Westerloo, Chevalier de la Toison d'Or, Capitaine de Trabans de l'Empereur Charles VI – 2 vols. 1840.

The Chronicles of an Old Campaigner – M.de la Colonie 1692–1717. Translated into English by Walter C. Horsley, 1904.

Index